THE AFRIKANERS

For Penelope

THE AFRIKANERS

AN HISTORICAL INTERPRETATION

G.H.L. LE MAY

BLACKWELL
Publishers

First published 1995
2 4 6 8 10 9 7 5 3 1

Blackwell Publishers Ltd
108 Cowley Road
Oxford OX4 1JF, UK

Blackwell Publishers Inc.
238 Main Street
Cambridge, Massachusetts 02142, USA

British Library Cataloguing in Publication Data
A CIP catalogue record for this book is available from the British Library.

Library of Congress Cataloging-in-Publication Data
Le May, G. H. L. (Godfrey Hugh Lancelot)
  The Afrikaners: an historical interpretation / G. H. L. Le May.
    p. cm.
  Includes bibliographical references and index.
  ISBN 0-631-18204-7 (acid-free paper)

  1. Afrikaners-History. 2. Afrikaners-Politics and government. 3. South Africa-
History. 4. South Africa-Politics and government. 5. South Africa-Race relations-
History.
I. Title.
  DT1768. A57L4   1995   95–11584
  968–dc20   CIP

Typeset in 101/2 pt on 121/2 pt Sabon
by Pure Tech India Ltd., Pondicherry, India
Printed in Great Britain by Hartnolls Limited, Bodmin, Cornwall

This book is printed on acid-free paper

CONTENTS

PLATES

MAPS

A NOTE ON NAMES

The naming of the diverse peoples who have populated South Africa in the past and the present is a matter of both difficulty and delicacy. The first settlers were a mixture of various European servants of the Dutch East India Company. With the passage of time, and the development of a sense of separate identity, the name Afrikaander, Afrikaaner, and Afrikaner came into use. I have used the modern spelling of Afrikaner. The name was sometimes used interchangeably with that of Boer, which literally meant a farmer, but then came to characterize a particular species of the genus Afrikaner. The early settlers called the first indigenous peoples whom they encountered Hottentots or Bushmen. Recent ethnologists have argued that these peoples should properly be called San or Khoisan or Khoikoi. I have kept to the old names because those were the ones which the Afrikaners used and to substitute the names favoured by later scholars would be misleading in this context. I am not trying to make a political point.

The Afrikaners sometimes called the Bantu-speaking peoples Kaffirs or Caffres, a word which originally meant unbeliever but quickly became a term of racial abuse. (One might make a comparison with the word nigger in the American experience.) I have done my best to avoid the word, except in direct quotation.

There is a particular difficulty in describing the Bantu-speaking peoples as a whole. Until well into this century it was common for Whites to refer to them, however inappositely, as natives. (There were some who saw nothing anomalous in talking about 'foreign natives' to refer to black immigrants.) It became common in English to refer to these people as Africans. But the translation of African is Afrikaner, and that was a word which Afrikaners were not prepared to use generically. More recently, the favoured term has been 'Black'. I have used all these terms according to the period under discussion. It would be anachronistic to change the names, for instance, of the myriad pieces of legislation which begin with the word Native.

Similarly, I have used 'Cape Coloured people' to describe those of mixed race who originated at the Cape. They sometimes called themselves *Bruinmense* – brown men. I have not used this term.

There is no single word for the South African English. I have avoided the clumsy term 'English speakers' or 'English-speaking South Africans', and have used 'English' when I am referring to those in South Africa and 'British' when I am referring to the citizens of the United Kingdom. I hope that the context makes it clear which is meant.

Finally, I have tried to avoid the word 'European' which was often used to distinguish between Whites and non-Whites. It has always seemed to be inappropriate as a description of those who have left their European origins far in the past.

INTRODUCTION

Anyone who is rash enough to attempt to interpret the Afrikaner people is perplexed at once by difficulties of definition. Who are the Afrikaners? Where did they come from? How did they become what they are? What values and characteristics do they have in common? When could they plausibly claim to have become a nation?

The 'definitive' Afrikaans dictionary published in 1950 has, under Afrikaner: 'One who is Afrikaans by descent or birth; one who belongs to the Afrikaans-speaking population group'. Definition by language alone is too broad; it would include, for example, the Cape Coloured people, or half-castes, who speak Afrikaans among themselves but would be surprised if they were classified as Afrikaners.* The *Shorter Oxford English Dictionary* defines an Afrikaner as a white native of South Africa. But when did a recognizably Afrikaans-speaking population group make its appearance? The first European settlers in South Africa (as distinct from castaways or transients) arrived at the Cape of Good Hope in 1652 as members of an expedition sent by the Dutch East India Company under Jan van Riebeeck to establish a refreshment station for the Company's ships on their way to and from the East Indies. Not all members of the expedition were Dutch, for the Company was not in the least exclusive in recruiting its servants. The settlement at the Cape was, officially at least, a God-fearing community. Its bibles were in High Dutch, which was the colony's language of record. It was not long before the original settlers were joined by others from east and west, both free men and women and slaves. In 1689, for

* I am grateful to my colleague, Gordon Lawrie, for this point.

instance, there arrived a contingent of Huguenots, Protestant refugees from France. High Dutch might be the official language, but as the settlement grew and the settlers dispersed a patois developed in which High Dutch became mingled with loan words from French, German, English and Portuguese–Creole, and was constantly influenced by the dialects of the indigenous inhabitants. By 1806, the year of permanent British occupation, the white population was estimated at 18,000, made up of Netherlanders (the largest group) and then, in order of size, of Germans, French and Scandinavians, with some Presbyterian teachers and preachers from Scotland. The 'tavern of the seas', one may cautiously assume, had a lingua franca that was distinctive but intelligible enough to the casual seeker after refreshment or entertainment. It was not until the 1870s that serious attempts were made to discipline this patois – commonly called the *taal* – into a literary language. It took another half-century before Afrikaans replaced High Dutch as an official language in South Africa.

But there were Afrikaners long before then. The first remembered use of the word was when Henry Bibault, in 1707, protested against a sentence of flogging imposed on him by order of the Company on the grounds that he was an Afrikaner and thus, in his opinion, not under the Company's jurisdiction. From the first, then, the word was associated with a protest. There are some who would contend that a feeling of resentment has been endemic in a people which felt itself to be perpetually subordinated or underrated, and that the language of protest, especially in demands for independence, has been an Afrikaner characteristic. For much of their history, so runs this contention, Afrikaners have felt threatened – by the Company, which ruled over them without their consent; by the British, who treated them as if they were under the occupation of a conqueror; by the possibility of being swamped by immigrants or having their way of life diluted by unwelcome intrusions. Furthermore, they were conscious from the beginning of being surrounded and outnumbered by indigenous peoples whom they regarded as barbarians; and they often felt that they were forever being misunderstood by a hostile world as a result of being traduced by those – such as English missionaries or foreign journalists – who did not understand them, their predicament or their just expectations. It is not difficult to visualize Afrikaners, like the Jews of the Old Testament, as those who had 'suffered under Pharaoh'. The principal manifesto of the Transvaal Republic, when it went to war with the British in 1899, was entitled 'A Century of Wrong'.

But this hypothesis is too simple to be accepted without all manner of qualifications; it is as delusive to make neat generalizations about the Afrikaners as it is to make them about any other nationality. There is a multiplicity of Afrikaner traditions, however much it might suit Afrikaner Nationalists to deny this plurality; in spite of all dragoonings, Afrikaners have never succumbed to that 'healthy unanimity' of opinion which some zealots have seen as desirable.

It is convenient to distinguish the words Afrikaner and Boer, which have sometimes been used interchangeably. Afrikaner merely means African, with a strong presumption of uniqueness. Afrikaners would certainly not include in that term the original inhabitants of South Africa, nor immigrants who spoke a different language; they would, however, have recognized those who called themselves Boers as a species of their own genus. Boer means farmer, and as early as the eighteenth century a different way of life was developing between the migrant Boer and the more sedentary Afrikaner. While the Boer was penetrating further and further into the interior there was developing in and around Cape Town, as the architecture demonstrated, a form of gracious living and the emergence of a class of country gentry. Many of these people regarded themselves, with justice, as the equals of the Company's higher officials. Later, with the coming of the British, their sons might find dignified employment in the governors' secretariat and become assimilated into a new society. A few became English in all but name but most retained their own identity. They would have spoken and written both English and High Dutch, and would have spoken the *taal* as well. They put their name to a particular attitude of mind – cultivated, tolerant and humane – that came to be called Cape Dutch liberalism and sometimes endured in individual members of families that had moved far from their original areas of settlement. Some examples may stand for many.

Jacques de Villiers and his two brothers, Pierre and Abraham, arrived at the Cape in 1689; all three were French Huguenots, born near La Rochelle, who had become refugees after the revocation of the Edict of Nantes in 1685. They prospered as farmers. Jacques de Villiers was one of the founders of the Cape wine industry and it was he who laid out the manor house of Boschendal in the Cape Dutch style of architecture. Directly, and through the ramifications of marriage, the de Villiers family has been woven into the fabric of South African history; in its diversity it is typical of the Afrikaner experience. Piet Retief, later revered as a Voortrekker hero, was a direct descendant of Jacques de Villiers through his mother's line.

Another relative by marriage was murdered at Retief's side in Natal, impaled on a stake by order of Dingaan, king of the Zulus. Yet another relative was Andries Pretorius, the avenger of Retief and victor of the battle of Blood River in 1838. There was not much of the liberal spirit among the Voortrekkers but the family also produced the first chief justice of the Union of South Africa in 1910, John Henry, first Baron de Villiers. René de Villiers (1910–92) grew up in the Orange Free State; he became a distinguished journalist, edited *The Star* of Johannesburg, and was then elected to Parliament as a member of the Progressive Party.

Jan Hendrik Hofmeyr (1845–1909) was one of the founders of Afrikaner party politics as the effective controller of the Afrikander Bond in the Cape from its early years in the 1880s; he was at ease both in English and in Afrikaner circles. He was one of the Cape delegates to the first Colonial Conference in London in 1887 on the occasion of Queen Victoria's golden jubilee; there he moved a resolution in favour of 'a closer union between the various parts of the British empire, by means of an imperial tariff'. He could be regarded as the embodiment of constitutional Afrikanerdom, a tradition very different from that represented by President Kruger of the Transvaal who could be described as the leader of militant Afrikanerdom.

Hofmeyr's biography was written by his nephew, also Jan Hendrik Hofmeyr, when the author was still in his teens. J. H. Hofmeyr the younger (1894–1948) was the exemplar *par excellence* of the liberal spirit in South African politics. He was an academic wonderchild: by the age of fifteen he had taken an honours degree at the University of the Cape of Good Hope and added to it an honours degree in mathematics a year later. He was elected to a Rhodes Scholarship in 1910 but was considered too young to go immediately to Oxford, and it was then that he wrote the *Life* of his uncle. At Oxford he took a double first in classical moderations and *literae humaniores* from Balliol College. At the age of twenty-three he was Professor of Classics at the precursor of the University of the Witwatersrand in Johannesburg, of which he became Principal two years later. In 1924 General Smuts brought him into politics as Administrator of the Transvaal. Hofmeyr entered Parliament as a member of Smuts's South African Party in 1929 and then, after the fusion with Hertzog's Nationalists, became Minister of the Interior, Public Health and Education. He carried his liberal convictions with him into the cabinet, where they were not always welcome. He opposed the restriction of the African franchise in 1936; in 1938 he resigned in protest against what he called 'a prostitution of the constitution' when General Hertzog, then Prime Minister, appointed an unqualified crony to represent 'Native interests' in the Senate. He rejoined the cabinet as Minister of Finance and of Education under Smuts in 1939. He was then generally regarded as the natural successor to Smuts, for whom he deputized several times as Prime Minister. After the war Hofmeyr became the principal target of the Nationalists, who portrayed him as a negrophile and hence a menace to the 'traditional South African way of life' based on racial segregation. This propaganda was sufficiently successful for members of Hofmeyr's own party to cast him as scapegoat for the loss of the general election in 1948. It is possible that Hofmeyr's career might have been still more distinguished but for the stultifying effects of his mother who prowled around him throughout his life like a medieval dragon guarding a treasure.

One of the leading cases in martial law is known by the short title of *Ex parte* Marais, and was decided by the Privy Council in London in 1902. It was a Boer War case, and it concerned the arrest under martial law of D. F. Marais, who was regarded by the British military authorities in the Cape as a fomenter of rebellion. His son, Professor Johannes Stephanus (Etienne) Marais, became one of the most distinguished of South African historians and, as chairman of the Academic Freedom Committee of the University of the Witwatersrand, led the vigorous protests against the Nationalist government's decision to exclude non-White students. His wife, whose father had been chaplain to General Botha during the Boer War, was a prominent member of the Black Sash, a women's organization which opposed the policy of *apartheid*, or racial segregation. Etienne Marais' political views were in polar opposition to those of his brother-in-law, the Reverend Willem Nicol, who had been Administrator of the Transvaal and a founder member of the Broederbond, the Afrikaner secret society which sought to transform South African society in conformity with ideas of racial zealotry.

It cannot, however, be denied that Cape liberalism was the creed of a minority and that the Cape itself had more than one tradition. A convenient illustration may be found in the careers of two Cape politicians of the same name. François Stephanus Malan (1871–1941) was educated at Victoria College, Stellenbosch, and Cambridge University. In 1895 he became editor of *Ons Land*, a Cape Town newspaper which supported the Afrikander Bond. He sympathized with the republicans during the Boer War and was imprisoned for a year for publishing a letter smuggled out of a concentration camp. At the national convention which drafted what became the Act of Union, Malan argued unsuccessfully for the extension of the colour-blind franchise of the Cape to the rest of South Africa. In 1910 he joined General Botha's Cabinet and supported the policy of conciliation between Afrikaners and the South African English. In 1936, by then a member of the Senate and no longer a minister, he fought another unavailing struggle to retain the common franchise for the Africans in the Cape Province. He was an elder of the Dutch Reformed Church, and in that capacity he wrote and spoke in defence of a theologian who was under attack for what were regarded as liberal heresies.

By no extension of vocabulary could liberalism be ascribed to Daniel François Malan (1874–1959), leader of the National Party in the Cape from 1913 until 1953 and, as Prime Minister from 1948 until 1954, the promoter of *apartheid*. But he did represent one tradition that was common both to Afrikaner liberals and to his own brand of Nationalism – a belief in constitutional legality. Some of the hardest-fought and most bitter episodes of his career occurred during the Second World War when he outmanœuvred those fellow-Afrikaners who did not hide their admiration for National Socialism and favoured direct action as a means to political power. In his insistence on the pre-eminence of Parliament, D. F. Malan could claim some affinity with the elder J. H. Hofmeyr.

Some have portrayed Paul Kruger as representing the non-parliamentary traditions of naked force and resistance to compromise. But Kruger's character was more complex than some of his admirers have recognized, and a better example of intransigent nationalism could be found in Christiaan Rudolph de Wet of the Orange Free State, one of the legendary commando leaders of the Boer War. De Wet believed that 'armed protest' was a legitimate form of politics. He was one of the 'bitter-enders' who in 1902 wished to continue the war, even at the risk of the extinction of Afrikanerdom; he never forgave those, like his brother, who surrendered to the British; he remained irreconcilable after the Peace of Vereeniging; and he went into open rebellion in 1914. The 'generals' of the Ossewa Brandwag (Sentinels of the Ox-Wagon) who flirted with rebellion during the Second World War would have found de Wet a more appropriate model than Kruger. Something of the de Wet tradition may linger on in the antics of the Afrikaner Weerstandsbeweging (Resistance Movement) which came into being in the 1970s to combat any relaxation of *apartheid*.

Amid this diversity, where is the 'typical Afrikaner' to be found? The South African English have a stock figure of ridicule. His name is van der Merwe, and he is perpetually involved in predicaments in which he demonstrates a well-developed stupidity. Doubtless he would deny these accounts of his adventures if he were present when they were related; but he is seldom there to listen for, except at a superficial level, most of the English and the Afrikaners form their opinion of each other by reputation rather than personal knowledge. Stories very like those about van der Merwe are told in other countries about Poles, or Irish or any nationality other than the narrator's; some of them, bizarrely enough, may be found in a slender volume entitled *The North Dakota Joke Book*. There is a kindlier satire of the *backveld* Boer in two volumes of short stories by Herman Charles Bosman, *Mafeking Road* and *Unto Dust*. The setting is one of the remote country districts in what is called the Bushveld. The narrator is Oom Schalk Lourens, a Boer who is *slim* underneath an appearance of simplicity – that is, he is one from whom no person of sense would buy a second-hand ox-wagon. ('Oom', literally 'uncle', is an affectionate term of respect; General Jan Smuts was sometimes known to his admirers as Oom Jannie and often called by his opponents Slim Jannie.) But the world of Bosman's crafty backwoodsman has long vanished in the wake of the motor car and as a consequence of urbanization. Boer families no longer trek by ox-wagon to the nearest church – which might be thirty miles away – for *nagmaal*, or the quarterly communion. Until about the 1930s the environs of a village church at these times seemed to harbour a commando in laager, complete with wives, children, servants and animals. What was essentially a religious gathering also served for gossip, trade and courtship, with here and there admonishment for a backslider. There are now other occasions and other meeting places for these activities. Nowadays, except in pageants or political demonstrations, Boers seldom travel by ox-wagon, and the authority of the *predikant*, or minister of the church, is not what it used to be.

The 'average Afrikaner' is an abstraction rather than a creature of flesh and blood. However, the Afrikaners as a people have become notorious over the past half-century as the creators of *apartheid*, or government by racial oligarchy. More recently still, they have become celebrated for abandoning their creation, voting themselves out of power and submitting themselves to the uncertainties of democracy in a multiracial society.

This book is an attempt to explain the genesis, aims, struggles and strategies of a complex and often divided people. Its subject matter is essentially the Afrikaner as a political animal, and its concentration therefore has been on those who have made the significant decisions. This means that, particularly when it is concerned with the events of the twentieth century, its focus has been on the National Party, its leaders and its aspirations. Two main themes may be discerned in the history of the Afrikaners. One is the urge towards independence, first from the Dutch East India Company and then from the British; the second is the survival of the Afrikaner nation itself. Twice, at least, an agonizing choice has had to be made between independence and survival. One was in 1902 in the debate on whether the war should be ended on British terms; the other was in 1990 when President de Klerk announced the end of *apartheid* and the concession of universal suffrage. Both these decisions amounted to a recognition that the Afrikaners' best chance of survival was by abandoning independence, even if that meant a long leap in the dark.

1 ARRIVALS

The first Europeans to settle in South Africa came in 1652 to what is now the city of Cape Town in an expedition sent by the Dutch East India Company to establish a refreshment station for its ships. What is surprising is not that the Dutch came when they did but why other Europeans had not established themselves much earlier at what looked like an attractive place. Francis Drake described it as the finest cape that he had seen in his voyage of circumnavigation in 1580; but he made no attempt to take possession. The Portuguese navigators who had long preceded Drake round Africa regarded the towering table-topped mountain that marked the Cape as no more than a dangerous landmark; to them it was the 'cape of storms', inhabited by predators. An English passenger on a Portuguese ship in peril in 1579 reflected what was probably the common opinion: 'the shore so evil that nothing could take land, and the land itself so full of Tigers and people that are savage and killers of all strangers that we had no hope of life nor comfort, but only in God and a good conscience.'[1]

This mistrust of the Cape dated from the beginning of Portuguese maritime ventures. Vasco da Gama's men had quarrelled with the indigenous people, whom they called Hottentots, in 1497. An expedition under da Saldanha had a more dangerous encounter a few years later when a party of Portuguese was attacked and da Saldanha himself wounded. The final discouragement came in 1510 when the viceroy, d'Almeida, returning from the Portuguese Indies, was attacked and killed on the shores of Table Bay, along with sixty of his ship's company. Thereafter the Portuguese rounded the Cape at a respectful distance on their way to and from the Indies. It had little to offer them, for they were in search of precious objects, notably gold and ivory. Thus, when they established themselves in southern Africa, it was well up the east coast, at Sofala, in what is now the northern part of Mozambique; there were no quick riches to be had at the Cape. The British showed no effective interest either, although the advantages of a refreshment station on the way to India were recognized. In 1608, one official of the English East India Company recommended the establishment of a permanent settlement; in 1619 there was a suggestion that the English and Dutch might set up a joint station; in 1620 two Englishmen purported to annex the Cape but this empty gesture had no consequences. The Cape offered spectacular scenery but little else; like the Portuguese, the Dutch thought the Natives to be hostile and unsavoury in their habits. A witness with the first Dutch fleet in 1595 described the Hottentots thus:

> They are small in stature, ugly of countenance, the hair on their heads stands as though scorched by the sun, and looks like that of a thief who has been dried out by hanging a long while . . . With regard to their speech, it is as if one were to hear some turkey cocks making a noise . . . They would also without a doubt, as one could observe, have eaten any of our company, since they made little of eating raw guts after they had drained out the muck a little with a finger, from which it can readily be surmised that they must be man-eaters.[2]

There were no cannibals at the Cape, but one must not expect scientific observation from early travellers; and the habits of one race are not always appealing to others. A traveller twenty years later was briefer but little more complimentary: '*Zy stinken, als men onder de wind het van hen staan.*' ('They stink, as you will discover if you stand to windward of them.')

But it takes at least two to make a quarrel, and the Natives were not always hostile. The survivors of the *Haerlem*, a Dutch Indiaman wrecked in Table Bay in 1647, who lived on shore for a year, had a different tale to tell. They found the soil to be fertile and well watered, suitable for the growing of vegetables, and the inhabitants to be 'docile' and willing to trade their cattle and sheep. It is likely that hostility in the past had been provoked by some act of wantonness by Europeans; this was demonstrated by the Natives' anger towards crewmen of the rescuing fleet who had shot eight or nine of the Hottentots' cattle and carried off the carcasses without payment. All this was set down in the Remonstrance presented to the Council of XVII, the governing body of the Dutch East India Company, in July 1649, based on the experiences of the *Haerlem*'s survivors. This emphasized the advantages of a garden at the Cape, with a fort to protect it; then, switching the argument, it turned to the merits of religious conversion as a by-product of occupation: some of the Natives' children might be employed as servants and brought up as Christians. 'The proposed fort and garden will therefore not only tend to the advantage and profit of the Company, but to the salvation also of many lives'.[3]

Jan van Riebeeck, whom the Company chose to lead the expedition and found the settlement, was much less sanguine. The fort should be strongly built, he argued, since the Natives were naturally brutal, living without conscience and not to be trusted. No general conclusions could be drawn from the experiences of the *Haerlem*'s survivors, who were thankful merely to be alive and had the good sense to know that they had everything to gain by a show of meekness towards the Natives; but their problems and those of the leader of a settlement were quite different things. However, van Riebeeck was bound by his instructions, and those were emphatic on a display of benevolence towards the Natives. The Company's aims were not extensive; it wished to establish a refreshment station at minimum cost, which meant that it was dependent on local trade for fresh produce. Van Riebeeck was instructed to seek out the best cattle pastures in the neighbourhood of the fort,

> for which purpose a good understanding with the natives will be necessary in order to make them, in course of time, accustomed to intercourse with you, and so attract them. In this, great prudence is necessary, and you shall have to take special care not to injure their cattle which they are herding or bringing on, as this would repel them from us, as has often been shown.[4]

The Company had put its finger on the source of much discord to come – the ownership and distribution of cattle. Van Riebeeck's first proclamation closely followed his instructions and was intended to establish and maintain good relations with the Natives and to assure them of the benevolent intentions of the newcomers; like many in authority who were to follow him, he tried to limit provocation by the settlers and to reinforce his orders by the threat of punishment. Temptation was not to be put in the Natives' way: arms and tools were to be looked after carefully and, if any should be stolen, those suspected of the theft should not, without the commander's knowledge, 'be pursued, beaten, or frightened with a sour face by anyone'. A scale of punishments was prescribed for the careless or truculent servant of the Company.

All arms and tools . . . shall be debited to those who have
received them, and should anyone lose them, he shall receive
50 stripes at a post and forfeit his rations 8 days, or undergo
such heavier punishment as the importance of the case shall
require. And should anyone ill treat, beat, or push a native –
whether he be right or wrong – he shall in the presence of
the latter receive 50 lashes, that the natives may be made
to understand that the deed has been against our will, and
that we desire to associate with them in all friendliness
and kindliness, according to the orders and object of our
Lords Principal . . . Everyone is likewise expressly forbidden,
whatever his position or rank may be, to undertake the least
barter or trade with the savages without the consent of the
Commander.[5]

It is worth noting that the presumption of guilt against a Settler, in
any dispute with a Native, was introduced by van Riebeeck.

The first results of the settlement were meagre. The Natives were
disinclined to trade and van Riebeeck asked in vain for power to
coerce them. There was probably more to the reluctance of the
Natives to part with their cattle than discontent with the goods
which the Company offered in exchange; they were facing a threat
to their livelihood. From the first there was a profound difference
of understanding between Settlers and Natives on the possession
and usage of land. All the indigenous inhabitants which the European settlers were to encounter for the next century at least drew no
distinction between use and ownership. Those who were known to
van Riebeeck and his successors as Hottentots and Bushmen were
herders and hunters; the idea of the exclusive possession of a piece
of land was outside their experience. They pursued their livelihood
where the grasses grew and where game was to be found. To the
Europeans, occupation meant possession. In this, and in the absence of natural boundaries, lay much future conflict. This was the
South African version of the struggle between the farmer and the
cowman which was later to become one of the perennial discords in
the western expansion of the United States.

The Natives had long but sporadic experience of encounters with
the crews of passing ships, transients who would depart as myster-
iously as they had arrived; settlement was something new and
menacing. On the other side, van Riebeeck's tariff of punishments
indicates that those under his command were far from benevolently

disposed towards their new neighbours, whom they regarded with a mixture of abhorrence and fear. There was a Western superstition that barbarous peoples were descended from Ham, whose fault was to have seen Noah, his father, in his drunkenness and to have told his brothers about it. Noah's curse fell on Canaan, the son of Ham: 'Cursed be Canaan; a servant of servants shall he be unto his brethren'.[6] There were also those who believed in the great chain of being and would find a place for primitive man somewhere between the apes and civilized man. Whether any of van Riebeeck's company held such thoughts may be doubted; it is more likely that they simply regarded the Natives as stinking and thieving savages. There is some evidence that the line drawn at first was not one of colour but between heathen and Christian. There was a much-quoted event in 1664, when Pieter van Meerhoff, surgeon to the settlement, married a Hottentot woman named Eva who had been baptized a Christian. The wedding was celebrated in style: the bride was given a dowry, the bridegroom was promoted and the commander and his council were hosts at a marriage feast to signify their approval. Eva had been brought up in van Riebeeck's household where she had learnt Dutch and made herself useful as an interpreter. She was a woman of spirited, if wandering, affections, and her story did not have a happy ending. Van Meerhoff was killed on an expedition to Madagascar and his widow turned to prostitution. She was sentenced more than once to Robben Island, which was used from the first as a prison. She was dead by 1674; her children by van Meerhoff were educated at the Company's expense and one of her daughters married a successful European farmer.[7] Miscegenation existed within and without the bonds of wedlock.

However, the most important circumstance for what would much later be called race relations was that, from its beginnings, van Riebeeck's settlement was a slave society. Some slaves had come out as the personal property of members of the expedition. A consignment of slaves arrived in 1658 and another in 1659; from then onwards, throughout the Company's rule, coloured slaves outnumbered white settlers. A decision to rely on slaves rather than on sponsored immigration from Europe was taken in the second decade of the eighteenth century. Immigrants were not easy to find and when they could be found they had a tendency towards insubordination which made them troublesome subjects. The Company was a vast trading concern, perhaps the biggest that had yet existed in Europe. So far as the burghers of the Netherlands were concerned it was something in which they might invest their money but it was seldom regarded as a desirable career for their sons. The Company picked up its servants wherever it could find them; they were a cosmopolitan bunch, of mixed social antecedents. The Cape was well down in the hierarchy of the Company's stations abroad; it took what it could get. It was not a centre of enlightened thought. One consequence of slavery was that colour and social inferiority became associated in the minds of Whites.

> More than any other single factor, [slavery] established a presumption that whites were naturally masters and members of a privileged group . . . while non-whites were meant to be their servants and social inferiors . . . a slaveholding mentality remained the wellspring of white supremacist thought and action long after the institution . . . that originally sustained it had been relegated to the dustbin of history.[8]

Another consequence was that there was an increasing dependence on slaves or, failing them, on Hottentot servants for manual labour. There developed a form of European society without a substantial artisan class.

> The fact that 'White South Africa' started its career as a slave-owning community has had certain important results for the older (Afrikaans-speaking) part of the population. During the eighteenth century there were complaints on the part of officials and others that the burghers were losing the habit of working with their hands, since they considered such labour to be fit only for slaves. The Cape landowners, it was said, were not farmers at all, but owners of plantations. As on the farms, so in the towns. In Cape Town and the villages that gradually grew up in the western districts most of the labour, whether skilled, semi-skilled or unskilled, was done by slaves.[9]

The importation of slaves meant the addition of yet another layer to an already heterogeneous population. There were the Hottentots and Bushmen. There were the Europeans, some already domiciled at the Cape, others who were transients. There were now the slaves, themselves a polyglot mixture – some from the Guinea Coast, some from Madagascar, others from the Malay archipelago. From all this there emerged yet another layer, the half-breeds who would come to be called the Cape Coloureds. 'Bushmen, Hottentots, Slaves, Europeans – behold the ancestors of the Cape Coloured People . . . during the first twenty years of its existence no less than 75 per cent of the children born at the Cape of slave mothers were half-breeds.'[10]

A mild slave regime is a contradiction in terms, and the Cape was no exception. The records show a grisly schedule of punishments. Death by torture was the penalty for the more heinous crimes, murder and rape (especially when the victims were Whites). In 1713, a slave called Anthony of Mozambique, convicted of raping a white woman, was sentenced 'to be bound to a cross and to have his flesh pinched from his body by hot irons; his body was then to be broken without *coup de grâce*, decapitated, and finally exposed to the birds'[11] Andrew Sparrman, a Swede who visited Cape Town in 1786, thought that the town was disgraced by the spectacle of the gallows, with its instruments of torture, in a dominating position opposite the fort.[12] Earl Macartney, the first British governor, abolished death by torture in 1796 against the advice of the Company's administrators who claimed that the severest examples were necessary as a deterrent, for the security of the community.

In spite of manifold difficulties, van Riebeeck accomplished his mission of establishing a refreshment station; passing ships, with those of the Company given priority, could be supplied with fresh water, fruit, meat and vegetables. However, none of the Company's servants was ever allowed to forget that the Council of XVII never intended to spend more than an irreducible minimum on the station at the Cape. It wished to limit its territorial responsibilities; it was as much to keep the Company's servants in as to keep marauders out that van Riebeeck planted a boundary hedge along the Liesbeeck River (still to be seen in Kirstenbosch gardens), and the Council of XVII once thought seriously about trying to turn the Cape peninsula into an island by digging a canal from False Bay to Table Bay. Colonization was never the Company's policy, yet colonization was made necessary by the exercise of strict economy. Cattle could be acquired by barter from the Hottentots but fruit and vegetables had to be grown, and van Riebeeck thought it cheaper to buy them than to involve the Company in farming. In 1657 nine of the Company's servants were released from their indentures and allowed to farm as 'free burghers'. They were the first colonists, ancestors of the Afrikaner people. At first there was not much of freedom in their new condition; they had been emancipated because the Company needed what they could grow; they were instruments of production who were there because it was thought that they would be cheap. Also, since they could be taxed, they were a source of revenue. They were intended to be auxiliaries

of the Company and not its competitors; they were to sell their
produce at fixed prices to the Company and might trade with
passing ships on their own account only to supply what deficiencies
there might be after the Company had done its own business. But
what was intended as a limited expedient had irrevocable consequences. One was the first of the Company's wars against the
Hottentots, provoked by the settlement of free burghers in the
Liesbeeck valley on land which the Hottentots regarded as grazing
pastures.

The free burghers grew in numbers and formed a potentially
discordant minority. Scarcely a year after the first emancipation
they had staged their first 'strike', withholding their produce and
declaring that 'we will not be slaves to the Company'. Some decamped, leaving their debts unpaid; others found it easier to make
a living by tavern keeping, or cattle trading on the black market
than by arable farming. Those who still remained as farmers tended
to move inland in search of fresh fields where the Company's
supervision would be less onerous. The *trek boer*, the itinerant
farmer, was making his appearance.

In 1671 the system of private farming was extended on instructions from the Netherlands. Official farming was to be run down
and transferred as far as possible to free burghers. It took some time
for the new policy to take effect: there were not enough free
burghers, there was too little immigration and there was the dis-
traction of another Hottentot war which dragged on for four years
from 1673 until 1677. It was not until the appointment of Simon
van der Stel as commander in 1679 that the settlement began to
expand rapidly. Van der Stel recruited farmers by freeing indentured servants of the Company before their time had expired. Some
of them were settled fifty miles inland, on a site of van der Stel's
choosing, which became the new town and district of Stellenbosch;
the noble avenue of oaks which he planted still adds distinction to
the town. (He also built Groot Constantia, which remains as one of
the grandest of mansions in what came to be called the Cape Dutch
style of architecture.) In 1689 there arrived the first substantial
batch of immigrants – nearly two hundred Huguenots, refugees
from France after the revocation of the Edict of Nantes in 1685 and
sent out by the Company. Van der Stel had no intention of letting
them become an immiscible minority: they were scattered among
the existing population, some around Stellenbosch, some in yet
another new district at Drakenstein and some at what came to be
called Fransch Hoek from their presence. The official use of French

was not permitted. The Huguenots made excellent colonists. Within a few generations they and their descendants had stirred and diversified Cape society. They were of a higher social class than most of the free burghers and they brought with them new skills, notably the cultivation of the vine; they were the founders of what was to become a prosperous wine industry. The transformation of many names of French origin is evidence of assimilation: Colberts, for instance, became Grobelaars, Villons became Viljoens, and Pinards became Pienaars. 'The old sluggish Batavian stock (not of the best quality, for the first settlers were as a rule of the poorest and least respectable class) was leavened with a finer French strain, and tinctured with a little native blood.'[13]

However limited its original aims may have been, the Company had now acquired a colony at the Cape and with it problems of governance that did not always harmonize with the purposes of a commercial enterprise; its critics would say that it could never make up its mind whether its first duty was towards its shareholders or its dependants. It had acquired subjects – the free burghers had taken an oath to the Company as well as to the States–General – and it was constrained to formulate something like a foreign policy with regard to an expanding frontier zone, leading to increased contact and points of friction with the native tribes. Violence on the frontier was seldom far from the surface of life. There were disputes with the Natives over land and over cattle. Cattle-rustling, proven or alleged, would be followed by punitive expeditions in which aggrieved farmers would band together in a *posse*; later this would be called a commando and regularized into a system which came close to that of compulsory military service in time of need. In time, a new word would be added to the English language.

But all was not hostility between the races. More and more Hottentots were becoming servants of the Europeans. These were regarded as 'tame', by contrast with their wilder compatriots in the frontier zones. The Company havered between contrasting attitudes: on the one hand the Hottentots were cozened as providers of cattle; at the same time they were regarded as potentially dangerous. It was easier to take a benevolent attitude towards the Hottentots from the prospect of Cape Town than in the frontier zone, and it was a constant complaint by farmers that the Company was biased in the Hottentots' favour. If travellers' tales are to be believed, it is difficult to see in the Hottentots the lineaments of the noble savage; at close quarters they looked more like the Yahoos whom Gulliver encountered in the country of the Houyhnhnms.

Barlow's *Journal* is typical: 'They are the heathenest people that I have ever seen, neither knowing good nor worshipping neither God nor Devil, going about more like brute beasts than mortal men, and they will eat any raw fish or guts of beasts which are thrown away.'[14] There were some who saw a depressing convergence of manners between some of the white frontier dwellers and their Hottentot neighbours. These strictures may refer to some of the relatively small class of knechts, landless Whites. Simon van der Stel complained of the existence of frontier vagabonds, some of them trading illicitly in cattle and some living with native concubines.

European settlement was in the end fatal to the Hottentots as a separate community. There was a severe epidemic of smallpox in 1713; the virus, it was said, came in the laundry sent ashore by a visiting ship. There was a second serious epidemic in 1755. Most of the Hottentots were eventually driven into European employment as herdsmen, wagon drivers or farm labourers; some served in the Company's militia. The Bushmen proved more formidable adversaries: they possessed the bow and the poisoned arrow. At times the settlers hunted them like vermin; often both men and women were killed and the children taken into what was called apprenticeship but which differed little from servitude.

The settlement soon spread outwards from the Cape peninsula. The available land there was quickly taken up or exhausted. New farmers would have to seek their fortune inland; but that diaspora frustrated the purpose for which colonization was needed – the ready supply of cheap provisions. What the colonist–farmers lacked was a stable market: the arrival of ships was uncertain and their demand irregular; booms and slumps followed each other in random sequence. Officials often traded illicitly, using their status to take the cream of the market. Much depended on the zeal and integrity of the men at the top; corruption was an added temptation when officials knew themselves to be months away from enquiry or rebuke. Beyond Cape Town, governance was uncertain; and in time its absence bred a contempt for authority on those occasions when it attempted to exert itself, in the outer districts usually in the form of the magistrate or the mixed force of armed Company servants and Hottentot militiamen. The country was habitually under-governed. The magisterial district of Graaff-Reinet was the size of Portugal, and the landdrost or magistrate in charge was assisted only by a secretary and a force of half-a-dozen mounted police. There was a board of heemraden or local councillors, but these were colonists who were seldom on the side of authority in any dispute which involved men like themselves. The trek boer, the wandering farmer, was beginning to regard himself as a man outside, or perhaps above, authority. There was usually tension between those who regarded the Cape as their permanent home and those who were waiting or hoping to go somewhere else; the latter included practically all the Company's servants, and among them morale was seldom high. The Cape was low in the Company hierarchy, so that the ambitious looked for promotion elsewhere and the less fortunate had often come to regard themselves as failures.

The Cape had already acquired a reputation as the 'tavern of the seas'; the word tavern was a metaphor for something more robust than mere good-fellowship. Cape Town alternated between a backwater and a thoroughfare, depending on how many ships were in port and how many sailors, passengers, hangers-on and the like were experiencing the various attractions which the tavern of the seas offered to its patrons. One contemporary observer detailed the provenance of the inhabitants of Cape Town: there were Netherlanders, English, French, High Germans, Savoyards, Hungarians, Malays, men of Malabar, Cingalese, Javanese, men of Macassar, Bengal, Amboyna, Bambana, China, Madagascar, Angola, Guinea. The Dutch language was already becoming encrusted with loan words from languages spoken to the East and the West; year by year the spoken tongue differed more and more from that of the Netherlands. This was particularly so in the world of the *trek boer* as he ventured further and further into the interior. Simon van der Stel did something to systematize the occupation of land by instituting the 'loan farm', usually of 6,000 acres, which could be taken up for a modest sum payable in Cape Town. The loan farm was easy to occupy and not very difficult to leave. Sir Keith Hancock was to describe the 6,000-acre farm as 'the basic fact' of South African history. It meant a constantly moving pastoral frontier, where 'the Boers developed as a class of land occupiers, hunters, and stock owners'.[15] The word 'boer' was to become a term of art. Literally, it meant 'farmer'; it was now more characteristic of the frontiersman, leading a peripatetic rather than static existence. Later still the word would be used to identify a species of the genus Afrikaner.

Cape Town itself was looking less and less like an outpost of the Netherlands. The free burghers enjoyed few of the political rights that were assumed by the colonists of North America, for instance, nor did they either possess or develop any representative institutions of their own. They were under the rule of the Company. There is little to be found here of Calvin's respect for authority; too much has been made, by later historians, of Calvinist influence during the formative years of Cape history. The Cape lacked schools, churches and an institutionalized intellectual life. The Company existed to make money. It now found itself required to provide government and the scaffolding of civilized life to subjects who were not always willing to welcome its attentions. Religious services were held at first in the fort at Cape Town, according to the rites of the Nederduitse Gereformeerde Kerk. The foundations of a church building were not laid until 1678. Ministers of the Church were employees of the Company, usually preaching to other employees for whom Sunday services were compulsory. The beginnings of schooling were entrusted to an official called the *sieckentrooster* or 'sick comforter'. The holders of this office do not seem to have been of intellectual distinction; it was not, after all, a calling which offered much hope of advancement. The first school was closed because all the pupils had run away; the second was nearly ruined by the habitual drunkenness of the reigning *sieckentrooster*, Ernestus Beck. However, the fortunate appearance of a comet was interpreted as a sign of the Almighty's particular displeasure, and Beck was deported to Batavia in 1665.[16] This is one of the first of many examples of the Company's authority; until well into the eighteenth century it used its power to deport free burghers who had infringed its rules or displeased its servants. The Cape was a victualling station, and one of the central questions was who was to provide the victuals. This was the issue in a quarrel between Willem Adriaan van der Stel, Simon's son and successor, and some of the more prominent free burghers which ended with van der Stel's recall in 1707. This episode has been described, rather too exuberantly, as a constitutional episode of seminal importance. (South Africa has not lacked its Whig historians.) A more sceptical enquiry reveals it as a less elevated matter of markets and monopolies. Van der Stel had abused his official position to corner what was already an oversupplied market. Protests began in 1705, and the dispute rumbled on for two years. The dissidents were led by Henning Huising, a former soldier turned meat marketeer, who was rich by local standards. Most of his followers were prosperous men who found their fortunes threatened. Van der Stel used his legal powers to attempt to stifle the protests: one of the protesters, Johannes Rotterdam, was deported to Batavia; another, Adam Tas, was imprisoned and on his release called his house 'Libertas'. This pun found its way into all the schoolbooks used by white South Africans and gave the affair a retrospective constitutional significance.

The affair generated considerable resentment in Cape Town and it had its consequences. For the first time the word Afrikaner was used to distinguish resident Whites from Company servants. Hendrik Bibault, of Stellenbosch, who was to be flogged for public rowdiness, denied that the Company had any rights over him because he was an Afrikaner. This was not the *Civis Romanus sum* of one who appealed to higher authority, but rather the outraged cry of a disturber of the peace who denied that he was subject to any authority. It is not easy to find heroes in the early history of the Cape. Van der Stel's mistake was to deport some of his critics to the Netherlands, where they could petition the Council of XVII directly; they did not rely on any principles of justice or freedom, but merely accused van der Stel of cheating the Company by trading on his own account. This was an effective argument, and van der Stel was recalled.

The episode did bring to the Council's attention some of the conditions which made the Company's trading account less profitable than it ought to have been. It also demonstrated the capacity of free burghers to make trouble for the authorities and may therefore have had something to do with the decision in 1717 to abandon assisted immigration from Europe: the Cape would have to supply its labour needs from the natural increase of its inhabitants and by such slaves as it could breed or acquire. For once the Council of XVII had the Cape high on their agenda; in 1716 they posed a set of questions to be answered by the local administration. Could more white immigrants be absorbed? Would European farmers be cheaper and more efficient than slaves? How many artisans were needed? If existing industries could not support the existing white population, what new industries could be devised? The answers were defeatist and despondent; only one respondent thought there was a future for white immigrants. His colleagues thought otherwise, that the Cape could not absorb a larger white population than it already possessed, that few artisans were needed, and there was no prosperous future for wine or grain farmers. It would be neither wise nor profitable to substitute white labourers for slaves; they would be insubordinate and prone to drunkenness; significantly enough, it was argued that their role would be limited, since unskilled labour could by custom be performed only by slaves. Indeed, the replies confirmed everything that the retired Governor-General van Hoorn had said when he passed through in 1610: 'and here is such a mess and everything so unfinished that I am at times reminded of the saying . . . that truly God Almighty neither cares for nor preserves the Company . . . Your Highness can have no conception of the miserable state in which everything is in this place.'[17]

By 1710, however, the Cape was already a slave society in which, it was reported, there were 995 free adults and 1,554 slaves.

2 DISPERSAL

It is important to keep in mind the geography of South Africa. There is an excellent short description in James Bryce's *Impressions of South Africa*, published in 1897, to which I am indebted.

Roughly speaking, Africa south of the Zambesi River consists of three regions. First there is a strip of lowland running round the coast from Cape Town, eastward past Durban and then turning north along the coast of Mozambique until it reaches the mouth of the Zambesi. Between Cape Town and Durban, a distance of about 1,000 miles, this strip is often very narrow where the hills, such as Table Mountain, descend close to the sea. Beyond Durban the strip widens until north of Mozambique it extends from sixty to eighty miles. The wider the strip, the more unhealthy becomes the land – swampy, mosquito-ridden and malarious.

Behind the coastal strip rise the hills. Between them, in the Cape peninsula, there are fertile valleys running for about sixty miles inland. This is good arable land; here may be found vineyards and intensive fruit farming. Unlike the rest of South Africa the western Cape has a Mediterranean climate. Then the ground rises sharply to a plateau running from about 3,000 to nearly 6,000 feet above sea level. This is the high *veld* which stretches through the central and northern Cape province, the Orange Free State and the central and northern Transvaal. The great plateau ends in the eastern Transvaal where the land descends to what is called the bush *veld*.

Through the plateau, running for nearly 1,600 miles north-east-wards, is the range of mountains known as the Drakensberg, the mountains of the dragon. On the borders of Lesotho, the country that lies at the junction of the Cape province, the Orange Free State and Natal, the mountains rise up to 11,000 feet and swoop down in spectacular disorder on the eastern side. (Some romantics have

classified mountains into the bland and the diabolical. In Africa,
Kilimanjaro viewed from afar is as bland as a Christmas pudding;
the summit of its neighbour, Mount Kenya, is a diabolical fang of
rock and ice. The Drakensberg are diabolical and, as their name
suggests, they have their legendary demons; the Mont aux Sources
is reputed to be haunted by a ghostly leopard.) The Drakensberg
encompass the land of the Sotho people on three sides; there they
are at their highest and form for sixty miles or so the one natural
boundary in South Africa. Elsewhere they are an obstacle rather
than a barrier; there are passes, and they can be circumvented.

> These great and dominant physical facts – a low coast belt, a
> high interior plateau, a lofty, rugged mountain-range running
> nearly parallel to, and not very far from, the shore of the
> ocean, whence the rain-clouds come, a strong sun, a dry
> climate – have determined the character of South Africa in
> many ways. They explain the very remarkable fact that South
> Africa has, broadly speaking, no rivers.[1]

There are rivers, but none of them is navigable and many of them
shrink to mere trickles in the rainless winter months. Thus the country
lacks any means of easy transportation and possesses no natural
internal boundaries except the high peaks of the Drakensberg. The
Orange and the Limpopo rivers, as marked on the map, run for
impressive lengths but they contain little water for three-quarters of
the year and most of their tributaries shrink in the dry season to a
chain of pools. These features were particularly significant in the
history of the ever-moving eastern frontier of the early Cape settlement, the friction points where the trek boers jarred up against the
Bantu-speaking peoples, tribes as nomadic as themselves and much
more populous. In this region there existed what was called, with
some hyperbole, the Great Fish River; but the straggling course of this
erratic stream, which meanders now from north to south, now from
east to west, and which could normally be forded anywhere along its
length, was no effective frontier – as useless, politically, as the cairn
erected by Governor van Plettenberg in 1778 to mark the point
beyond which trek boers were forbidden to venture.

South African rivers formed neither boundaries nor natural lines
of penetration into the interior. Thus the usual method of transport
was the ox-wagon; it could serve as a carrier of goods and as a
mobile home, and when a number were formed into a circle – the
laager – they became a formidable defensive rampart. Much later,
the ox-wagon would be adopted by some Nationalist Afrikaners as

the symbol of their people, the *Volk*. It was slow, but it was reliable and it got there in the end. It was not the symbol that would appeal instinctively to all men, but it was thought to reflect certain facets of the Boer character. By the end of the eighteenth century, the word *boer*, which originally meant 'farmer', had been adopted as a generic name for those Afrikaners who were colonizing the high *veld*. A distinction could already be drawn between the Boer frontiersman and his sedentary kinsmen who were making the Cape peninsula bloom. In the western Cape the tradition was that families settled on the land, developed it and then passed it on to their children and their children's children. Groot Constantia, originally the property of Simon van der Stel, resembled one of the greater mansions of the American South, except that its riches came from wine rather than cotton. Constantia wine was said to have been

PLATE 1. *Groot Constantia, Cape Peninsula* (Courtesy of S. V. Maxwell © 1993).

appreciated by Baudelaire; another wine farmer, Cloete by name, corresponded with Frederick the Great. There was developing in Cape Town and its neighbouring districts a settled society, graced in its upper tiers by an elegance of life. An inventory from Boschendal, owned by the de Villiers family, mentioned 'sofas, easy chairs and dining chairs with horsehair upholstery, mahogany-framed mirrors, a grandfather clock, cabinets with silver inlays, sideboards, paintings with gilded frames, several dining tables, a four-poster and other bed with drapery, carpets, curtains, cuspidors and kettles, a large collection of silverware and crockery'.[2] The Cape possessed within its diversity of peoples a sophisticated society which could be called Afrikaner, no more out of touch with Europe than the American colonists and a great deal closer than the Company's servants in the Dutch East Indies.

Thus two types of Afrikaner were developing – the settled bourgeoisie of the western Cape and the Boers of the plateau. It was the Boers who benefited from the system of 'loan farms' which could, by prescriptive right, be regarded as settled possession; they found it easy to obtain loan farms for their sons. It was easy, too, to move onwards if grazing was exhausted, the soil eroded or neighbours became tiresome. Boer dwellings were often of adobe, akin to the 'soddy' of the Western pioneers in the United States and for the same reason, the scarcity of timber. One set of Afrikaners built substantial houses and churches; another took the family bible with it into the wilderness. Architecture, it was said, ended at Swellendam.

One is dependent on travellers' descriptions of the Boer way of life, and since their tendency is to emphasize the rare or the abnormal it is not easy to reconstruct the everyday life of the Boer. But certain recurrent themes emerge. One is the hospitality of the Boer to the White stranger – a reaction, perhaps, to a land in which there were no carvanserais, but a sign of warm- heartedness none the less. On the less favourable side, there are accounts of the cramped narrowness of life – the single room for daytime use, often shared with servants and animals; the absence of all but the crudest pieces of furniture; the unglazed windows, sometimes closed by hide screens; the floor of stamped cow-dung, seldom polished; the sombre, bearded men of the household with their unlettered children and frequently pregnant wives. Each Boer household – on trek, each group of wagons – formed a small society of its own. There would be the head of the family and his wife. There would probably be sons and daughters-in-law, with their progeny, and perhaps a grandfather or grandmother. Then there would be the servants –

Hottentots mostly, with perhaps an 'apprentice' Bushman young-
ster and sometimes, but by no means always, a slave or two. It was
the servants or slaves who would do the manual work, including
the herding of stock and the milking of cows; the Boer women
would supervise the household while the men habitually hunted,
for the country abounded in wild animals.

As the Boers moved further and further into the interior so the
Company's authority over them diminished. There developed not so
much a contempt for the law as a disposition to regard it as irrelevant;
they administered their own form of rough justice to their retainers
and regarded this as nobody's business but their own. However, the
link with Cape Town would never quite be broken; its markets were
needed for the sale of cattle and the purchase of lead and gunpowder,
salt, sugar, tobacco and cloth. Sometimes household necessities could
be bought or bartered from smouses (pedlars, often Jewish) who made
irregular appearances. There might be visits from itinerant ministers
of the Church, useful for marriages and christenings. Simple funerals
might be performed by the head of the household and ended with a
psalm; by all accounts the Boers were devout and greatly addicted to
psalm-singing.

It could be argued that the Boers practised the worst form of
agriculture, very different from that of the settled farmers of the
western Cape who regarded their land as something to be developed rather than merely exploited. The Hottentots had destructive ways but they usually moved on before their stock-grazing
permanently damaged the soil. Some have thought the Boer to be
more destructive than the Hottentot because he stayed longer and
caused more erosion before he was forced to move on by his own
wasteful methods. It could be said that he had a craving for land in
general but a liking for no land in particular. There was little to
distinguish one square mile of the high *veld* from another.

How lawless was the frontier? First, it must be remembered that
the frontier was a zone rather than a clearly demarcated barrier.
There were certainly outlaw bands, some of mixed black and white
parentage. They were likely to be stock thieves and even more likely
to be regarded as outcasts both from Boer and tribal society. The
Boers themselves were lawless only in the sense that they tended to
substitute practices of their own for the regulations of the Company. There were customary codes of conduct which they observed
in relations with each other. They practised a rough egalitarianism;
in the frontier zones everyone was somebody though few were
anybody in particular.

It was different in Cape Town where a stratified society had developed. At the apex came the senior officials – those who had access to the governor – and their ladies. Most of these were, by the middle of the eighteenth century, expatriates themselves, coming to the Cape from the Company's stations in the east and often choosing, on retirement, to go to Java rather than Holland. Below the class of higher officials came the wealthier merchants and farmers. Below them, not well thought of but still superior to any persons of colour, came the remainder of the resident Whites, themselves divided by intricate gradations of status. There were the proprietors of taverns and boarding houses; lesser merchants and shopkeepers; not many artisans, but some who had established themselves as foremen and sometimes as employers of coloured workmen. Among the lower ranks of the Company's servants were gaolers and officers of the forces of law and order. Lower down still, there was a stratum, not very numerous, of 'free Blacks'; some were manumitted slaves. At the bottom came all other persons of colour – servants, slaves, apprentices and Hottentots in Company employment. The word Afrikaner, in a variety of spellings, had become a term of art to distinguish the settled inhabitants from officials, travellers, passing sailors and other transients. It is possible, thus early, to recognize a certain exclusiveness in those who used the word to describe themselves: it distinguished those who had a stake in the country. There was already an ambiguity of attitude towards the Company and its officials. On the one hand they were regarded with a certain suspicion (envy might not be too strong a word) as persons with different interests whose futures and fortunes lay in places other than the Cape and who were, moreover, possessed of authority which could cramp the Afrikaner's freedom to do as he chose. On the other hand, the Company was a shield against enemies within; its penal code might be a scourge to errant Whites, but it was also a protection against the recurrent nightmare of a slave uprising. Within Afrikaner society, in the last resort, colour was more important than class. There was already the beginnings of a substratum of 'poor Whites' – those without visible means of support, ignorant, degenerate and occasionally dangerous. They were sometimes joined by runaway slaves, deserters from ships or from the Company's service; if they were White there was a limit to the caste that they could lose; they would still be regarded as Afrikaners.

Territorial expansion had never been part of the Company's purpose, but in a land without natural frontiers it was impossible to prevent the eastward movement of the *trek* Boers, until they found their path impeded by the westward movement of the Bantu-speaking peoples. It is one of the myths of South African history that the *veld* was vacant land, ready for first occupation. The eastern Cape frontier in the early eighteenth century was a vaguely defined area lying beyond the Gamtoos river; it was there or thereabouts that black Africans, Bantu-speaking as distinct from Hottentots, first encounted Afrikaners (as distinct from the more adventurous traders or missionaries). Whites usually called them Caffres or Kaffirs; the word is of Arabic origin and means 'unbelievers'. Later it was to become a pejorative term in Afrikaans and was deeply resented by the people to whom it was applied. It is used here in the same spirit as the use of the words Hottentot and Bushman – part of the idiom of the times.

Early in the eighteenth century trade in ivory and cattle began between Whites and Africans across the frontier; there were also gun-runners and liquor sellers. The Company disapproved of the trade, but found it impossible to stop it. There was a scandal in 1702 when a party of forty-five young white men from Stellenbosch, each with a Hottentot servant, rode eastwards and fought with a party of Xhosa tribesmen whom they encountered near the present town of Somerset West. They got no cattle from the Xhosa but compensated themselves for their failure by rustling cattle and sheep from Hottentot encampments. This affair was given wide publicity during the inquiry into the conduct of Willem Adriaan van der Stel; there is some evidence that he was privy to the expedition. The Company might not like such cross-frontier traffic but its disapproval had little effect; men came and went without any record of their movements. By 1770 there was a regular wagon road as far as the Fish River, well into territory officially forbidden to Whites.

The wagon-road to the frontier has profound significance. South Africa differed radically from the greater part of Africa to the north in this one respect: the facility of transport. Horses flourished, and south of the Vaal [river] there was no tsetse fly to impede the movement of stock to the coast, or prevent ox transport. The most lucrative trade was in cattle, and these were driven to market. Every hunting and trading party was mounted, and many of them were accompanied by ox-wagons which carried metal, beads, and tobacco to exchange, and brought back ivory. The implications of this were far-reaching. Horses and ox-wagons gave a mobility to the colonists which was absent further north, and it made possible trade without dependence on slavery. On Lake Malawi until the late nineteenth century ivory was of little value without slaves to carry it to the coast, but, except from Lourenço Marques, the safari with head loads was rare in the south. Instead, there was the ox-wagon. Trade seven hundred miles from the Cape was thus profitable, and whole families, not only single men, could move readily.[3]

Boers and Xhosas had similar needs as they migrated towards each other; they were in search of hunting and grazing grounds. The horse does not seem to have been indigenous to southern Africa until introduced there by Europeans; there are drawings of Xhosa riding on oxen and some evidence that they used them as primitive cavalry in their own internal wars. The white man's possession of the horse and its use in combat proved to be of decisive importance; the horse and the gun in combination made the white tribe more formidable than any of the other tribes which it met in its wanderings. Thus far, a history of the horse in South Africa does not exist. Later it was domesticated and bred by the Sotho people and the Basuto pony became famous for its hardiness and surefootedness. It is significant that the Sotho people, who also had the horse and the gun, preserved themselves (though with difficulty) from conquest and eventually exchanged independence for security by placing themselves under British protection.

In the frontier zone there was constant competition for land, stock and game. Latent hostility could easily erupt into open conflict; in all, there were nine Kaffir wars in which Cape colonists were involved. The land was not empty but the Boers sometimes behaved as if it were; the north exerted a sort of magnetic pull as the vanguard of the Boer dispersion tried to outflank the Xhosa to the east.

By the time substantial contact was made with the Xhosa masses, the preconditions for Afrikaner nationalism had been set: the rejection of cosmopolitanism from the Cape . . . the notion that Boers and their descendants were by natural right entitled to as much land as they wanted . . . the belief that political superiority was theirs by natural right; the by now developed notion that the land was 'empty' and therefore ownerless; the assumption that black cultures would give way before superior white will; the belief that retreat into the interior was the way to solve the problem of harassment by law or native.[4]

The assertion here is that the preconditions of nationalism were to be found on the frontiers and that there already existed among the Boers of the interior a different way of life from that of the solidly established inhabitants of the western Cape. What these two wings of the Afrikaner people did share was a common colour-consciousness which was characteristic of most European colonists in all parts of the world. That consciousness was not formed on the frontier; it was one of the consequences of a slave society and was held as firmly and equally without questioning in Cape Town as in the interior. What divided the two segments of the Afrikaner people was a difference in culture between the relatively sophisticated Cape Dutchman, literate, urbanized and in touch with Europe, and the rough-hewed Boer. It needed a common aspiration, or a common grievance, to link together these two diverging parts of the Afrikaner people. That link was eventually made through a distaste for British rule; the precipitants of Nationalism existed when a sufficient number of Afrikaners, wherever they lived, began to feel a communal resentment at what they regarded as a foreign occupation. Afrikaner Nationalism did not have a steady and homogeneous growth. There were periods when it went, as it were, into remission until stimulated by some fresh grievance. But some of the preconditions had existed before the coming of the British and could be found in Boer resentment at aspects of the Company's rule.

What sort of people were the frontier Boers? It is hard to generalize; there is no great corpus of diaries or correspondence on which to draw. A distinction must be made between the true nomads – always a minority – and those who settled down to farm in reasonable proximity to their neighbours. Too much can be made of the myth of the Boer as a rugged individualist – his supposed craving for solitude, his aversion to the sight of the smoke from his neighbour's chimney. Love of space came close to covetousness of land; the dislike of meddlesome neighbours, who might be competitors for water, game, grazing land or all three, had to be balanced against the quest for suitable sons-in-law and the need for protection against Kaffir raids. The closer one lived to the frontier zone, the greater the potential riches in cattle or ivory; the greater, too, the risk. The frontier was not a scene of constant violence but one in which the expectation of violence was never wholly absent. On the eastern frontier, cattle raiding from both sides of the national boundaries was endemic. The Boers' response to raiders was usually the commando – a posse of vigilantes – following the track of the rustled beasts (the 'spoor law'), and engaging in what was partly punitive expedition and partly counter-rustling. Any Xhosa cattle which the commando happened upon might be regarded as fair game; here and there *kraals* would be burnt and Xhosa men, and sometimes women, killed. Where there were killings there would usually be Xhosa reprisals. The reaction of the Company in its latter days, and of the British thereafter, was to attempt to prevent strife by keeping the antagonists apart; neither the Company nor the British succeeded. If the presence of the Xhosas prevented Boers from going eastwards they would divert themselves to the north.

The farmer of the western Cape, with his land, his slaves, his substantial house built to last and his distaste for manual labour, might be compared to a primitive aristocracy; there was not much that was aristocratic about the Boer of the high *veld*. In his dwelling, most of his household might be found, by day at least, in a single large room – his family, his dogs (if they were not with him on the hunt), some of his servants. There is a strong tradition that no family was without its bible; if so, it was probably the only book in the house. To what extent the Boers compared themselves to the children of Israel, both as wanderers and as a chosen people, is a matter of later conjecture; certainly there were parts of the Old Testament that were perennially quoted, especially that which purported to provide a justification for the superiority of the white man. As early as 1706, during the disputes over Willem Adriaan van der Stel, a petition from Stellenbosch was addressed to the Council of XVII complaining that free Blacks had been issued with firearms and had taken part in military exercises. (What is referred to is probably the nucleus of what was to become the Cape Regiment, a mixed force of black and white Company servants, used for arresting malefactors and generally keeping the peace.) 'For there is no trusting the blood of Ham', the petition claimed, 'especially as the black people are constantly being favoured and pushed forward.'[5]

The petitioners of Cape Town may have been more literate and better read than their kith and kin on plateau and frontier, but their racial sentiments were much the same. The similarity of sentiment is evidence against the contention of Professor MacCrone, one of the first scholars to attempt a systematic study of the racial attitudes of white South Africans, that the colour-consciousness of the Afrikaner originated in the conditions of a frontier society.[6] That consciousness was to be found also in the settled areas of the western Cape; it was quickly assumed by most white immigrants. MacCrone's contention can be accepted only if *all* South Africa were to be regarded as frontier, which is to stretch the theory until it becomes meaningless.

Racial prejudice, by definition and experience, is based on instinct, not reason. It may be an instinctive reaction towards the stranger; early descriptions of the Hottentots are an example. At the Cape it was reinforced by slavery, was extended from the slave to any person of colour and was passed on through the generations. There was no need for reasoned justification; the inferiority of the black man was regarded as self-evident. What is difficult to find, either in the settled areas or among the wandering frontiersmen, is any coherent ideology or anything resembling political theory. There were grievances against authority in plenty, but they were specific and they were asserted rather than justified by reference to principles. The grievances from the outlying districts were repetitive. Why could not loan farms be obtained more easily, instead of needing tedious journeys to Cape Town? Why was stock-bartering with the Natives prohibited to farmers but permitted to the Company's servants? Why must farmers pay high prices at Company stores while their own produce was bought at fixed, low prices? Why were taxes not used directly for the farmers' benefit? Why did the Company accept so readily complaints made by Hottentots and Xhosas, and why was a black man's word so often preferred to a white man's?

It is against this background that one must appraise the various burgher rebellions at the end of the eighteenth century. They had little to do with the spread of the Enlightenment in Europe, and those who argue that they were influenced by the French Revolution have a great deal to prove: there is nothing except a rough approximation of dates to link what happened in Paris with what happened in Swellendam and Graaff-Reinet. What was probably an important factor was the Company's decision, in 1789, to reduce its garrison at the Cape. The Boers of the eastern districts were quick to realize that the Company could neither effectively protect them nor punish them. The causes which produced the rebellions which began in 1795 (if rebellion is not too strong a word for insubordination) were local and particular. The epicentre of discontent was at the farthest rim of 'civilization', in the district of Graaff-Reinet. In 1792 the Company had tried to increase the rents of loan farms. The unpopularity which this produced was

compounded by the losses suffered by the Boers in the Kaffir war of
1793.

Their wrath fell principally on the *landdrost*, H. C. D. Maynier;
his most heinous crime, in the mouths of his accusers, was that he
had taken the Hottentots' side in disputes, thus preferring heathens
to Christians. It was a well-worn accusation that was to become
even more familiar in the next half-century. There was a revolt in
the Swellendam district, in sympathy with Graaff-Reinet and with
much the same complaints.

> Some of the demands addressed to the Government by the
> 'Nationals' of the Swellendam district . . . showed clearly
> enough the position in which many Boers would have liked to
> have the aborigines placed. They asked *inter alia* that all
> Bushmen captured by commandos or by private individuals
> might be retained in perpetual slavery by the Boers – they and
> their children after them; that the custom, recently abolished,
> according to which Boers retained in their service Hottentot
> children born on their farms till their twenty-fifth year, might
> be restored; and that no Hottentot who left his employment
> should in future be allowed to take refuge in any 'colony', i.e.
> village, but that after his complaints had been noted down he
> should forthwith be returned to his 'lord and master'.[7]

It was the strategic importance of the Cape on the sea route to the
Indies that had led to its occupation by the Dutch. The same reason
brought the British in 1795, a reaction to the overrunning of the
Netherlands by the French revolutionary armies. The British would
not risk the Cape's falling into French hands: there were bleak
memories of the damage to the East Indian trade when a French
squadron had operated from the Cape during the American War of
Independence. The British returned the Cape to the Dutch under the
Treaty of Amiens in 1802; in 1806 they came again, after the treaty
had been broken and the war with the French resumed, and this
time they were there to stay. The peace settlement in 1815 confirmed the Cape as a British colony.

British administration was efficient compared with that of the
Company in its latter days – too efficient for some of those who had
now, without their desire or consent, become British subjects. At
first the British governed in the spirit of the Quebec Act of 1774,
that existing laws and customs should be retained 'as nearly as
circumstances would permit'. But the new Government meant to be
obeyed, and after the last days of a moribund Company this came

as a novelty, and sometimes an unwelcome one. The British Governor could, if he chose, behave as an autocrat (at least until he was superseded from home); his style and titles were 'Governor and Captain–General of His Majesty's Castle, Town and Settlement, of the Cape of Good Hope, in South Africa, and of the Territories and Dependencies thereof, and Ordinary and Vice–Admiral of the same'. The British had always tried, nearly always successfully, to enlist local collaborators in the administration of their colonies, and the Cape was no exception. E. T. Bird, who wrote *State of the Cape of Good Hope in 1822*, noted that young men from the most prominent families were being trained for administration in the office of the colonial secretary. Bird referred to them as 'Cape-born Dutch', for 'it would be thought an affront to call them Afrikaners'.

Like the Company before them, the British made use of Hottentot troops; they were part of the force sent to suppress the continuing troubles at Graaff-Reinet in 1799, and there they attracted as camp-followers a number of Hottentots who had formerly been farm labourers – a fair indication of the unpopularity of their employers. But the presence of these refugees was thought to be dangerous, and when the British general attempted to disarm them a rumour spread that they were about to be returned to their former masters, at which many of them fled to the Xhosas and threw in their lot with them. As the Xhosas were then invading the colony the British were faced with both an invasion and a rebellion: the revolting Hottentots numbered 700, and some of them were mounted and armed with muskets. The British regarded the situation as potentially very serious indeed: if the revolt spread to the Hottentots in the west, and they were joined by the slaves, the position of the white man in South Africa would be in jeopardy. There was a grisly precedent in British experience in the slave insurrection on the island of St Domingo in 1791; the Governor at the Cape, Sir George Yonge, 'feared with great reason the most serious consequences if the progress of this evil were not speedily repressed'. This is the first evidence from British sources of the fear of a concerted Native uprising to sweep the white man into the sea. The Boers, who could claim to know the indigenous inhabitants rather better, always remained sceptical of a pan-African combination against them.

The British tried to remove Hottentot grievances in two ways. The first was by trying to find land for those who refused to go back into Boer service; this was difficult, because most eligible land had already been occupied or claimed by the Boers. Some Hottentots were entrusted to a missionary, Dr J. T. van der Kemp of the London Missionary Society, and settled at a mission station named Bethel near Algoa Bay. The coming of the London missionaries, and especially Dr John Philip, van der Kemp's colleague, was to provide Boer mythology with new demon figures. The second way of improving the condition of the Hottentots was by reforming their terms of service. In 1809 Governor Caledon proclaimed extensive regulations; there was not much that was new about them except the will to enforce them. The Government tried to explain its policy to those to whom it would apply, both in Cape Town and the districts. What Caledon was trying to do was to establish equality before the law for all British subjects within the colony. In 1812 Governor Cradock added some important provisions to Caledon's labour code, regulating apprenticeship. In future Hottentot children who had been maintained by their parents' employer up to the age of eight could be apprenticed to that employer for a further ten years without pay, but with food and clothing; to ensure that apprenticeship did not last beyond the age of eighteen, employers were required to inform local officials of the birth of Hottentot children on their farms and to submit these details to a resident magistrate every quarter.

The London Missionary Society added a new hazard to Boer life. Little love was lost on either side. Dr Philip, regarded as the arch-villain among the missionaries, considered that: 'The habits of the Boers . . . are perfectly Scythian in their character'.[8] Among the complaints brought forward by the instigators of the troubles at Graaff-Reinet was that Hottentots were allowed to worship in the local church and that they were being taught to read and write by missionaries, 'and thereby put upon an equal footing with Christians'.

From the Boer point of view the appearance of meddlesome missionaries and Hottentots claiming rights were symptoms of something more serious for the future. What was beginning was a revolution in government that would eventually transform the whole nature of frontier society in the Cape Colony (to give it what was now its official name). For those on the fringes of settlement, a way of life was coming to an end. One sign of this was the establishment of circuit courts of law, a form of assize. Missionaries saw to it that Hottentots knew when the court would be sitting in their district, and some Hottentots were certainly encouraged to put forward complaints. It was as a consequence of attempts to enforce the rule of law that there occurred two episodes that entered the demonology of Afrikaner oppression – the Black Circuit of 1812 and the Slagtersnek rebellion of 1815.

The Black Circuit was the name given to court proceedings in the districts of George, Uitenhage and Graaff-Reinet, when many Hottentots made allegations of ill-treatment by their employers. The court found that some of the complaints were without foundation and others had been exaggerated. The storm of protest that resulted was a result of feelings of outrage that Hottentots should have been admitted to the processes of the court at all and that, once there, they should have been treated as equals of the white man.

The Slagtersnek rebellion was a complicated affair. In 1813 a Hottentot named Booy complained to the assistant magistrate at Cradock that his employer, Freek Bezuidenhout, was withholding part of his pay and would not let him take away his cattle even though his contract of employment had expired. In spite of repeated summons Bezuidenhout refused to leave his farm to answer the complaints, nor would he release the disputed cattle. At this point Booy fades from the story; he was killed in 1814 by another Hottentot whose wife he was accused of seducing. However, the merits of Booy's character or conduct had no legal relevance; what was at issue was Bezuidenhout's refusal to respond to a summons. In October 1815 the circuit court at Cradock sentenced him *in absentia* to one month's imprisonment for contempt of court. The under-sheriff, with a detachment of the Cape Regiment, went to arrest Bezuidenhout, who refused to submit, took refuge in a cave and opened fire; fire was returned and he was shot dead by a 'Hottentot bullet'. At the wake after Freek Bezuidenhout's funeral his brother Hans swore to be revenged; his proposed vengeance was ambitious enough, for it involved nothing less than fomenting a rebellion to expel the British from Cape Colony, with the help of friendly Xhosa. A look at the curricula vitae of some of Hans Bezuidenhout's co-conspirators indicates the existence of a set of frontier outlaws, some with black common-law wives. Among them was 'Kasteel' Prinsloo, so-called because his father had been imprisoned in the *kasteel* or castle in Cape Town for taking part in the Graaff-Reinet insurrection of 1799; Stephanus Botha, a convicted forger; and Cornelis Faber, Hans Bezuidenhout's brother-in-law, who had taken refuge with the Xhosa after the troubles of 1799. They attempted to mobilize the frontier Boers and managed to collect a band of about a hundred like-minded men; their overtures to the Xhosa were less successful.

On 13 November 1815 Kasteel Prinsloo was arrested and taken to a military post at Vanaardtspos. This seems to have stimulated recruiting, because Bezuidenhout was able to demand his release at the head of about 200 armed men. The demand was refused, and about sixty men, armed, then gathered at the pass known as Slagtersnek. (*Slagter* means butcher, and the pass was so named because butchers' agents from the villages used it as a place of assignation where they might buy cattle from Boer farmers; it was a trading post without sinister significance.) On 18 November this gathering was confronted by a force of British dragoons supplemented by loyalist Boers. There were some arrests there and then, and the gathering dispersed; but Bezuidenhout, Bothma and some others fled northwards into Xhosa territory, pursued by a mixed force of Boers and members of the Cape Regiment. Bezuidenhout, his wife and his twelve-year-old son were cornered beyond the Winterberg mountains, fifty miles away, and resisted. In the skirmish that followed one Coloured soldier was killed and all three Bezuidenhouts were wounded, Hans so severely that he died in captivity that same day.

The Government took the affair seriously, probably because of attempts to stimulate the Xhosa to invasion. Forty-seven of the conspirators were tried before a special commission at Uitenhage; thirty-eight were found guilty and of those six were sentenced to death. The Governor, Lord Charles Somerset, commuted one of the death sentences; the other five condemned men – Prinsloo, two Bothmas, Faber, and de Klerk – were to be hanged at Vanaardtspos on 9 March 1816. The executions became a spectacle of unexpected horror. The public hangman of the district lived at George, nearly 150 miles away. When he was summoned, he thought that he had only one hanging to carry out and brought with him only one rope; when he discovered his mistake, he procured four more ropes locally. All of them were rotten and broke under the weight of their victims, leaving four partly-hanged men still alive. The crowd appealed for the executions to be stopped; but the four were hanged again, this time in succession with the one sound rope. Gruesome though the executions were, the British reaction to the 'rebellion' marked the end of the frontier risings or 'armed protests', and demonstrated that the Government was not prepared to tolerate those who regarded themselves as above the law. Had it not been for the botched hangings it is probable that there would have been no aftermath: the conspirators were not men who were widely respected in their district and many people thought that it was unpardonable to try to stir up the Xhosas against white men. It was not until nearly two generations later that Slagtersnek, as it came to be known, took its place in the martyrology of persecuted Afrikanerdom.[9] Before then there is only one piece of evidence that the episode was remembered with especial bitterness. This came in a lecture given in the 1850s by one Henry Cloete in which he repeated a remark attributed to a Boer emigrant in Natal: 'We can never forget Slagtersnek'. It is doubtful whether this was a general sentiment. The Natal emigrants were especially bitter after the British had annexed their fledgling republic of Natalia; it was their women who were reputed to have said that they would rather walk back barefooted over the Drakensberg than submit to British rule. Cloete, one may note, got some of his facts wrong and put the hangings at Slagtersnek instead of Vanaardtspos.

It was not until anti-British feeling had revived in the 1860s in consequence of the protectorate over Basutoland and the annexation of the newly discovered diamond field that Slagtersnek was retrospectively transformed into a struggle for freedom. There was a play about it performed in Cape Town. In 1877, S. J. du Toit, the protagonist of the first language movement to popularize Afrikaans as a national language instead of High Dutch, revived the memory of Slagtersnek once again; in his version both Bezuidenhouts and their associates were patriots and martyrs. (Not for the first or last time in South African history, those who had suffered were, on that account, endowed with nobility of character. That was how some English liberals regarded the burghers of the Transvaal and Orange Free State during the Anglo–Boer war of 1899–1902. In the latter part of the twentieth century liberals took a similar view of the Africans' suffering under *apartheid*.) In 1880, the Revd J. D. Kestell wrote a monograph on Slagtersnek, and in 1881 a play in five acts, *The Struggle for Freedom*, was published in London; this coincided with the 'First Freedom War', the Boer name for the rebellion of the Transvaal against British rule. By the end of the century the legend had become both anti-British and anti-Black and was used as a manifesto against both oppression and gelykstelling or racial equality. It was forgotten that Freek Bezuidenhout lived with a coloured woman and had a half-caste son, and forgotten, too, that his brother had tried to bring on a Xhosa invasion. In 1896 what was reputed to be the beam of the gallows used at the hangings was sent to Pretoria in the hope that it could be used for the members of the Johannesburg Reform Committee who were on trial for their part in the Jameson Raid. One of them wrote:

The *Volksstem*, the Hollander–Boer organ [in Pretoria], in an extremely violent article, described in detail the Slagter's Nek executions, and called upon the burghers to avenge on the persons of the Reformers their murdered countrymen; and it is a fact vouched for by persons by no means friendly to the Uitlander that certain Boers approached President Kruger, intimating to him that the beam had arrived, that it would not be necessary to bother about a trial, but that the four men should be hanged out of hand from the same scaffold which had served for their compatriots. It is but right to say that President Kruger's reply was a severe reprimand, and a reminder that they were not a barbarous people, but should comply with the law.[10]

The final transfiguration of Slagtersnek came with Langenhoven's poem in *Die Pad van Suid-Afrika*, in which there appeared the apotheosis of Freek Bezuidenhout, now represented as one man standing for the freedom of the Afrikaner against the British Empire on 'the road of South Africa' (a favourite pilgrimage for ardent patriots, the more attractive since it could lead anywhere that fancy dictated). On 9 March 1916, the centenary of the hangings, a thousand Afrikaner Nationalists assembled to unveil a monument at Vanaardtspos; their country was then involved in a 'British war' in which their sympathies lay with Britain's enemies. General Hertzog and General de Wet (the latter on parole after conviction for rebellion) sent messages of goodwill. Dr D. F. Malan, the principal speaker, thought it proper to criticize the appeal to the Xhosas, but found nothing to excite his disapproval at rebellion. There were more speeches, in the same tone, at Vanaardtspos in 1938 during the centenary celebrations of what had long been called the Great Trek, at which grievances against the British were diligently recalled. But if patient investigation could find no better martyrs than the Bezuidenhout brothers, the oppression of the Boer frontiersmen could not have been insupportably onerous.

The fame of Slagtersnek, then, was posthumous, and the Boers did not mention it twenty years later as one of the grievances which impelled so many of them to *trek* out of the colony in the 1830s.

As one of its attempts to bring peace to the frontier, the British Government had settled about 4,000 English immigrants in the eastern Cape in 1820. The newcomers were neither docile nor grateful to authority; they demanded the same rights in their new domicile as they believed had been their due at home. Freedom of the press was one of their achievements, and the *Grahamstown Journal* became an outlet for frontier opinion and the rehearsal of both English and Boer grievances. There was no overt hostility between Boers and 1820 Settlers, but the new English presence probably deepened the Boers' feeling that they were becoming foreigners in their own land. They had never been noted for subservience to authority, and now they were faced with a government that was much more effective than its predecessor and much less intelligible. In 1822 it had been proclaimed that English would become the exclusive language of the courts in five years time. The abolition of the slave trade in 1807 did not make much difference to the Cape, but the abolition of slavery itself in 1833 was a different matter; it entailed loss of property, since compensation to slave-owners was to be paid only in London, which meant that middlemen demanded a heavy premium for acting as collecting agents. There was also the gloomy prospect of former slaves now enjoying equality before the law. In the opinion of some Boers it was all the fault of English missionaries.

Dr John Philip was the most hated missionary of them all. Like many zealots he took a simple view: the Boers were persecutors and their slaves and their servants were their innocent victims. It is likely that Philip has been given more blame, or credit, than he deserved; missionaries seldom had much influence on imperial policy, although their testimony could be used in justification of decisions taken for other reasons. British policy towards Natives was two-handed: they should be protected against ill-treatment but they should also be pushed into the white man's employment. Those men who were not white were required to carry passes, a means both of identification and of controlling vagrancy; those who were unemployed might be drafted into work. There was a new code regulating apprenticeship. Then in 1828 came the most controversial measure of all, which is still the subject of debate. This was Ordinance 50. It was promulgated in Cape Town, but it was a measure imposed from without on a hostile colony. It owed much to the propaganda of the London Missionary Society and its principal representative in South Africa, Dr Philip. It was his crowning, and perhaps his only, lasting achievement. What it did was to repeal the legislation relating to the non-White peoples passed from 1809 to 1819, and make 'Hottentots and other free persons of colour' equal with Europeans in the eyes of the law. Professor Marais, the historian of the Coloured peoples, commented thus:

In the history of European colonisation in South Africa there have been two determinations of outstanding importance. The first, taken at the very beginning, was the decision to make South Africa a slave-owning country. The second was Ordinance 50. The second decision, followed up as it was by the abolition of slavery, came too late to undo all the evils of the first. It was impossible, by a single piece of legislation, to destroy the slave-owning mentality, or to make the Hottentots and the slaves worthy of the freedom which had been suddenly thrust upon them. Time alone could cure the evils which time had wrought.[11]

Ordinance 50 was the foundation of what would later be called Cape liberalism, an attitude which favoured equality in public, if not in private, matters. The Cape differed from the other territories which later made up the Union of South Africa in that legislation which discriminated against persons solely on grounds of race or colour was prohibited. However, to many Boers it was the final provocation. They might be powerless to prevent legal equality between White and Black in the land of their birth; they would seek other lands in which they would make sure that white supremacy would last for ever.

3 BOER INDEPENDENCE GAINED AND LOST

In the 1830s there was a mass migration of Boers out of the Cape Colony. This was a deliberate and premeditated exodus from British rule. In the course of a decade about 10,000 Boers left, taking with them their household goods, their retainers and their livestock. Later this would be known as the Great Trek, and those who took part in it as the Voortrekkers, the pioneers; at the time, they called themselves the 'emigrant farmers'. They may have been of one mind, but they were not of one body. There were piecemeal departures by self-sufficient groups, each forming something like an extended family. There was no single directing figure, and most of the group leaders found it hard to co-operate with any other leaders; the exodus lacked its Moses.

The clearest statement of motives is in the remonstrance issued by Piet Retief, whose party left from Grahamstown in 1837. The first complaints were of frontier disorder and the turbulence of vagrants; second came the losses sustained through emancipation of slaves; third was 'the continual system of plunder which we have for years endured from the Kaffirs and other coloured classes'; fourth was the 'unjustifiable odium' which they had suffered because of what missionaries had said about them. Then came a statement of purpose. They would 'uphold the just principles of liberty'; that is, they would have no truck with slavery but would 'establish such regulations as may suppress crime, and preserve proper relations between master and servant'. They would 'on arrival at the country in which we shall permanently reside . . . make known to the native tribes our intentions, and our desire to live in peace and friendly intercourse with them'. That sentence gives an insight into the outlook of the *trek boer*: he assumed that his new permanent home was ready for occupation, whatever the Native tribes might think about his assumption of ownership.

The remonstrance concluded: 'We quit this country under the full assurance that the English Government has nothing more to require of us, and will allow us to govern ourselves without interference in future.' This statement disposes of the contention that the migration was not a consequence of discontent but the natural consequence of the exhaustion of grazing through erosion, or the land hunger of young men who found the eastern frontier blocked by Xhosa tribesmen. One reason why the wilderness was attractive was because it was there, offering to the pioneer a land of his own, free from foreign magistrates and missionaries. But the migration was not the product either of youthful ambition or mere wanderlust: it was a long-pondered decision made at substantial cost, for many of the emigrants were settled farmers who now had to dispose of their possessions for what they could get at what amounted to a forced sale.

PLATE 2. *The Great Trek: crossing the Drakensberg, 1836* (Courtesy of R. Caton Woodville, *Harper's* Magazine).

PLATE 3. *Voortrekker Monument* (Courtesy of the South African High Commission).

The country beyond the colony was not wholly unknown, for scouting parties, oddly called 'commissions', had been spying out the land for some time past. The migration was the ultimate protest by men and women tired of living under foreign occupation, beset by laws with which they did not agree promulgated in a language which some of them did not understand. Anna Steenkamp, Retief's niece, recalled forty years later the emotions with which she left her home in the colony. The emancipation of the slaves, she wrote, was the final grievance; but 'it is not so much their freedom that drove us to such lengths, as their being placed on an equal footing with the Christians, contrary to the laws of God and the natural distinction of race and religion . . . wherefore we rather withdrew in order thus to preserve our doctrines in purity'. She was claiming, whether she knew it or not, one of the natural rights of man asserted by John Locke – 'liberty to go and incorporate himself into any other commonwealth, or to agree with others to begin a new one, *in vacuis locis*, in any part of the world they can find free and unpossessed'[1].

Free and unpossessed . . . That was the critical question: how empty was the land behind the horizon? Emptier, probably, than it would have been had the migration occurred some years earlier. In the first third of the nineteenth century there had been immense disturbances among the Bantu-speaking peoples in consequence of the and massacres by the armies of the Zulu kingdom under Shaka. The Boers were moving into what had been a whirling flux, over much of which the terms aggressor and victim of aggression had no meaning, and where they arrived as the last and most formidable tribe of them all. The Boers were conquerors: their use of the horse and the musket in combination, reinforced here and there by cannon, made them irresistible against Native opponents. One consequence of the migration was that the area of contact between Boers and tribesmen was immensely enlarged. So were the possibilities of conflict.

The British Government at the Cape let the Boers go, for the simple reason that there was no way of stopping them; as the Attorney – General put it, 'is there any effectual means of arresting persons determined to run away, short of shooting them as they pass the boundary line? I apprehend not'. But the British were not of a mind to let the Boers do what they liked wherever they chose to go. One immediate reaction was the Cape of Good Hope Punishment Act of 1836 which asserted a claim to British jurisdiction over all European settlers or travellers in southern Africa as far as the twenty-third degree of latitude, about fifty miles north of the modern Pretoria. Thus the Boers had instigated a change in the British policy of limited commitment. Like the Dutch East India Company, the British Government had little interest in the Cape except as an outpost on the way to India; again, like the Company, it visualized the Cape as a seascape rather than a landscape. It had been assumed that the energies of British subjects in those parts would be confined to 'cultivating to their highest capacity the terraced shores of the Southern Ocean'. The Boers had left the terraced shores far behind them. They had repudiated British authority, but the British Government still claimed a notional jurisdiction over them – this would later be expanded to a claim of paramountcy over all of southern Africa. The Boers could not be permitted to endanger the European presence by provoking new Kaffir wars on new frontiers. It was the British who feared the possibility of a concerted Native rising against the white man – fears which John Buchan expressed in imaginative prose when he wrote *Prester John* sixty years later.

The Boers had no such fears, nor did it seem that they had set any boundaries to their expansion. Their first major battles with hostile tribes occurred in 1837 and 1838. In two campaigns in 1837, commandos under Hendrik Potgieter and Piet Uys defeated the Matabele (an offshoot of the Zulu) so comprehensively that the whole tribe decamped northwards across the Limpopo River. Meanwhile Piet Retief and his party had crossed the Drakensberg and had negotiated what was believed to be a treaty with Dingaan, half-brother, murderer and successor of Shaka. In spite of warnings of treachery, Retief trusted Dingaan, unwisely as it turned out, for he was murdered, with his entourage, at what he had believed to be a ceremony in his honour. Thereafter Dingaan's warriors massacred all those Boers and their Native retainers whom they could find in unfortified positions, perhaps six hundred in all. The village of Weenen – 'the place of weeping' – commemorates those days of disaster. Retribution followed swiftly: a punitive commando under Andries Pretorius defeated Dingaan's army at what was then christened the Battle of Blood River. It is said that over 3,000 Zulus were killed and that the stream which ran across the battlefield ran red with their blood. No Boers were killed, and only three wounded. This was a triumph for Boer tactics – well-aimed musket fire from a laager of wagons, and some rounds from an ancient cannon, and then charges by mounted Boers firing from the saddle. The anniversary of the battle of Blood River, 16 December 1838, was to become the most celebrated festival in the Boers' patriotic calendar. According to legend, the Boers, in their prayers on the eve of battle, had vowed to build a commemorative church if the Almighty granted them victory. The church was duly built, in Pietermaritzburg, a newly-founded Boer settlement named after Piet Retief and Gert Maritz, two heroes of the *Volk*, in what was now occupied as the Republic of Natalia.

Thus, within two years, the Boers had broken the power of two of the most formidable military monarchies in southern Africa. The defeat of the Zulus, like that of the Matabele, was decisive: when the Boers advanced to Dingaan's 'great place' they found it deserted; the king and his warriors had fled to the north. The Boers had not yet, however, found for themselves a home where they could preserve their doctrines in purity. The Republic of Natalia had only a brief life before the British annexed it in 1843 along with Durban, its port. It became a British interest to keep the Boers away from the sea lest they should attract the sympathetic attention of one of Britain's maritime rivals. In 1848 the Governor of the Cape, Sir Harry Smith (a hero both of the Peninsular and Sikh wars), extended British rule northwards by proclaiming the Queen's sovereignty over the area between the Orange and Vaal rivers which was later to become the Orange Free State; he disposed of Boer opposition at a 'severe skirmish' at Boomplaats. Those Boers who still refused to accept British rule trekked still further to the north across the Vaal River, where for the time being they were safe from British territorial advance.

What has been described as 'the strangest race ever run by mortal man' between the fleeing Boers and the pursuing Colonial Office, was nearly over. There was a change of opinion in London, which had little to do with the exertions of the Boers and much to do with demands for economy. In 1850 there had been yet another Kaffir war on the eastern frontier of the Cape, which cost the British taxpayer £3,000,000 and brought the affairs of southern Africa to the critical attention of Parliament. The outcome was an attempt to return to the policy of limited commitment. The Colonial Secretary reminded the Governor of the Cape that 'beyond the very limited extent of territory required for the security of the Cape of Good Hope as a naval station, the British Crown and nation have no interest whatever in maintaining a territorial dominion in southern Africa'. In the opinion of *The Times*, 'a private and peculiar war, like that now raging at the Cape, seems to fall fairly within the province of the local government to manage and of the local exchequer to support'.[2] William Ewart Gladstone thought that local responsibility was the way to peaceful coexistence between colonists and their tribal neighbours, and he saw in official parsimony the operation of a beneficial principle. 'The plague and scourge of these colonial wars', he said in the House of Commons, would never be destroyed until 'the community which is exposed to the war is likewise responsible for its expenses. For the burdens of war are the providential preventives of war, and operate as a check upon the passions of mankind, the lust of territorial acquisition, and the heats of international hatred.'[3]

One result of the change of opinion in Parliament was the granting of representative government to the Cape Colony. Another was the formal recognition of the independence of the remotest of the Boer republics. By the Sand River Convention of 1852, British commissioners recognized 'the fullest right of the emigrant farmers beyond the Vaal River to manage their own affairs and govern themselves according to their own laws, without any interference on the part of the British Government'. They were also assured of access to supplies of ammunition.[4] One of the commissioners, Major W. S. Hogge, expressed the mood of the moment.

> The history of the Cape is already written in that of America, and the gradual increase of the white race must eventually though surely ensure the disappearance of the black. Providence vindicates this its unalterable law by rendering all the philanthropic efforts that have been made to avert such a destiny subservient to its fulfilment.[5] What had been granted

to one group of Boers could hardly be refused to another, especially as the British Resident in the Orange River Sovereignty reported: 'The fact is that two-thirds of the Boers in this Sovereignty are in their hearts decided rebels, and consequently do all in their power to thwart Government'. Sir Harry Smith argued in vain for the retention of British rule by depicting the alternative as one of lurid disaster:

If Her Majesty's sovereignty over this territory were now rescinded, the step would be regarded by every man of colour in South Africa as an unprecedented and an unlooked-for victory to his race, and be the signal of revolt or continued resistance to British authority from Cape Town to the territory of Panda [*sc.* Mpande, Dingaan's successor] and from thence to the Great Lake.[6]

In 1854, by the Bloemfontein Convention, Britain renounced the sovereignty proclaimed by Sir Harry Smith over the territory between the Orange and the Vaal rivers. There were now new states in South Africa, the Orange Free State and in the Transvaal, which eventually consolidated itself into the South African Republic. Boers with long memories might reflect with satisfaction that the influence of Dr John Philip had at last been buried.

Compared with the turbulence of the rough and ready communities of the Transvaal, the Orange Free State appeared as an oasis of pastoral calm and peaceful administration. It had equipped itself with a simple but effective constitution. Legislative power lay in the Volksraad, or elected assembly, executive power with a president elected for five years and assisted by an executive council. A high court of justice was established in 1867 and a court of appeal in 1874. The burghers of the Orange Free State combined a wary suspicion of the British Government with tolerance towards individual Englishmen who settled in their midst and conformed to their ways. They were fortunate, or wise, in their choice of presidents. The longest in office was Johannes Henricus Brand who was imported from the Cape Colony. He was born and educated in Cape Town, became a doctor of laws of the University of Leyden, was called to the English bar from the Inner Temple and had been a member of the Cape House of Assembly and a professor of law at the South African College, the predecessor of the University of Cape Town. He became president in 1864 and was re-elected until his death in office in 1888; in 1886 he was knighted by Queen Victoria.

James Bryce, who visited the Orange Free State in 1895, described it as the kind of commonwealth depicted 'in fond fancy' by the philosophers of the eighteenth century.

> No great industries have come into the Free State to raise economic strife. No capitalists tempt the virtue of legislators, or are forced to buy off the attacks of blackmailers. No religious animosities divide Christians, for there is perfect religious freedom. No difficulties as to British suzerainty exist, for the Republic is completely independent. No native troubles have arisen. No prize is offered to ambition. No political parties have sprung up. Taxation is low, and there is no public debt. The arms of the State are a lion and a lamb standing on opposite sides of an orange tree with the motto 'Freedom, Immigration, Patience, Courage', and though the lion has, since 1871, ceased to range over the plains, his pacific attitude beside the lamb on this device happily typifies the harmony which exists between the British and Dutch elements . . . It is an ideal commonwealth.[7]

It was ironic that within five years of the painting of this idyllic picture, the Orange Free State should be involved in a devastating war that was none of its making, which it had entered to fulfil its treaty obligations to the South African Republic.

Bryce counted the Orange Free State to be fortunate in its lack of capitalists. (In the South African context, 'capitalist' meant 'mining magnate'.) Things would have been otherwise had its claim to the newly-discovered diamond fields been successful; if there were no capitalists in the land it was not for want of trying to get them. The dispute over the diamond fields was put to the arbitration of the lieutenant-governor of Natal, who decided it in favour of a Griqua tribe which immediately offered the territory, known as Griqualand West, to the British as a protectorate. The British accepted and then tried to pass the territory over to the Cape Colony, whose government was unwilling to accept it: it hoped to profit from the new mines without the responsibility of policing them. Cape politicians were learning of the advantages of informal empire. The British Government, on the other hand, had been constrained to take formal control, an action that was inconsistent with the policy of limited commitment.

The discovery of diamonds marked a new stage in South African history. It was the beginning of industrialization. The new diggings attracted fortune-seekers of all colours, from inside and outside South Africa. In the early days, Whites and Natives competed and squabbled over rival claims, until the Whites were able to obtain a virtual colour-bar which reserved ownership of the diggings for themselves. Natives were employed in large numbers as labourers. There was no shortage of recruits: wages were relatively high and could be spent on guns and liquor. The new town of Kimberley became notorious as the centre of prosperous gun-running and bootlegging industries which existed side by side with mining operations that became increasingly sophisticated and required more and more capital investment. Some great fortunes were made, notably by Cecil Rhodes. The two Boer republics were fortunate not to have to try to regulate the industry or govern the discordant horde of magnates and diggers. For this relief the Orange Free State offered no thanks. It felt that it had been cheated by the arbitration award and thought the sum of £90,000 that it accepted as compensation from the British Government was too little. Justice may have been done by the arbitration, but it had not manifestly been seen to be done. The British asserted, with much truth, that their sole interest in the diamond fields was the preservation of order; the Boers did not believe them. The aftermath of the diamond discoveries led to a revival of anti-British feeling which did something to bridge the gap that was developing between the settled south and the wilder north. There was another side to the smiling face that Bryce saw in the Orange Free State. The country had its own frontier wars, with the Sotho and Rolong peoples; and the Free Staters considered it an unfriendly act when Basutoland was placed out of their reach by becoming a British protectorate. The first indigenous history – H. J. Hofstede's *Geschiedenis van den Oranje-Vrystaat* published in 1876 – was a tale of woe and oppression, which the Volksraad welcomed 'since it made known to the world the numerous grievances of the Afrikaners, and of this people in particular'.[8]

The Transvaalers, too, had their grievances, but in the absence of the British these were held against other Transvaalers. There were ten *émeutes* between 1847 and 1864. It would be an exaggeration to class these as rebellions; they were, rather, angry disputes between extended families. General de la Rey, one of the heroes of the Boer War, recalled in 1913 the early days of independence in the Transvaal:

You talk about Union of all the states; *of one* country; *one* Parliament; *one* flag; *one* king! What does this signify to the

Boer? . . . Why, I can remember the time when we had five governments in the up-country [*sc.* the Transvaal] – all our own, too! and *that* was not enough. No sooner did we start a new Government than there would be two parties again and each would want its own Government and Parliament, and we would take up our rifles and break up again. It is the way of the Boer.[9]

While the Boer population was still sparse enough for habitations to be changed at will, distance was sometimes a solvent of animosity, as it had been between Abram and Lot:

And there was a strife between the herdmen of Abram's cattle and the herdmen of Lot's cattle . . . And Abram said unto Lot, Let there be no strife, I pray thee, between me and thee; for we be brethren. Is not the whole land before us? separate thyself, I pray thee, from me: if thou wilt take the left hand, then I will go to the right; or if thou depart to the right hand then I will go to the left . . . Then Lot chose him all the plain of Jordan; and Lot journeyed east, and they separated themselves the one from the other.[10]

But even if there were no separation, and burghers brought their rifles with them to their bickerings, this did not necessarily mean that they had any intention of shooting one another. The *wapende protes*, the protest in arms, was sometimes regarded as no more than an especially emphatic method of expressing disagreement. Christiaan de Wet, a turbulent personality who was later to become a legendary commando leader, tried unsuccessfully by armed protest to prevent the building of a railway between the Orange Free State and the Cape Colony, because he thought that it would make the Free State more vulnerable to invasion.

Where differences of principle emerged, they were often on matters of religion – there were three branches of the Dutch Reformed Church in the Transvaal – but even then what was usually at issue was not doctrine, but status or personalities. Attachment to particular leaders could be as much a source of discord as of cohesion. In the Boer commination, the *broedertwis*, strife between brothers, stood high in priority, as well it might considering its popularity.

It could be argued that Boer society was stunted at both ends: at the bottom, there was over-dependence on black labour for manual work; at the top there was practically no professional class. Thus the Boers were constrained to import presidents from the Cape, ministers of religion from Scotland and bureaucrats from Holland.

The *grondwet*, or constitution, of the Transvaal was largely the work of a Hollander, Jacobus Stuart. It was a muddled document, but the intentions of those who adopted it were clear enough on two points: one was the emphasis on the *volkswil*, or voice of the people, as the source of authority; the other was that 'the *Volk* desire to permit no equality between people of colour and the white inhabitants, either in Church or State'. The word *volk* was used restrictively in the sense of 'our own people' or, in the fullness of time, 'we the Afrikaners'.

The Boers of the Transvaal had thought that the Sand River Convention of 1852 meant what it said, that the British Government had renounced its interest in their affairs; it proved, however, to be merely another halting-place in what Sir William Molesworth, a Liberal member of the House of Commons, called 'the strangest race that ever was run by mortal man' between the flying Boer and the pursuing Colonial Office. The British had found that changed circumstances meant new commitments. First had come the discovery of diamonds, which attracted the attention of the Western

PLATE 4. *Trekking Home: the last of the Boer Commando* (Courtesy of the Hansell Collection).

world to the new town of Kimberley where the population reached 50,000 within four years. Then came the first discoveries of gold in the eastern Transvaal, around Lydenburg, which brought the Transvaal back to the attention of British politicians. Prospectors were attracted to the new gold fields, and with them came a supporting cast of shopkeepers, speculators, publicans and sinners of both sexes, establishing soon-forgotten settlements with names like Revolver Creek and Last Chance Creek. There was now a British interest group in the Transvaal, using against the Boers the same language of disaffection and complaint that the Boers had for so long been accustomed to use about the British.

The second circumstance was that the activities of the Transvaal Government had awakened British suspicions both of Boer intentions and their consequences. The Boers had long wished for an outlet to the sea. Now they were seeking for the next best thing by trying to build a railway line through Portuguese territory to Delagoa Bay. The whole business was mismanaged, not least by the over-sanguine President Burgers, a politician–clergyman whom the Transvaalers had imported from the Cape as their head of state. The Transvaal Government sank still deeper into debt, while such rolling stock and other railway equipment as had already been bought had either never left Europe or else lay rusting on the quayside at Lourenço Marques.

To compound their toll of mismanagement, the Boers had just fought an unsuccessful little war within their own borders against the Pedi tribesmen of chief Sekukuni. The Boers were not in search of new territory; in their own opinion, they were chastising a rebel. Sekukuni, on the other hand, regarded his tribal territory as his own. The immediate quarrel began when Sekukuni objected to the Lydenburg miners felling what he claimed to be his timber. This does not, taken by itself, appear to be a sufficient *casus belli*, but the Boers might have regarded it as one more example that Sekukuni was insufficiently deferential and needed a lesson. In the middle of 1876 President Burgers called out the commandos.

Burgers had an aptitude for failure, and his military adventure was no exception. He had lost the confidence of influential burghers before he took the field. Doppers (members of the most fundamentalist of the Dutch Reformed Churches) thought him frivolous in matters of religion. He had allowed his likeness to be minted on the first coins to be struck from the Lydenburg gold, thus breaching the Second Commandment. (It was also said that he had denied that the Devil had a tail, but that may have been either slander or heavy humour.) The commandos gathered, but had no stomach for battle. Burgers led them to an attack on Sekukuni's mountain stronghold, but when he failed to storm it he was unable to sustain the fighting spirit of his burghers, who became mutinously discouraged and went back to their farms, sped on their way, it was said, by wild stories that the Zulus were coming to attack them in the rear.

There were no Zulus, and Burgers's repulse by Sekukuni could hardly be said to have jeopardized the existence of the Transvaal republic, but the importance of the episode was inflated by rumours, some of them spread by those who either knew little about what the military situation actually was, or else had reasons of their own for their prophecies of doom. The English inhabitants of Lydenburg met and passed a resolution inviting the British Government to take over the Transvaal to protect them from massacre. Once again, the British raised the fear of the concerted Native uprising; Boer fecklessness had imperilled the future of the white man through South Africa by a display of military incompetence. Sir Henry Bulwer, Governor of Natal, thought that the effect upon the Zulu kingdom, adjacent both to Natal and the Transvaal, would be a critical change in Zulu opinion.

> The Boers were no longer to be hated and feared; they were to be hated and despised. Henceforth, the English might be friends or not, so far as it suited the interests of both nations to be friends; but their friendship was no longer needed as a shield of protection against the aggression or injustice of the Government of the [Transvaal] Republic. In future the [Zulu] King could breathe more freely and act more independently.[11]

This was to attribute a great deal to the effects of a single military reverse under irresolute leadership, but it could not be called an extravagant appreciation. But there were others who pushed extravagance to the brink of hysteria. Sir Theophilus Shepstone was accounted as one of the foremost authorities in South Africa on Native affairs; he wrote to the Secretary of State for the Colonies that the botched attack on Sekukuni

> had sent the thrilling intelligence through all the immense masses of natives between the Zambesi on the north and, the Cape Colony on the south, that the relative positions of the white and black man had become seriously changed, and had

prompted the thought that the supremacy of barbarism was
no longer hopeless, provided only that the effort be well-
planned and simultaneously executed.[12]

The embarrassments of the Transvaal offered a new opportunity
to those who had been hoping for confederation of the British
colonies and the Boer republics. Paradoxically, this was not intended in the Colonial Office to be a forward step in the acquisition
of empire but a return to the policy of limited commitment after the
untoward event of the annexation of the diamond fields. The
colonies and republics of southern Africa, once they had been
brought into association, could both support and restrain each
other, and a burden would be removed from the British taxpayer.
Confederation had been canvassed in London for over twenty
years; what stood in the way was that the colonies were lukewarm
and the republics were hostile: confederation meant some sort of
British rule, and British rule was what the Boers had gone on their
travels to escape. Confederation had a special appeal to Lord
Carnarvon, now Secretary of State for the Colonies for the second
time. Carnarvon looked on the federation of Canada, achieved by
the British North America Act of 1867 during his first spell as
Colonial Secretary, as his supreme achievement thus far, and one
that he would like to repeat. (In 1885 he was to float the idea of
confederation before Charles Stewart Parnell as an answer to the
'damnable question' of Ireland.) Thus far Carnarvon's efforts had
achieved no success, but the sudden slump in the Transvaal's fortunes seemed to offer a fresh chance; the Transvaal's difficulty
might be Britain's opportunity.

Carnarvon had talks in London with Shepstone, who seems to
have persuaded him that the Transvaalers were in a mood to invite
the British Government to save them from themselves. A temporary
British occupation of the Transvaal might remove one of the obstacles to closer association. The hoped-for sequence of events
would be annexation of the Transvaal, by consent; confederation;
and then a removal of direct British responsibility from those South
African matters that did not directly involve imperial interests. One
step forward would be followed by two steps back. But what if the
Transvaal refused to agree to the first step, annexation? That would
depend on whether the internal condition of the Transvaal was in
such chaos as to threaten the stability of southern Africa. If this
were so – and the decision was to be delegated to Shepstone,
Carnarvon's agent – then Great Britain would disregard the Sand

River Convention on the grounds that the paramount power must act in the interests of South Africa as a whole.

Certainly the Transvaal was in a condition of administrative disorder that came close to paralysis; but even administrative paralysis meant less to the burghers of a pastoral republic than it would have done to the citizens of an urbanized state. Whether this state of affairs justified outside intervention was a matter of opinion. The Boers themselves took a relaxed view. The failure of the campaign against Sekukuni had been followed by the shortest session of the Volksraad in the republic's brief history. President Burgers had asked for a special tax to pay for the costs of the war; he got his way, after the Volksraad had indulged itself in criticism of his conduct. But it was one thing to vote a tax and another to collect it; most burghers simply did not pay. Technically, the Transvaal was bankrupt. Certainly, voices were to be heard asking for British intervention, but most of those belonged to English traders or miners who could hardly be regarded as representative. Carnarvon had sent Shepstone back to South Africa to annex the Transvaal, provided that he was invited to do so by the Boers themselves or could find a pretext that would satisfy opinion both in Britain and South Africa. Carnarvon had made this clear in a private letter to Shepstone on 4 October 1876.

> On the one hand it is of great consequence to secure the Transvaal; on the other, it is most desirable to make the cession as far as possible the act of the Dutch part of the population. If they think or have it in their power to say that they have been coerced into union, most of the good of the annexation will be lost for they will remain a discontented element in the body politic, troublesome and anti-English . . . [It] is extremely desirable to have the consent of the Volksraad to a cession of the State, and it would be dangerous to take over the country against their desire except under circumstances so grave as to justify us on the ground of unquestionable safety.[13]

What circumstances did Carnarvon consider grave enough to justify a breach of the Sand River Convention? Shepstone had warned him that the weakness of the Transvaal might provoke a Native rising against the white man all over southern Africa. This was highly unlikely. The Pedi might be a nuisance, but they were hardly a mortal peril even to the Transvaalers. To the south-east of the Transvaal lay the kingdom of the Zulus, much revived since the

battle of Blood River. As an official in the Colonial Office put it,
the Boers and the Zulus 'employ and expend their strength in an
attitude of suspicious observation which is not exactly either war or
peace.'[14] The same could have been said, during the past century, of
any frontier zone in southern Africa at almost any time. There was
no evidence in 1876 that aggression was likely from either side of
the Transvaal's boundary.

Had the Boers known what had passed between Carnarvon and
Shepstone they might reasonably have concluded that there was a
conspiracy against their independence. Shepstone had his own
agents in the Transvaal whom he used to sound out what he called
'the real feelings of the Boer population'. These men told him what
he wanted to hear: one of them, Percy Whitehead, wrote to him on
7 December 1876 that 'there is not a Boer who in his heart will not
welcome you and your Government, but that their fear of the
present Government and want of moral courage will prevent them
from memorializing or taking an active part in the change'. This
was having it both ways: if the Boers asked for annexation, Shepstone's road was clear; if they objected, the road was equally clear
since he could assume that no meant yes.

On 20 December 1876 Shepstone told President Burgers that he
was coming to the Transvaal as the Queen's representative to hold
'a special inquiry into the origin, nature, and circumstances' of the
Transvaal's recent difficulties and to try to find a settlement. Surprisingly, Burgers did not at once object to this intrusion; he may
have thought that he needed all the help he could get, since it was
clear that he had lost the support and respect of his own Volksraad.
Shepstone crossed into the Transvaal from Natal in January 1877,
bringing with him a small staff and an escort of twenty-five
mounted policemen. He had, however, British troops in reserve,
though at a distance: the 3rd Buffs, on their way to India, were
stopped at Cape Town and diverted to Newcastle in Natal, 160
miles from Pretoria. Shepstone's initial reception was encouraging.
There were volleys of welcome fired by Boers on horseback, and
there were triumphal arches and cordial speeches. But the address
presented to him by the burghers of Heidelberg was expressed in
terms of modified rapture:

So far as we know, you are the representative of Her Majesty
the Queen of England, and as such your message will, no
doubt, be one of peace and friendship. Be assured that we
burghers now assembled cherish the most friendly feeling

towards your Government, and that we shall concede to everything you might arrange with our Government for the well-being of our State.[15]

Shepstone entered Pretoria on 22 January 1877. President Burgers, mindful of European protocol, had sent his carriage to the outskirts of the town. The horses were taken out of the shafts and Shepstone dragged along by 'working men' who sang God Save the Queen with enthusiasm. But it was the immigrant English, and not the Boers, who gathered in welcome. Once lodged in Pretoria, Shepstone canvassed the possibility of annexation very widely. By one count, there were fifty-nine parties in the next ten weeks, given either for Shepstone or by him. Burgers was particularly susceptible to Shepstone's entertainments; after his tribulations among the children of nature he probably found it a welcome change to talk to someone more sophisticated. Shepstone said later that 3,000 people had declared themselves to be in favour of annexation. If this figure is to be accepted, and it seems very high, it must have included all those who accepted his hospitality – a form of acquiescence by association. He had convinced himself either that the real will of the Transvaalers was for annexation or, at least, that they would like him to make up their minds for them: 'many – I believe most – of the people see the impossibility of carrying on the Government, but they have not the courage to say so and wish me to act as if I did so against their wish.'[16]

Once Shepstone had come to this conclusion any expression of disapproval could be interpreted as a coded form of encouragement. But there was one Transvaaler whom he explicitly exempted from any shuffling or equivocal behaviour: 'Mr Paul Kruger positively declined to enter upon the discussion of any subject that might involve in any way the independence of the State as a Republic.' Kruger's intransigence was not buttressed by any practical suggestions: he merely expressed a 'strong hope' or a 'confident belief' that things would come right; how, he could not say.

This was Shepstone's first meeting with the man who was to become, later in life and even more emphatically after death, the avatar of one form of Afrikaner nationalism. Stephanus Johannes Paulus Kruger was then fifty-one. He had trekked out of the Cape Colony with his parents when he was ten. Responsibility had come to him early, and by seventeen he was a field-cornet. He had been prominent as a conciliator among the squabbling factions in the early years of the republic. He had also won the reputation of being

a mighty hunter and trusted fighter. He had been elected commandant–general and a member of the executive council. To the end of
his life his mastering purpose was the retention of the Transvaal's
independence.

Shepstone had made no secret of the fact that he had annexation
in mind, and he had probably linked this with the question of
confederation, since the Volksraad passed resolutions against confederation and for independence as soon as it met in emergency
session at Burgers's summons. It showed little enthusiasm for Burgers's proposals for reform of the constitution, although it was
proposed that failure to pay the war tax should be treated as high
treason – a measure which, if taken seriously, would have empowered Burgers to have hanged most of the population. Shepstone
kept in the background, dispensing food and drink and awaiting the

PLATE 5. *Paul Kruger* (Courtesy of the South African High Commission).

moment when it would be propitious to take the step upon which he had already resolved. He had convinced himself either that annexation would be popular, or at least that it would not be resisted. Evidence of opposition was dismissed as being the result of intrigue or intimidation. He thought that the Hollanders in the civil service were more in favour of independence than the Boers, because they feared for their jobs. The Volksraad itself, he said, was meeting under coercion: 'A system of terrorism represses every independent utterance, even in the council chamber. Many of the members have warmly but privately wished success to my mission, and declared their conviction that it is the only possible solution of their difficulties, but they dare not utter such sentiments openly.'[17]

However one interprets this, it is clear that Pretoria was a town of mistrust and unrest. Henry Rider Haggard, who was on Shepstone's staff, corroborated part, at least, of the tale of double-dealing:

> Members of the Volksraad and other prominent individuals in the country who had during the day been denouncing the Commissioner in no measured terms, and even proposing that he and his staff should be shot as a warning to the English Government, might be seen arriving at his house under cover of the shades of evening, to have a little talk with him, and express the earnest hope that it was his intention to annex the country as soon as possible. It is necessary to assist at a peaceable annexation to learn the depths of meanness human nature is capable of.[18]

But whatever individual members did or did not say in private, the Volksraad, as a body, did not vote itself out of existence. It acted at last at the beginning of March, after Shepstone had told the President and his executive council that he was sending for British troops, in that it postponed the forthcoming presidential election, appointed Kruger as vice-president, gave a general blessing to Burgers's proposals for constitutional reform, and instructed the executive council to negotiate with Shepstone, 'with the object of maintaining the independence of the State'. It then adjourned until May. The executive council had a single inconclusive meeting with Shepstone, and then its members voted an adjournment and went home, leaving Burgers as the solitary guardian of the State. On 11 March, Burgers formally asked Shepstone in a 'memorandum of questions' whether the British Government intended that the Transvaal should remain a separate state, retaining its autonomy, and with a popularly elected legislature. Shepstone replied:

> The Transvaal will remain a separate State in the sense that it will become a separate British Colony, with its own Laws and Legislature. It is the wish of Her Majesty's Government that the Transvaal should enjoy the fullest legislative privileges compatible with the circumstances of the country and the intelligence of its people; but much must of necessity depend upon the manner and spirit in which Her Majesty's benevolent intentions are received.[19]

Shepstone had failed to obtain the assent of the Boers to the annexation of their country. Apart from dubious interpretations of cryptic utterances by unnamed worthies, he had so far achieved the open backing only of English immigrants, mostly traders and miners. The Volksraad and executive council, by adjourning, had effectively refused to deal with him. He had little direct knowledge of the feeling in the country districts, apart from the impressions formed during his original journey to Pretoria; but his lack of popularity might have been deduced from the actions of a commando of about fifty armed burghers which had come to town and was dominating the streets and talking of violent actions, of which pulling down Shepstone's commissioner's flag was among the mildest. Burgers and Kruger both counselled against violence. Having failed to achieve assent, Shepstone was thrown back upon the second part of his instructions which permitted him to annex if the alternative were clear and pressing danger. But no such danger impended, and Shepstone was constrained to justify himself by arguing from the possible consequences of a collapse of the Transvaal economy, seasoned with allegations that might not have fared well under cross-examination. Thus he wrote on 3 April 1877:

> it is impossible for me to retreat now, come what may. If I were to leave the country, civil war would at once take place and the Natives would consider it the sunshine in which they should make hay in the Transvaal. The gold fields are in a state of rebellion against the Transvaal Government, and they are kept free from overt action only by my warnings and entreaties[20]

He added that 'the active opposition of the President is a serious matter, and must first be overcome, if possible'.

That opposition never was overcome. However, Shepstone had already selected his moment. Easter fell that year on 1 April, a highly unpropitious day since Boers from all over the country would have gathered in their districts for *naghtmaal*, corporate communion. Thereafter the Boers would scatter, since it was their custom at the beginning of autumn to move their cattle from the bleak and unsheltered high *veld* to lower and warmer altitudes. If he timed his *coup* for that period, Shepstone reasoned, the Boers would be too busy with their pastoral affairs to have any time for political resistance. Burgers was privately told that annexation would be proclaimed on 12 April. He replied that he would be bound to make a public protest, and he showed the text of this to Shepstone on 11 April. Next morning Melmoth Osborn, secretary to the mission, and seven other members of Shepstone's staff walked down to Church Square, the centre of Pretoria, where the proclamation of annexation was read to a small crowd, mostly English. There was no resistance whatsoever, but Shepstone thought it prudent to leave the ceremonial flagstaff bare until the arrival of the first British troops. Then on 24 May, Queen Victoria's birthday, the Union flag was hoisted by Colonel Brooke, RA and Rider Haggard.

The Transvaal had been annexed under protest. All that could be said, as evidence that Shepstone's action had been in accordance with the real will of the Boers, was that there was no immediate violent reaction – the argument of tacit consent. To argue that it was a popular move required diplomatic gymnastics which taxed Shepstone's skill. It was, he wrote to Robert Herbert, the permanent secretary at the Colonial Office, a difficult task. 'I had to steer clear on the one hand of giving the Boers the idea that the Government (Burgers and Company) were consenting parties, and on the other of conveying the notion to readers at a distance that in fact they were not so.'[21]

On this note of duplicity the Transvaal passed under British rule.

4 THE FIRST 'FREEDOM WAR'

Shepstone had been told to annex the Transvaal on one of two conditions – an invitation from the Boers, or an internal crisis serious enough to threaten other South African communities. He had gone ahead in the absence of either condition. Instead of an invitation he had received a solemn protest from President Burgers which could be said to legitimize the recalcitrance of those Boers who refused to recognize British authority. The internal troubles of the Transvaal were essentially domestic, and it could not plausibly be argued that the Transvaal's lack of money imperilled anyone except its officials and its debtors. Shepstone therefore asserted that the annexation had been popular and that opposition was confined to a few malcontents. He had come to the conclusion, moreover, that the Boer was not by nature a political animal:

> The great majority of voters, say nine-tenths, are Dutch–Africander farmers, slow in appreciating the bearing of political questions, phlegmatic in all political movements, very amenable to the representations, however absurd, of clever adventurers, and constitutionally averse to the struggles of political life.[1]

Shepstone's diagnosis showed little knowledge of the Boers' capacity for internal strife, nor did he seem to realize that the annexation had revived old animosities against the British. The Colonial Office also received encouraging reports from Shepstone's immediate superior in South Africa, Sir Bartle Frere, High Commissioner and Governor of Cape Colony. The annexation, Frere said, had been received in the Transvaal with 'acquiescence, relief, and satisfaction ... there has been no expression of opinion ... from any class whatever indicating the slightest desire to undo what has been done'. Looking further afield, Frere found positive approval among the native tribes, and in Natal, Kaffraria, Griqualand West and the eastern districts of the Cape. What he was saying was that it had been welcomed, hardly surprisingly, by the African tribes and the English. It had not been welcomed by the Afrikaners of the western Cape, where a protest had received 5,400 signatures; but Frere thought that this represented merely sentimental regret, such as the 'attachment to the Stuart line among many loyal English and Scotch people at the present day'. There was discontent in the Orange Free State, but it was not dangerous. In short, the Colonial Office was told by its men on the spot that what opposition existed was shallow-rooted and would wither away as the benefits of British rule became apparent.[2] One official wrote that 'whatever may have been the valour of a past generation, the present race of Boers are of an unwarlike disposition'.[3]

The Boers were resentful, but not despairing. It seemed to them incomprehensible that the British Government could believe that they had consented to the surrender of their independence, unless it had wilfully been deceived; surely, when it learnt the truth, it would return what it had taken away. The Volksraad had decided, in its dying days, that Paul Kruger, the newly appointed vice-president, and E. P. Jorissen, a Hollander official, should go to London to tell the Colonial Secretary exactly what Boer opinion was. The Volksraad had no money, and the expenses of the deputation, estimated at £2000, would have to be paid by public subscription. About half this sum had been subscribed by the time the deputation left; the rest was advanced by the new British administration. The sum subscribed was small but significant; the Boers were more willing to pay for a deputation to argue for independence than they had been to pay the tax for the war against Sekukuni – this time they were voting with their purses.

The deputies were received with cordial condescension in London. Lord Carnarvon invited them to Highclere, his country house, where Kruger made wassail with his host's home-brewed ale and told stories of lion hunting, with noises and gestures. (One of his favourite stories was how, as a boy, he had jumped on a newly-slain lioness so that the expulsion of air from the lungs made the carcase seem to roar; his elders first ran away and then came back and beat him.) Otherwise, their journey was a failure. Carnarvon told them that what was done could not be undone and, anyway, they did not represent the true feelings of their own people; his information was that the annexation had generally been welcomed. He would not allow them to hold a plebiscite because that would be 'calling into question the act which Sir Theophilus Shepstone did with the sanction of the Queen and in her name'. If they wanted a vote, they could have it on some issue that did not call the annexation into question, such as some aspect of the prospective constitution, 'so as to give the Dutch population the power of indirectly expressing their acquiescence in the new order of things'; but a direct vote on the annexation itself there could not be.

> I am altogether unable to consent to any such arrangement. Not only is it impossible for me to allow the act done in the name of the Queen by her fully-authorized officer to be now questioned, but if this were possible I should consider it in the highest degree inexpedient to place on record that an extremely small minority of the community, as I believe you agree with me in estimating it to be, is opposed to an acceptance of the Queen's rule.

The deputation's formal reply was that there was no more that could profitably be said:

> Although we may have perhaps a different idea as to the number of the inhabitants of the Transvaal who should have preferred independence to the acceptance of Her Majesty's sovereignty, we think it quite useless after your Lordship's decision to dwell any longer upon this matter.[4]

These published accounts seem to record a dialogue of the deaf. The deputation reported back to a public meeting held at Potchefstroom on 28 January 1878. The atmosphere was not always friendly, and Kruger was called on to deny that he had said that he accepted the annexation. He was then asked whether he still considered himself to be vice-president, a question that amounted to asking him whether he was ready to rebel. Kruger fenced skilfully. The answer to that question, he said, depended on the feeling within the Transvaal. If the majority of the burghers wanted independence, then he was vice-president still; but until they had won their case he was nothing. It was a shrewd answer: what Kruger was saying was that he was not going to be cast either as a catspaw or as the leader of a forlorn hope, but that he would do his duty to his people if circumstances permitted; at the same time there was nothing in his words that could put him in peril with the British Government.

In the same spirit he opposed a proposal by M. W. Pretorius that the old Volksraad and executive committee should be reconstituted; this was not the time for so drastic a defiance. But he supported Pretorius's next proposal, which was that a committee should be appointed to collect signatures. Carnarvon was to be met on ground of his own choosing. He had said that only a minority of the Boers was opposed to annexation. Very well; the Boers would prove him to be wrong, and they would do so without a a formal plebiscite.

The committee was chosen at once – Pretorius as chairman, Kruger and M. F. Viljoen. In an atmosphere of growing excitement during the next few weeks, it set about the collection of signatures for and against annexation. Shepstone reported that revolt was openly spoken of as the committee's agents toured the country. He remonstrated with Kruger who replied that he was a man of peace who merely wanted to find out what the facts were. 'What civilized being', he asked, 'could consider it a transgression to make known an untruth?' He meant no offence to Her Majesty's Government which, he felt confident, would allow truth to prevail. 'In this belief I shall confide until I am persuaded to the contrary; but I feel sure that when barbarous kaffir tribes complain to the Government and obtain their rights, why should not white people enjoy the same privilege?' He insisted, this time in a letter to Melmoth Osborn, Shepstone's secretary, that his was a pacifying influence. On his return from England, he wrote, he had found that some Boers were ready to fight but he had calmed them and persuaded them to trust in peaceful measures. As for himself, if he were shown that there was a majority for the annexation he would accept the Queen's sovereignty. Osborn warned him that his actions might have serious consequences: 'you must be equally well aware that the signatures to such a memorial will not represent the true feelings of those who sign it'.[5]

There was some justification for Osborn's scepticism, for the committee had decided that no abstentions would be permitted and those who refused to sign would be written down as favouring annexation. This decision could be interpreted in two ways – either that the Boers had given every chance to their opponents or that those who would have preferred to give silent consent were to be publicly exposed as enemies of the *Volk*. Shepstone issued a proclamation against sedition and warned the members of the committee that, although he would not prohibit the meeting called for the counting of signatures, he would hold them personally responsible for its transactions. This had some effect, for on 28 March the committee appealed to the *Volk* to stay away, 'armed or unarmed', from the meeting, which would deal only with the count, and would publish the result. This appeal went unheeded. The meeting was held at a farm named Doornfontein, midway between Pretoria and Potchefstroom, lasted for three days, and attracted a floating congregation of Boers estimated at different times at between 500 and 1,100. Feelings ran high, and the committee members had to defend themselves against accusations that they had been bought by the British and had taken an oath of allegiance to the Queen. These produced hot denials; but Shepstone must have found it ominous that any Boers who had dealings with him, however official, might be accused of disaffection from the *Volk*.

The lists of signatures were scrutinized, and it was announced that 6,591 were against the annexation and 591 in its favour. Since it was generally agreed that the white adult male population was about 8,000, this was a massive majority against British rule. The meeting then decided to send a second deputation of two to London, to present these figures to the Colonial Secretary in person. Election by district representatives produced thirty-six votes out of a possible thirty-seven for P. J. Joubert, with Kruger as runner-up with twenty-nine. Eduard Bok, another Hollander, was to go with them as secretary.

The number of signatures against annexation could hardly be shrugged off, although Shepstone tried to diminish their significance by reporting that 'several burghers' had told him privately that they had voted 'no' for fear of victimization; anyway, majorities were not everything. 'The Boer population of the Transvaal consists of about thirty vast families, and even these for the most part are connected by intermarriage.' This meant undue patriarchal influence. On the other hand, a quarter of the property of the Transvaal was in English hands, and there were also the interests of the Natives, who had not been consulted, to be considered. He advised the Colonial Secretary to give 'a decided no' to the new deputation. He also conducted a brisk exchange of accusations with Kruger and Joubert, who had written to tell him that some of their countrymen who had originally welcomed him had now repented. 'The deplorable state in which the country was then declared to be in has in every respect more than double increased, and the future is more than dark.' If that were so, Shepstone retorted, then it was their own fault. 'No two men in the Transvaal have done more to make the general ruin you deprecate possible than you have, and upon no shoulders will the responsibility of averting it press so heavily as upon yours.'[6] On 21 May 1878 Shepstone terminated Kruger's appointment as a member of the executive council of the former republic which he had held, rather oddly, without duties but with salary since the annexation; there was no point, Shepstone said, in 'retaining services which are detrimental rather than otherwise to the peace of the country'.[7] This dismissal redounded to Kruger's credit in Boer eyes.

Sir Bartle Frere, the High Commissioner, saw the deputation in Cape Town and offered soothing words. His advice was 'that they and their countrymen should address themselves to the more practical point of assisting us, under the British flag, to arrange such a constitution and system of administration for the Transvaal as would satisfy the reasonable wants and desires of the people'.[8] The Boers must by now have despaired of finding words which would make a British official comprehend that the 'wants and desires' of the Boers were to be rid of British rule.

The deputation's reception at the Colonial Office was chillier this time. There was, to begin with, a new Colonial Secretary, Sir Michael Hicks Beach, a bleaker man than his predecessor and, being new to the office, even more disposed to listen to his officials. Their advice was that the deputation should be dismissed as quickly as courtesy would permit; Robert Herbert, the permanent secretary, described Kruger and Joubert as 'bitterly anti-English dopper Boers who cannot be "civilized" '.[9] This time, therefore, there was no jolly private hospitality. Kruger and Joubert said that they now had the evidence of the signatures to show that seven-eighths of the white population were opposed to the annexation. Hicks Beach told them that they were wrong. Some signatures had been obtained under duress; furthermore, he was 'unable to regard the memorial as representing the true and deliberate opinions of those inhabitants of the Transvaal who are capable of forming a judgement on such a question'. Anyway, there were other interests to be considered: Britain, as the paramount power, must govern in the interests of the whole of South Africa and all its peoples, and therefore the fate of the Transvaal was a matter for the British Government and nobody else. The matter was *chose jugée*.[10]

Donald Currie, founder of the Castle steamship line, who had extensive interests in Cape Colony and had acted as an unofficial adviser to the deputation, warned Hicks Beach that if the Boers did not get what they wanted they would either fight or trek out of the Transvaal. There was no point in trying to woo them with promises of future material advantages for their country because they were simply not interested in British ideas of economic development.[11]

Hicks Beach took Currie's warning seriously; he persuaded the Cabinet to strengthen the garrison in South Africa and spun out the discussions to give time for the troops to arrive before the deputation returned. Kruger and Joubert left England in October; there had been no change of attitude on either side. Hicks Beach told them formally that it was the British Government's unalterable intention that the Transvaal should become 'an integral and separate State' within a South African confederation, 'possessing a Constitution securing, to the utmost practical extent, its individuality and powers of self-government under the sovereignty of the Queen'. The deputation replied that, without independence, the Transvaal would never voluntarily enter any confederation. Their last word was 'We should consider it an unfriendly act did we not inform you that we feel much disappointment at being forced to return without carrying with us any the least hope or prospect for our countrymen in respect of the future'.[12]

On 10 January 1879 the deputation reported on the failure of its mission to a public meeting. The outcome could be summed up as no co-operation without independence. The meeting authorized the 'signatures committee' of three (Pretorius, Kruger and Viljoen) to remain in being, to continue to protest and 'with the people to concert further measures towards the achievement of their object'. The first of these measures was the summoning of an 'assembly of the people' to meet in March, with an invitation to the High Commissioner to attend.

Sir Bartle Frere was willing enough, but for the moment he had other matters on his mind. He had brought on a war with the Zulus, the first result of which was the annihilation of a British regiment at Isandhlwana, a disaster partly redeemed by the defence of Rorke's Drift and by victory at Ulundi. War against black enemies usually evoked white solidarity; this time it did not. Kruger refused Shepstone's appeal to him to take the field against the Zulus with whatever forces he could raise: 'I am sorry to inform you . . . that the annexation has caused a breach between the people of the Transvaal, who have protested against the annexation, and the British Government; a breach of so serious a nature, that for many years to come no friendly co-operation can be thought of.'[13]

Shepstone was replaced as Administrator early in 1879 by Colonel Owen Lanyon. He had served in Jamaica, and that and his swarthy complexion persuaded some Boers to believe that he was of Coloured blood and that his appointment was therefore intended as an insult to themselves. He arrived at a time of crisis; the mass meeting summoned by the Boer committee had assembled at Klein-fontein, thirty-six miles from Pretoria, and was waiting for the promised visit of the High Commissioner. It had to wait for nearly a month, and tempers began to rise. This was a *wapende protes*, a protest under arms, and the younger Boers beguiled the tedium with what Lanyon called 'reviews, parades, and sham fights'. Not all was playful: post-carts were held up and wayfarers molested. The committee disavowed these activities, but they went on none the less. Meanwhile, as grazing became exhausted and the environs were befouled – for about 5,000 Boers stayed at the camp at one time or another, with their wagons and ox-teams – the whole assembly moved gradually in the direction of Pretoria, to the alarm of the town, which prepared itself for a siege.

By argument, vote and now by their physical presence – in itself a formidable feat of organization – the Boers had tried to make it clear that they did not want British rule. They had not succeeded. Lanyon reported to Frere that the assembly could not be regarded as representative because many who were there had been forced to come, and that even the volunteers did not accurately reflect 'either the intelligence or the vested interests of the Transvaal'. Agitation, he thought, had been fomented by foreigners – he meant the much-maligned Hollanders – and 'were it not for their evil influence, by far the greater portion of the people would gladly accept the peace and sense of security which Her Majesty's rule affords them'.[14]

Frere came at last in the second week of April, when the moving assembly had reached Erasmus's Spruit, fourteen miles from Pretoria. He was received with hostile silence when he rode into the camp. He had long discussions with the committee. He offered concessions within the framework of British rule, and the Boers replied that they wanted nothing at all until they had got their independence back.[15] Frere accused them of intimidating dissidents, and said that his information was that those who had been reluctant to join the assembly had been told they would otherwise be shot, cut in pieces and made into *biltong* (raw flesh dried in the sun, and accounted a delicacy in South Africa). The Boers professed to be much wounded by this imputation, which they repeatedly denied. Frere tried to define what he understood by independence – freedom of speech, protection of life and property, votes for all white men who paid taxes; they replied that they were not interested and what they meant by independence was what they had possessed before Shepstone had taken it away. Kruger talked of the Sand River Convention and of stolen goods that they would like to have restored. Frere said that they might have 'all the liberty which any Englishmen may have'. The Boers said that they were not Englishmen. Frere said that he had no power to undo the annexation; Joubert replied that the committee had no power to undo 'the will of the people', and he appealed to Frere to be the Boers' advocate and to explain to the British Government that the people of the Transvaal abhorred an annexation 'brought about by perjury and deceit'. An extract from the published version gives some idea of the temper of a meeting that was becoming increasingly heated.

FRERE : If I had taken Mr Kruger's tobacco fields from him and he were to see cattle destroying them, he would not be able to stand quietly by; he would drive them out.

KRUGER : No; and I would put it more strongly still. If Your Excellency had taken my house from me and I saw it on fire, I would let it burn down without moving a hand; if I may not have the use of it, neither shall you.

Frere met the committee twice, once in the camp and once in Pretoria. In between he sent an urgent appeal for troops to General Lord Chelmsford, commanding the British army in Zululand; the Boer camp, he said, was now in laager and could be dispersed only by artillery fire. During the meeting in Pretoria the Boers asked that this time their opinions should be accurately reported to London; in the past, they said, they had been misrepresented. Frere showed them a draft of his dispatch, over which they argued for hours. After much talk at cross-purpose Frere said that if they gave him a memorial, setting out their views, he would send it to the British Government and commend it to 'serious consideration'. The Boers took this to mean that, at last, they had won Frere over. They were wrong. He had come to the Transvaal to reconcile the Boers to the inevitability of British rule, if he could; and if he could not, to force them to endure it. On 23 April he reported to London that he had given a warning that no more armed gatherings would be allowed: 'the Government will not again permit itself to be menaced by an armed malcontent force.'[16] He asked for reinforcements, including cavalry and at least two field guns. Frere's impressions of the people with whom he had been dealing deserves extensive quotation:

If I may judge from the gentlemen composing the deputation, and others of their class whom I have had the honor of meeting since coming to the Transvaal, the leaders are, with few exceptions, men who deserve respect and regard for may valuable and amiable qualities, as citizens and subjects. In simple faith, in fidelity to all obligations of family, race and kindred, in reverential observance of all scriptural obligations and precepts, as understood by them from the word of God which is their sole text-book and written authority, they strongly remind me of the Puritans and Covenanters of earlier days. In education and the refinements which go with it, they are obviously behind the better class of Dutch farmers in the old Colony [*sc.* the Cape], who belong to the same original stock. The Transvaal farmer is generally the son or grandson of a 'Voor-trekker' whose descendants have lived perforce in the wilderness, far from schools and all means of education; comparatively few have had the advantages of a whole year's schooling of any kind. But this to my mind makes more meritorious the amount of education, almost self-acquired, to be found among them, and more touching their earnest desire to give to their children advantages, in the way of education, which have been denied to themselves . . .

The few exceptions are mostly foreign adventurers of various sorts and nations – English, Irish and Scotch, Jews, Americans, Hollanders, Germans, Belgians, and Portuguese – who though often well educated and naturally able, are rarely men of high character or disinterested aims. They acquire great influence among the less educated Boers, but foster the tendency towards suspicion which, mixed with extraordinary credulity in many things, is a marked feature in the Boer character, and makes them very difficult to manage by anyone who does not enjoy their entire confidence.

They are extremely sensitive to ridicule and to opprobrious or slanderous imputations, feeling most keenly unjust charges against their race by any in authority. Hence perhaps they are very liable to be deceived by men who, for their own ends, flatter and pretend to sympathize with them.'[17]

The final sentence might have been applied to all those British officials who continued to assert, on the evidence of unnamed Boer informants, that the annexation was popular. Frere's character sketch, sympathetic though it is in some respects, failed to understand the Boer desire for independence. His reference to foreign agitators avoids the question whether their influence was based on their ability to revive resentments that already existed. Nor did he seem to be aware of the implications of his statement that the Boers could not be managed by those whom they did not trust. The members of the Boer committee considered themselves as the 'voice of the people'; to Frere they were malcontents, whose followers had either been dragooned or had their true feelings warped by agitators.

No British administrator at this stage would admit that the mass of the Boers regarded British rule as abhorrent. On 11 May 1879 Frere telegraphed to the Colonial Secretary that 'the malcontent party, though large and active, does not represent general Transvaal opinion'; the Boers in the western districts, he said, were 'loyal'. If there were discontent, it could be removed by administrative reform. The first requisite, however, was to set at rest any doubts that might exist about Britain's determination not to withdraw. The second was to establish the machinery of responsible government, as Shepstone had promised, and persuade the Boers to accept it and work it. Here one may discern two of the underlying strands of British imperialism, one of objective and the other of method. The objective was efficient administration or, to put it another way, civilized government. The method was by enlisting local collaborators. In the main, the method had produced converts, and the objective could sometimes serve as a sufficient justification for imperial occupation, as Alfred Milner justified the British presence in Egypt. The British had brought to the Egyptians 'the ordinary methods and principles of civilized government . . . As this has been the nature of our influence, it is evident that it could never be out of place'.[18]

The difficulty in the Transvaal was that Boer collaborators were hard to find, and those who existed were generally rejected by the rest of the *Volk*. In the middle of 1879, Lanyon reported that four field cornets had been intimidated into refusing to take an oath of allegiance, and he quoted an affidavit sworn to by one of them, of the Gatsrand ward, who had suffered a discouraging experience at the Kleinfontein meeting in March. He had gone there, he said, not because he was disaffected but because he had a wagon to sell. He was accosted by the leader of a posse of about fifty armed men and told that he was not welcome at a patriotic gathering. 'You are a British subject and field cornet; what do you want here? I give you ten minutes to inspan and go away, and you must not talk much or I'll cut your ears off.'[19] But whatever bizarre influences beat upon the lesser folk, there could be no question of intimidation in the attitude of P. J. Joubert, who wrote to the public prosecutor in response to a tax demand: 'Under the legal government of the South African Republic I was always willing and obedient to the laws. Since the arbitrary, artful and illegal annexation of the country and the transgression and violation of the laws and rights of the people, I have considered myself under protest.'[20]

Joubert would neither take the oath of allegiance nor give up his office as justice of the peace, the equivalent of which he had held under the republic. His original oath, he said:

> does not in the least bind me to any individual person, but tells me how to act as a faithful and upright justice of the peace for the benefit and welfare of the people of the Republic, to advance its progress and to maintain its independence. The country being deprived of this independence by treachery and fraud under solemn protest has not left me at liberty to take the oath demanded by you without a violation of my first oath and without committing perjury.[21]

No action was taken against Joubert; Lanyon reported that he could not take the risk of arresting him until there was a stronger armed force in the country. He added, inconsistently, that the spirit of resistance represented 'neither the intelligence, the majority, nor the property-holders of the territory'.

Lanyon's travails were compounded by a judgment delivered by J. G. Kotze, a judge of the High Court of the Transvaal, in the case of *White and Tucker* v. *Rudolph*, in May 1879. Rudolph, *landdrost* of Utrecht, had been ordered to seize all spirits in his district to prevent drunkenness among the British soldiery. Kotze's judgment denied the legality of the order. Seizure of property would ordinarily require the sanction of the legislature. Thus the question arose, had the Crown power to legislate for the Transvaal? Kotze decided that the Transvaal had become British not by occupancy, conquest or cession, but by a proclamation of annexation that was a solemn treaty in which it was stated that the Transvaal would remain a separate government with its own laws and legislature; and the laws then in force would remain until altered by a competent authority. 'At the time of the annexation, the Transvaal had a legislature of its own, and the Proclamation expressly guaranteed the continuance of the local Legislature, although perhaps not necessarily constituted in the same form as previously.' He argued from *Campbell* v. *Hall* (1774) that if the Crown once divested itself of the power of legislation it could not exercise it again. Therefore the Crown could not legislate for the Transvaal, although the

Transvaal as part of the British Empire was subject to the legislation of the Imperial Parliament. The Administrator's Minute of 10 March 1879 had said: 'Critical times require prompt remedies, and if the law enacts anything which may be contrary to the safety of the country, we must act contrary to the law so long as the public safety is endangered.' In this instance, Kotze ruled, the argument of *salus populi* failed because the circumstances did not justify strong action.[22]

The Administration could neither issue emergency orders nor collect its revenue. Joubert's example in refusing to pay taxes was widely followed; this was a matter in which self-interest and patriotism walked hand in hand. Nor could the laws always be enforced; it needed an officer and ten troopers of the Kimberley Horse to escort the sheriff serving an order of the court on J. P. Maré, a member of the Boer committee, who had refused to recognize the court's jurisdiction. Lanyon asked for reinforcements; he needed a force strong enough to support the civil power.

> I feel confident that firmness backed up by the knowledge that such a force is available, will bring about a peaceful solution of all the difficulties connected with this disaffected spirit on the part of this section of the Boers, for they have not the sympathy of the majority of their countrymen. But at the present moment, and in existing circumstances, the Government would be acting unadvisedly to invite opposition by the enforced collection of taxes.[23]

This dispatch was addressed not to Frere, whose authority had now been confined to the Cape Colony, but to Sir Garnet Wolseley, the most celebrated of living British soldiers, who was now responsible, as high commissioner and governor, for the affairs of the Transvaal. The troops which Lanyon had asked for arrived with promptness – a battalion of infantry, a battery of artillery and a squadron of the King's Dragoon Guards – and hard on their heels came Wolseley himself. Joubert, who met him at Standerton, warned him not to take at face value such addresses of welcome as he might receive, or even what some Boers might say to him in private, 'as many who would not dispute with him, and even seem to agree with him, would be as determined as ever in their opposition as soon as they had left him'. Wolseley replied, with breathtaking confidence, that he knew better, and rebuked Joubert for 'lowering his countrymen in an Englishman's eyes'; Boers always spoke frankly to him, Wolseley said.[24]

Whatever Wolseley did was likely to be brisk; not for him the strategy of the long haul. The advice of the men on the spot was that the malcontents must not be confused with a majority that remained silent because of fear of British inconstancy. Both Frere and Lanyon had assured him, he reported to the Colonial Secretary, 'that there is in this territory a strong if not a preponderating body who are in favour of our rule, but who from fears engendered by uncertainty as to whether they might not be abandoned before long to a return of Dutch Government, have hesitated to raise their voices on the side of peace and order.'[25]

Thus, certainty should replace doubt. At a banquet in Pretoria, attended mostly by the English community, Wolseley announced that the Transvaal would remain British as long as the sun shone, and the Vaal River would flow backwards to its source before it regained its independence. He followed this up, on 29 September 1879, with a proclamation of the British Government's firm intention that the Transvaal should be 'for ever an integral part of Her Majesty's Dominions in South Africa'. In October he expanded the machinery of government, in standard Crown Colony style, by an ordinance which created an executive council consisting of the governor and five official and three unofficial members. None of this had much effect; administration was carried on without friction only in the towns, and not always there. Edward Fairfield, an official in the Colonial Office, commented mordantly: 'In a country where our own paid officers actively conspire against the Queen's rule, and where a man need not pay taxes unless he likes, the finances cannot be expected to be carried out with much regularity.'[26]

Lanyon tried sanctions; he withdrew permits to buy sporting ammunition from all those who could not produce tax receipts. The result was open defiance; the occasion was the trial of J. H. Jacobs, a member of the Boer committee, summoned to appear before the magistrate of Middelburg to answer a charge that he had hung up a native servant by his hands from a beam for trying to leave his employment. Jacobs brought with him an escort of fifty friends, all of whom crowded into the court room. The magistrate, John Scoble, thought it propitious to read from the bench Wolseley's proclamation on the retention of the Transvaal. He was howled down, at which he adjourned the trial after remarking, unpersuasively, that politics should not be discussed in court. Whooping with triumph, Jacobs's escort streamed from the court house into the streets of Middelburg, descended on the town's two general stores and helped themselves to the entire stock of ammunition; they offered payment which was refused when they presented neither tax receipts nor permits. When the trial was resumed next day the prosecutor asked for an adjournment *sine die* lest the public peace be endangered. Lanyon sent a troop of cavalry to Middelburg, backed up by a detachment of infantry, and ordered Jacobs's trial to be resumed and summonses issued to those of the ammunition takers who could be identified. Lanyon went there himself and found the town in a state of semi-siege, with Jacobs and his friends in a *laager* on its outskirts. Jacobs did not appear when his name was called in court, and a warrant was issued for his arrest. The military was there in force, and Jacobs submitted himself to the court, pleaded a misunderstanding and was bound over to come up for trial when called upon to do so. Three ammunition takers were convicted and fined £5 each, three others were acquitted, and the remainder pleaded guilty and paid their £5 fines.

In private, Wolseley was having doubts, which he aired in a protracted correspondence with the Colonial Secretary.[27] Was the Transvaal worth keeping? The Boer committee had summoned another mass meeting for December, and he wondered what would happen when, as seemed likely, it declared for independence. Were those who wanted independence fit to have it? 'There can be little doubt in the minds of men who know the Boers that they are, in their present ignorant state, utterly incapable of governing themselves.' The country would revert to anarchy, banks would close, traders would be ruined; surely the British Government owed something to those who had been attracted to the country precisely because it was under British rule? 'If nine shopkeepers out of ten in any town were to actively assist the Government and the tenth man to remain cowardly inactive, expressing no opinion or traitorously advocating the Boer cause, he would monopolize all the Boers' business . . . to the ruin of the nine others.' A majority of the white population probably wanted the British to go; but what sort of a majority was it? It would 'include all the most ignorant and illiterate of the population, whilst on the other side the minority would represent the intelligence of the Transvaal'. What, then, was to be done? There seemed no middle way between retrocession, with all its humiliations, and effective military occupation. The balance of advantage probably lay on the side of occupation.

[T]here can be little doubt that larger and still more valuable goldfields will sooner or later be discovered. Any such discovery would soon bring a large British population. The time must eventually come when the Boers will be in a small minority ... Would it not, therefore, be a very near-sighted policy to recede now from the position we have taken up here, because for a few years to come the retention of 2000 or 3000 troops may be necessary ...?

Frere, who was invited to comment on Wolseley's views, agreed that the Transvaal ought to be retained, not for advantage but for peace.

When one's neighbour's house is burning, a man has a proverbial right to put out the fire. Such was the state of the Transvaal. Practical anarchy and paralysis of all governing power had reached a pass which threatened the peace of all South Africa. No one can judge of the necessity for interference in such cases save the neighbouring community whose peace is threatened. No sane man waits to call the fire engines to his neighbour's burning house till the bewildered tenants have decided, by a show of hands, that without external aid the house must be burnt.'

Presumably, the danger to the neighbours lay in the possibility of a Native uprising; surprisingly, Frere defended the Boer treatment of the Natives and contrasted it favourably with that of the South African English.

[The Boers'] general feeling seems to me much like that of the less educated class of farmers in remote districts of our own country towards the labouring class; it is a hard and unsympathetic, but not intentionally cruel feeling.

There are, of course, terrible exceptions in South Africa as elsewhere on the outskirts of civilization, where there is a chronic kind of race antagonism; but as regards the Native races within the Colonial border, the tendency of the Boer farmer is not generally to 'bully' the natives who are his workpeople but to treat them often, I think, with more real kindness than they would experience from European employers of the ruder class; certainly the Dutch, as a rule, seem to me to retain the voluntary services of their native servants for longer periods, and with less occasional friction, than English colonists of the same class.[28]

The British Government decided that there would be no second thoughts and, in reaffirming its decision to keep the Transvaal, modified retrospectively the Sand River Convention to mean that

Boer independence was intended to be conditional on their governing in such a way as to preserve the common safety of the white
communities in southern Africa; and this, in the opinion of the
British Government, the Boers had sufficiently demonstrated that
they could not do. Thus they must endure the loss of their independence with such stoicism as they could muster. If they wished to
be contented they must change their attitudes. Hicks Beach hoped,
he concluded in his dispatch to Wolseley, that

> even the Boers themselves may yet see that their natural
> desires for self-government will most surely be realized by that
> cordial co-operation with Her Majesty's Government which I
> have so often invited, rather than persisting in demands which
> cannot be complied with for the restoration of an isolated
> independence which has already failed to ensure the peace of
> the country or the safety of its inhabitants.[29]

There was no sign, as 1879 drew to a close, of Hicks Beach's hopes
being fulfilled. Magistrates' reports from district after district told
the same story – disaffection, the need for troops to compel com-
pliance with even civil judgments of the courts, and open talk of
rebellion to come after the next mass meeting. In the face of all this
Wolseley tried boldness – an expedition of his own against the
still-contumacious Sekukuni. This was one of the 'little wars' in
which Wolseley excelled, where success depended on speed, energy
and ruthlessness. The gamble succeeded: a British force with Swazi
auxiliaries stormed Sekukuni's stronghold and brought Sekukuni
himself back as a prisoner to Pretoria. It was a demonstration of
what British troops could do when properly led, and it probably
had some effect in damping down belligerent spirits among the
Boers at the next mass meeting.

Wolseley took the threat of rebellion seriously. Before he left
for his whirlwind campaign against Sekukuni he issued a proclamation warning that the laws of the South African Republic
against treason and sedition were still in force and reminding the
population that it was an offence to threaten, coerce or intimid-
ate others for political purposes. The garrison, after its tuning-up
campaign in the north, was concentrated around Pretoria. Privately, Wolseley was pessimistic; he could see no sign that Boer
hostility was diminishing.

The long-awaited mass meeting began at Wonderfontein, seventy
miles from Pretoria, on 11 December 1879 and lasted for three
days. The temper was threatening but the mastering fact was that

British troops were mobilized in force. But there was more to the meeting than angry rhetoric. A common sense of injury was generating a feeling of solidarity which had not been present in the days of the republic. This was noted at the time by a correspondent writing in *De Volkstem*:

> When I walked back to my tent and once more cast my eye on that assembled crowd, come together here from near and far, it seemed to me that the annexation after all had had a beneficial result for the Transvaal people. It called into existence the mass meetings, of which we have now the fifth, and by that very means the various elements of the country were, as it were, securely knit together; and where formerly speaking about the Transvaal we could mention only a thinly-populated country, whose inhabitants were severed by many divergent interests and, as it were, bound together by no single bond of union, these same inhabitants now come together as one people, with their own history, and indissolubly bound together by the highest virtue – patriotism. Thus a bad cause sometimes brings good results.

Pretorius presided over the meeting, but the dominant figure was Paul Kruger, now appearing more and more as the embodiment of the *Volk* in conclave. He counselled moderation; not, he said, because he favoured British rule but because he thought that immediate resistance would be futile. It was all very well to fly the old republican flag and to talk about war, but he doubted the resolution of some of those present. 'You put up your hats; but when the strife commences, will you not say then that your business calls you away, that your farms require your presence?'

The meeting passed resolutions which stopped just short of open defiance but showed hostility not only to the administration but to all that was English in the Transvaal. Members of the *Volk*, 'except under coercion', would not appear in court. When the time was ripe Kruger as vice-president would convene the old *volksraad* according to the constitution of the old republic. In the meantime, if nothing were done 'in a friendly way' before 6 April 1880, right-thinking Boers should boycott all English supporters of the government, destroy all English books and documents within reach, remove their children from English schools, refuse to have English spoken in their homes, refuse hospitality to or from the English, and give neither assistance nor protection to English travellers. A final resolution condemned the British Government and its ministers and high commissioners as being 'deaf to right and justice'. On this note the meeting adjourned until 12 April 1880, a significant date since it would mark the third anniversary of the annexation.

Wolseley was relieved; it could all, he thought, have been a great deal worse. However, the Boers must be taught that subversive talk would not go unnoticed. He arrested Pretorius, chairman of the meeting, and Bok, its secretary. Kruger claimed that he had prevented violence then and there by galloping after a party of Boers that was on its way to rescue Pretorius by force and persuading it to give up the attempt. Neither of the arrested men came to trial. Wolseley had Pretorius brought before him and appealed to him to use his influence to persuade his countrymen to turn away from agitation and settle down under British rule. Pretorius was cagey: he did not, he said, know how much influence he had, for he was only the chairman of the committee and thus bound to do whatever the people wanted. But he would try. Wolseley gave him a spider with horse and driver, put money in his purse for expenses and set him loose on his travels. They were not extensive. He addressed one meeting, near Potchefstroom, found the audience unresponsive, and then retired, discouraged, to his farm; no more was heard from him until the Transvaal was at war.

Wolseley turned easily from gloom to optimism; this may have been a sign of his eagerness to shake the dust of the Transvaal from his feet. Once the Boer meeting had dispersed he began to talk about reducing the garrison. Then the Boers cancelled the April meeting, and Wolseley galloped out of the Transvaal, congratulating himself that his firmness in arresting Pretorius had dampened the Boers' seditious ardour.

A lull had fallen over the Transvaal, but it was not the result of anything that Wolseley had either said or done. The beginning of autumn was the natural end of the agitating season as the Boers busied themselves with the seasonal migration of their cattle to the low *veld*. Moreover, British politics seemed to be turning in their favour, and they had reason to believe that what a Conservative Government had done a Liberal Government would undo. Echoes of Gladstone's Midlothian campaign had reached the Transvaal, with the news that the greatest Liberal of them all had publicly described the annexation of the Transvaal as insane. Gladstone's was not the only Liberal voice: Lord Hartington, leader of the party in the House of Commons, had apparently accepted the argument that the Boers had put so fruitlessly to Carnarvon and Hicks Beach.

We were informed that a large majority . . . were in favour of
the annexation. It is now proved conclusively that a large
majority, at all events of the Boers, are bitterly against it. We
are now told that the annexation was rendered necessary
because we could not permit the foreign policy of the Government of the Transvaal in their dealings with the Natives; but
we have been ourselves compelled to adopt almost the same
line of policy . . . Our true dignity would be best consulted by
acknowledging that we have made a mistake, if indeed it is
found that a mistake has been made, and restoring the Government of the Transvaal.[30]

The Boers could hardly have put it better themselves. If they had
known rather more about Gladstone they might have noticed an
ominous qualification in his speech of 17 March 1880: 'We have no
power to relieve you from engagements of honour and good faith
entered into by the present Government'. What this meant became
clear when Gladstone became Prime Minister again in April 1880,
and it was announced that the Queen's authority over the Transvaal would be maintained. The Boers might be excused if they
thought that they had been double-crossed once again by a British
politician. This time they were not told that it was their real will to
be British subjects; the reasons for retention were stated to be
obligations to British settlers who had entered the Transvaal since
1877 and the duty which Great Britain owed to the Natives. Moreover, there still remained the faint and fading hopes of some closer
union in South Africa, described sometimes as federation and sometimes as confederation. It is doubtful whether these hopes had ever
been justified; they were dead now. Kruger and Joubert had
campaigned vigorously in the Cape against federation; Gladstone's Colonial Secretary told him that the matter was 'adjourned
sine die'.

It might be thought puzzling that Lanyon was still convinced that
the Transvaal was settling down. True, taxes were not being col-
lected, but he saw no political motivation there: it was in the
nature of the Boer to object to government in general and taxes in
particular. But summonses could not be delivered without military
protection, and the King's Dragoon Guards, much to their disgust,
found themselves escorts to process–servers. It was upon Lanyon's
sanguine reports that Wolseley, now back at his headquarters in
Natal, relied. In August 1880, after some prodding from the War

Office, Wolseley agreed that the King's Dragoon Guards could be
sent to India. This meant that the Transvaal would be denuded of
regular cavalry. In retrospect this seems to have been a strange
decision. However, service in the Transvaal was not the King's
Dragoon Guards' finest hour. In a year, sixty troopers and seven
non-commissioned officers had deserted. Mostly they slipped across
the border with the Orange Free State where they settled down to
pastoral pursuits, often married to the daughters of local farmers.
One of the regiment's officers, hunting in the Orange Free State on
leave, found that the local blacksmith was the former farrier of his
own troop, who told him that the usual charge for replacing a cast
shoe was five shillings but for this customer it would be one pound.

Rebellion came at last at the end of 1880. It was touched off by a
bungled court case out of which emerged a dubious and reluctant
martyr. A farmer named Bezuidenhout from the Potchefstroom
district was served with a tax demand for £27 5s., the rate for two
'full farms' of 6,000 acres each. Bezuidenhout claimed that he only
owned 'half farms' and offered to pay £14. This offer was refused;
Bezuidenhout was taken to court, where judgment was given for
£14 but with the addition of £8 in costs. Bezuidenhout felt that he
had been unjustly treated for proving that he had been in the right
and refused to pay the costs. His wagon was attached in execution
and put up for auction in Potchefstroom on 11 November. The sale
was interrupted by the arrival of about a hundred armed and
mounted men, led by Piet Cronje, who seized the wagon and then
encamped outside the town. From then on events moved swiftly.
The old *volksraad* was summoned to meet at Paardekraal on
8 December. There each member took a vow to uphold independence, in the manner of the vow on the eve of the battle of Blood
River, and placed a stone on a cairn as a sign of resolution. Kruger
resumed the title of vice-president and he, Joubert and Pretorius
were elected as a triumvirate at the head of a provisional government. Three commandos were mobilized: one, under Cronje, went
to Potchefstroom to print the proclamation of republican independence; a second, under Frans Joubert, went to the north-east to
prevent reinforcements from outlying garrisons from reaching
Pretoria; and the third and largest went to Heidelberg, where the
vierkleur, the old republican flag, was hoisted on 16 December –
Dingaan's Day, the anniversary of the battle of Blood River – and
an ultimatum was sent to Lanyon requiring him to hand over the
state to the triumvirate within forty-eight hours. The first shots
were fired at Potchefstroom on that day.

Colonel Bellairs, the officer commanding the British forces in the Transvaal, had begun to take precautions after the Bezuidenhout affair in November, and among them was the recall to Pretoria of the outlying detachments of the 94th Regiment from the northern and eastern districts. One detachment, which had been delayed by bad roads and flooded rivers, was still on the march from Middelburg to Pretoria when the rebellion began. On 15 December Bellairs sent a warning to its commanding officer, Lieutenant–Colonel Anstruther, that he was likely to be attacked. Anstruther received this on the morning of the 17th; a second warning reached him on the morning of the 20th, which told him to be especially careful 'at the Botha's Hill range or defile' about twenty miles east of Pretoria. Anstruther apparently interpreted this as meaning that he need not be careful anywhere else. At about 1 p.m. on 20 December his column was approaching a small stream, the Bronkhorstspruit, where he intended to bivouac. His force consisted of nine offices and 254 other ranks, and there were also three soldiers' wives. The disposition of the troops did not suggest that Anstruther thought himself in any danger. His train of thirty-four wagons stretched for

PLATE 6. *Boers during the war* (Courtesy of Popperfoto).

half a mile. The troops carried thirty rounds of ammunition each, instead of the seventy laid down in regulations for those about to go into action; the lids of the ammunition chests in the wagons were screwed down. The band was playing at the head of the column. About 150 mounted Boers appeared over a crest 300 yards away on the column's left. A herald under a white flag came forward and gave Anstruther a letter from the triumvirate saying that until they heard from Lanyon they did not know whether they were at war or not, but in the meantime they would not permit any troop movements and Anstruther was to stay where he was. Anstruther replied: 'I am going to Pretoria. You must do as you like.' He also asked to see the Boer commandant. The herald rejoined his own people, and Anstruther began to put his command into fighting order. The Boers – they were of Frans Joubert's commando – advanced about 150 yards, took cover, and opened fire with rifles.

This was the first serious action fought by British troops against white opponents since the Crimean War. It was also the last fight in which the British wore scarlet: khaki uniforms had recently been issued but had not reached the 94th in their isolation. The action lasted for about ten minutes before Anstruther surrendered; he had lost one officer and fifty-six other ranks killed, and seven officers and ninety-two other ranks wounded. Eight out of nine officers had been put out of action. The Boer losses were two men killed and five wounded.

A paramount power can ill afford to lose battles, however insignificant, and Bronkhorstspruit was both a military humiliation and a political embarrassment. The Government of the Orange Free State remained impeccably aloof, but there were rumours that volunteers from the Free State were preparing to join the Transvaalers. Sympathy among Afrikaners in the Cape Colony was overwhelmingly pro-Boer; Lord Kimberley, the Colonial Secretary, said: 'Every blow we strike in the Transvaal is a blow felt by our own Dutch subjects in the Cape Colony.' For the moment, the British were receiving rather than striking blows; there was a defeat to be avenged and troops to be rescued, for the Boers had besieged all the garrison towns in the Transvaal.

These tasks fell to Sir George Colley, Wolseley's successor as High Commissioner, Governor and General Commanding in Natal and the Transvaal. Colley was then forty-five, and was looked on as one of the most distinguished of the younger generation of general officers. He had passed out of Sandhurst first in his year; at the staff college he had passed out first with the highest aggregate of marks ever obtained until then by any candidate. He was one of the brilliant collection of promising officers whom Wolseley had taken with him to the Ashanti War in 1873. Colley was in his fifth tour of duty in southern Africa; he was therefore a soldier of proven ability with local knowledge. What he did not have were first-rate troops. He advanced towards the Transvaal with a scratch force. It was particularly deficient in cavalry; of his 120 mounted men, some were from the headquarters staff of the King's Dragoon Guards that had not yet embarked for India, some were from the Natal police and some were infantrymen who had only just been taught to ride. For the rest, he had twelve companies of infantry, drawn from four different battalions, 120 sailors and six guns – in all about 1200 men.

Lanyon had given Colley a disparaging view of Boer military competence: 'They are incapable of any united military action, and they are moral cowards, so anything they may do will be but a spark in the pan.'[31] A very different opinion was expressed in a confidential memorandum by Sir Archibald Alison, Deputy Quartermaster-General for Intelligence in the War Office:

> The Boers are an enemy different from any with whom we have had hitherto to contend. Mounted upon active, hardy little horses, provided with the best firearms, and accustomed from their earliest years to their use, they combine the rapidity of Asiatic cavalry with more than the precision of fire of the most highly trained European infantry. They are thus probably the most perfected Mounted Infantry in the world. These peculiarities render them especially dangerous in (1) the defence of mountain passes and (2) in the attack of long trailing convoys bringing up supplies to an army in the field.[32]

Colley was to offer the Boers ample opportunity for the exercise of their peculiar skills. He had chosen the direct route from Natal, which involved crossing a mountain pass at Laing's Nek; reports from the Transvaal were that Potchefstroom's supplies might last until the middle of February but no longer. Thus, if he were to reach Potchefstroom in time, Colley could afford neither to wait for promised reinforcements from India nor to take a longer route that would avoid the mountains. On 28 January 1881 he attempted to storm Laing's Nek and was repulsed with the loss of seven officers and seventy-six men killed, and two officers and 110 men wounded. Eleven days later, after the Boers had begun to threaten his communications, he moved out from his fortified camp at

Mount Prospect to bring in a convoy coming from Newcastle. He
was intercepted by the Boers at the Ingogo River, and was able to
retire and take with him his guns only with difficulty; his losses
there were five officers and sixty-one men killed, and four officers
and 68 men wounded. More than a quarter of his effective force
had been put out of action in two engagements before he had
crossed the Transvaal border.

The Liberal Government in Britain had no wish for a long war for
the sake of keeping the Transvaal. President Brand, of the Orange
Free State, offered himself as a peacemaker, and early in January he
and Lord Kimberley began to correspond. Colley had only spas-
modic knowledge of the negotiations, partly because his telegraph
lines were repeatedly being cut. On 13 February Kruger wrote to
Colley saying that the Boers were so certain of the justice of their
cause that they were prepared to submit their case to a Royal
Commission. Colley referred this to London and was told that the
British Government would be willing to appoint commissioners; if
the Boers accepted this offer, Colley was authorized to suspend
hostilities. On the same day, 20 February, he received a telegram
from the Secretary of State for War, which said that 'as respects the
interval before reply from the Boers is received, we do not bind your
discretion; but we are anxious to avoid the effusion of blood'. On
21 February Colley wrote to Kruger saying that a commission
would be appointed if the Boers ceased armed resistance: 'I am to
add that upon this proposal being accepted with 48 hours, I have
authority to agree to a suspension of hostilities.'

Colley's letter was received by General Nicolaas Smit at Laing's
Nek on 24 February. Smit replied on the same day, saying that he
had forwarded the letter to Kruger at Heidelberg and adding that
the letter could not reach Kruger is less than two days nor the
answer arrive in less than four. On the 26th, Colley was told that
Kruger was not at Heidelberg but at Rustenburg and that there
would be a still longer delay.

Colley's state of mind may be conjectured from a letter which he
wrote to Sir Evelyn Wood on 21 February:

> I am now getting together a force with which I think I could
> command success, but the Home Government seem so anxious
> to terminate the contest, that I am daily expecting to find
> ourselves negotiating with the 'Triumvirate' as the acknow-
> ledged rulers of a victorious people; in which case my failure
> at Laing's Nek will have inflicted a deep and permanent injury

on the British power in South Africa which it is not pleasant to contemplate.

Colley had been beaten at the head of a scratch team, with political consequences that were lamentable; he now had a force strong enough to recover part, at least, of the lost prestige. He still had received no reply from Kruger and thus he considered himself free to act at his own discretion. On the night of 26/27 February, he made a night march to occupy Majuba Hill, overlooking Laing's Nek. He had with him a mixed force of about 700 men; there was no artillery. His last two signals were:

> 9.30 a.m. 27 February. Occupied Majuba Mountain last night, immediately overlooking Boer position. Boers firing at us from below.
> 12.10 p.m. Boers still firing heavily on hill, but have broken up their *laager* and begun to move away.[33]

Colley was mistaken: the Boers were not retreating, but preparing to storm his position. Under covering fire from the *laager*, marksmen swarmed up the hill, taking advantage of dead ground, occupied the crest and poured down a deadly fire on Colley's surprised and disorganized force. Colley was killed almost at once; his troops panicked and fled. Out of a total of 554 who had occupied Majuba, the British lost 280 killed, wounded and captured. The Boers lost one man killed and five men wounded.

The damage to British prestige was out of all proportion to the size of the forces engaged. The Boers could with sombre satisfaction give thanks to the Lord, mighty in battle, who had guided them to the humiliation of their oppressors and the restoration of their independence. By the Convention of Pretoria in 1881 the British Government restored to the Transvaal 'complete self-government subject to the suzerainty of Her Majesty'; that vague limitation was replaced by specific and limited obligations at the Convention of London in 1883, when the Transvaal resumed the name of South African Republic.

However, the British withdrawal from the Transvaal was by no means an inevitable result of a freakish defeat; it was partly a consequence of the quarrels in Gladstone's Liberal Government between Whigs and Radicals who were at odds, among other matters, on whether coercion or conciliation was the proper antidote to nationalist violence in Ireland. The Government's first reaction to the news of Majuba was that troops must be provided for the reconquest of the Transvaal. That decision had been taken by the Whig majority in the Cabinet in Gladstone's absence (he was recovering from a gashed forehead which he had suffered when he slipped on the snow outside his house), and it had been influenced by a memorandum from the Duke of Cambridge, Commander-in-Chief of the British Army, arguing that it would be disastrous for military morale if the shame of Majuba were not at once expunged; like a horse that had refused a fence, the Army should be put to the jump again, lest it lose its nerve. At this point, threats to resign from the Cabinet came from the principal Radicals, John Bright and Joseph Chamberlain, supported by Sir Charles Dilke, a junior minister. Dilke wrote in his Diary:

> Chamberlain had an hour and a half with Bright and got him to write a strong letter to Gladstone about the Transvaal, which we put forward as our ground for proposed resignation, although of course the strength of the [Irish] coercion measures ... and the predominance of the Whigs in the Cabinet are the real reasons.[34]

The threats of resignation were decisive. Gladstone asserted his authority, the Cabinet reversed its decision, and Sir Evelyn Wood, Colley's successor, found himself negotiating with the Transvaal Triumvirate instead of leading a conquering expedition. The Boers drew two conclusions from their 'Freedom War' – that the British Army had a poor fighting capacity, and that Liberal Governments in Britain restored what Conservative Governments had taken away. Both of these convictions were important when the next serious dispute arose with the British Government in 1899. Meanwhile, the fight on Majuba Hill passed into the Boer mythology of militant nationalism.

5 THE SECOND 'FREEDOM WAR'

The Conventions of Pretoria in 1881 and London in 1884 had, it seemed, settled two questions: there would be no South African confederation, and the Transvaal (or, as it preferred to call itself, the South African Republic) would be left to manage its own internal affairs. In the 1890s a new question arose – the part which the indigenous English should play in the governance of the Transvaal; later this question would be applied to the governance of South Africa. It was a question that was debated mostly by Afrikaners.

In 1884 the Transvaal had a pastoral economy, diversified by the small gold-mining industry around Lydenburg. This condition changed with the discovery of the vast gold deposits south of Pretoria under the Witwatersrand (the 'ridge of white waters', so called from the streaks of silicon which gave from afar a delusive appearance of running water on its arid cliffs). The town of Johannesburg was founded in the centre of the 'Rand' in 1886; ten years later its population was about 100,000, divided in roughly equal numbers between those of European and non-European descent. Of the Europeans, only about 6,000, or one in eight, were Boers. The rest came from all over the Western world. There were immigrants from North America, Germany, France, Holland, Australia and New Zealand. There was a community of Jews from Lithuania. There were other South African colonials from the Cape and Natal. The largest component of all came from the United Kingdom.

The new goldfields were no place for the lone prospector. The gold-bearing ore lay far below the surface; it required deep-level mining which in turn required very large sums of capital investment. Control was soon exercised by a small number of large companies, some of them controlled by capitalists who had already made fortunes from the diamond mines of Kimberley. Of these Cecil Rhodes was the most flamboyant but by no means the most financially important. The mining magnates – or 'randlords', as they were sometimes called – formed a cosmopolitan elite: they included such men as Julius Wernher and Alfred Beit, J. B. Robinson, Barney Barnato, Sammy Marks, Abe Bailey, Adolf Goertz and George Albu, to name some of the most prominent. By 1889 the leaders of the industry had come together to form the Chamber of Mines, which was recognized unofficially by the Transvaal Government as representing the industry.

The Transvaal had been subjected simultaneously to an industrial revolution, a population invasion, an advanced form of capitalism and a partial occupation by foreigners. Johannesburg and its environs became an English-speaking enclave within a Boer republic. Some of its inhabitants behaved as if the country were theirs, exhibited towards Britain the exaggerated loyalty of the expatriate and ignored the Boers except when they were complaining of the iniquities of the Government. They had grievances, although these were neither so numerous nor so intolerable as they liked to allege. The root of the matter was that, like the Armenians within the Ottoman Empire, they had become aliens of their own accord for the sake of making money, at the price of living under a government which they regarded as detestable.[1] The Boers called them 'Uitlanders'. Literally, this meant 'outlanders'; an Athenian would have recognized the connotation – somewhere between interloper and barbarian. To the burghers of the republic the Uitlanders were not only alien and unwelcome; they were also dangerous. They and their machinery, their stocks and shares (quoted as 'Kaffirs' on the London Stock Exchange), their newspapers and their music halls, their clubs and their race horses, their bars and their brothels, represented something that was both corrupt and seductive; mammon might be unrighteous, but it had its attractions for the weaker brethren of the *Volk*. But more was at stake than the virtue of the Boers. If the Uitlanders continued to flock into the Transvaal, at no far distant time they would outnumber the 'old population', as the Boers sometimes called themselves. If, by then, they had acquired the right to vote, what would become of the Boers' precious independence, so hardly gained? A horde of Uitlanders with ballots was scarcely less menacing than an invading army. To the Volksraad of the republic it appeared no more than an act of common prudence when, in 1890, it raised the residence qualification for the franchise from five to fourteen years.

The dominating personality in the Government of the Transvaal was the President, Stephanus Johannes Paulus Kruger, commonly known as Paul Kruger. Professor Marais, an outstanding historian of the last days of the South African Republic, and himself an Afrikaner in the mainstream of the Cape liberal tradition, wrote of Kruger: 'With the passage of time his stature grows steadily, so that the claim that he was the greatest Afrikaner of them all does not today appear preposterous'.[2] Kruger was a Voortrekker in his own right, having accompanied his parents out of the Cape Colony in 1835 when he was ten years old. He had been chosen as field cornet when he was seventeen, which was unusual. In outward appearance he was massive and uncomely, but the crudeness of his person concealed a solid intelligence and a natural aptitude for politics. He was personally devout, a religious fundamentalist who belonged to the 'Doppers', the most uncompromising of the three Dutch Reformed Churches. He had, Marais wrote, 'a childlike faith in the literal truth of the Bible, much of which he knew by heart . . . It was this intense religiousness, which reminded his contemporaries of a sixteenth-century zealot, that was responsible, as much as anything, for his being so often described as "an anachronism".'[3] He did not undervalue himself; in 1889 he had allowed the Volksraad to vote him an annual salary of £8,000, which made him among the best-paid heads of government anywhere in the world. When Shepstone had annexed the Transvaal in 1877 Kruger had never wavered in his determination to recover the independence of his country, and the maintenance of that independence remained the dominating purpose of the rest of his life. He was a skilful practitioner of the arts of politics in an arena where personal influence and local knowledge counted for more than ideology or manifestos. He was elected four times as president, a tribute not merely to his constancy but to his intuitive knowledge of what was in his burghers' minds. He was always accessible to those of his people who wanted to see him; important business was sometimes conducted on the *stoep* or porch of his house in Pretoria. He liked to portray himself as being no more than the mouthpiece of his people's will; in reality he combined some of the qualities of both the lion and the fox, with the addition of considerable histrionic ability. General Smit, the hero of Majuba, once described, in a tone of affectionate despair, his official encounters with Kruger:

> I do stand up against him, I know he is wrong and I tell him so; but first he argues with me, and if that is no good he gets

into a rage and jumps round the room roaring at me like a
wild beast . . . and if I do not give in then he fetches out the
Bible and . . . quotes that to help him out. And if all that fails,
he takes my hand and cries like a child and begs and prays me
to give in. Say, old friend, who can resist a man like that?[4]

Kruger's experiences with the British Government might reasonably have convinced him that the price of independence was
constant suspicion. He had much to be suspicious about. His republic was being hemmed in on all sides by the British – by annexations
in the east, Bechuanaland to the west and Rhodesia to the north;
few Boers would distinguish the niceties between colonies, protectorates and the possessions of chartered companies; the Union Jack
flew over them all. Although the word 'suzerainty' had been
omitted from the Convention of London, the British had not abandoned their assumption of paramountcy over southern Africa. The
assertion of Britain's claims became more frequent, and more strident, after the general election of 1895 resulted in the defeat of the
Liberal Government, and the appearance of Joseph Chamberlain as
Colonial Secretary. Chamberlain was not a man content to react to
events; he was an activator. With him, the ideas of imperial consolidation revived and took more ambitious forms. The Government of
President Kruger was an obstacle to any programme of consolidation in southern Africa; the ambitions of Kruger and Chamberlain
stood each in the way of the other. Kruger's determination was that
the Boers should remain masters in their own house; to Chamberlain, that house, whatever flag flew over it, ought to be contained
within the many mansions of the British Empire. British influence
over the Transvaal had been deliberately whittled away by the
Boers ever since 1881; therefore, he argued: 'We ought to keep our
hands clenched on what remains, and if possible magnify it by any
plausible interpretation of the Convention.'[5] This meant that the
actions of Kruger's Government would be under constant scrutiny
from London.

The presence in the Transvaal of a large number of British subjects who were becoming increasingly clamant in their grievances
against their hosts gave ample opportunities for British remonstrance. In 1895, Kruger's Government put itself clearly in the
wrong. In 1895 the completion of a railway line between Pretoria
and Lourenço Marques at last gave access to a port that was not
British. It was in the Transvaal's interests to favour the new line, the
more so as far more of it ran through Transvaal territory than the

lines of the railways originating in the Cape and Natal. It was the Transvaal which tried to negotiate an equitable division of freight among the three competitors and the Cape which chose to begin a tariff war by undercutting the other two lines. The Transvaal's reply was to raise the rates on the 51-mile section of the Cape line which ran through the Transvaal. The Cape refused to pay and began instead to shift its goods by using ox- wagons for the Transvaal stretch. The Transvaal then closed the drifts, or fords, across the Vaal River by presidential proclamation. Chamberlain, in response to an appeal from the Cape Government, sent Kruger a stiff protest. The proclamation was withdrawn and the drifts reopened. The impression formed in London was that Kruger was more likely to be influenced by threats than by reason.

In 1892 the Uitlanders within the Transvaal had formed a political organization of their own, the National Union, the object of which was to work through constitutional means for equal rights for all citizens of the republic and for 'the redress of all grievances'. Their grievances were summed up by one of the magnates of the Rand, the American John Hays Hammond, as

> comprising exorbitant taxation, Government grants to private monopolies, corrupt administration and legislation, the denial of personal rights . . . and the denial of representation upon reasonable conditions of franchise, for interests representing more than two-thirds of the population, more than one-half the land, more than nine-tenths of the assessed property, and more than nine-tenths the taxes paid in the Transvaal.[6]

The proportions of property owned and taxation borne by the Uitlanders may have been overstated but the underlying purpose behind the Uitlanders' claims was for freedom to shape the Transvaal to their own advantage and to justify their pretensions by their economic predominance. Chief among the grievances of the mining industry was the dynamite monopoly, granted to a German and French consortium. Dynamite was essential to deep-level mining operations, and the Chamber of Mines complained that the monopoly meant an unreasonable increase in costs to an industry which depended for its profits on the economical recovery of small quantities of gold from very large tonnages of low-grade ore. Kruger regarded the dynamite monopoly as 'the cornerstone of his independence'. If the worst happened and the republic had to fight for its independence once again, it would be important to have the manufacture of explosives in friendly hands. As for the Uitlanders'

demands for equal rights, which included the franchise, it would in
the opinion of many Boers have been more seemly if they had
shown themselves more willing to accommodate to the 'old population'. As things were, Uitlanders and Boers formed distinct communities which met only at the bottom, when Uitlanders came into
contact with the police, and at the top, when the magnates of the
Chamber of Mines parleyed with Kruger's officials. Bryce, who
visited Johannesburg in 1895, wrote:

> Although less than half the immigrants came from England,
> probably five-sixths spoke English and found themselves
> drawn together not only by language, but by community of
> ideas and habits. The Australians, the Americans, and the men
> from Cape Colony and Natal considered themselves for all
> practical . . . purposes to be English, and English became the
> general spoken tongue not only of Johannesburg, but of the
> mining districts generally. Hearing nothing but English
> spoken, seeing nothing all round them that was not far more
> English than Dutch, though with a half-colonial, half-Amer-
> ican tinge, it was natural that the bulk of the Uitlanders should
> deem themselves to be in a country which had become vir-
> tually English, and should see something unreasonable or even
> grotesque in the control of a small body of persons whom they
> deemed in every way their inferiors.[7]

The National Union had declared its intention of working for
reform by constitutional means. In 1895 some important persons in
the Uitlander community turned to conspiracy, to prepare for an
armed rising in Johannesburg. There is still much that remains
unclear in the murky story of the prelude to what came to be called
the Jameson Raid.[8] It is not clear what the conspirators' aims were
or whether they had any agreed purpose except to rid themselves of
Kruger's Government. There were some who thought that even an
unsuccessful rising might compel British intervention. Some may
have thought of an Uitlander republic taking in the goldfields.
Others, and these probably included Cecil Rhodes, may have
thought of another British annexation as a means to that most
elusive of dreams, a federation of southern Africa. Rhodes saw
nothing incompatible between the position which he then held as
Prime Minister of the Cape Colony and preparation to overthrow a
government with which the Cape was at peace. Rhodes was also
controller of three great joint stock companies – De Beers in
Kimberley, the Consolidated Goldfields on the Rand and the British

South Africa Company which governed Rhodesia and which had very recently acquired a strip of territory on the frontier of Bechuanaland, abutting the western boundary of the Transvaal. It was there that Rhodes stationed his friend and associate, Dr Leander Starr Jameson, with an irregular force of about 600 horsemen, ready to ride to the rescue of the Rand once an appeal came from the conspirators. Meanwhile, Rhodes used the organization of De Beers to smuggle arms to the Rand.

The conspirators were remarkably incompetent. There was little secrecy about what they were doing: anyone who visited the Rand Club in Johannesburg could hardly have been unaware that a plot was hatching. Kruger's intelligence department certainly knew the outlines of what was proposed. Kruger himself was prepared to wait; to those of his burghers who urged him to take pre-emptive action he replied: 'Wait till the time comes; for take a tortoise, if you want to kill it you must wait until it puts its head out.'

In December 1895 the tortoise obligingly did so. The rising planned for the Rand was repeatedly postponed; Jameson eventually lost patience and on 29 December rode into the Transvaal to 'rescue' persons who until then had been in no danger whatsoever. Kruger called out his commandos; Jameson was shadowed by superior forces and forced to surrender on 2 January 1896, fourteen miles from Johannesburg.

The question was asked then, and may still be asked now, whether the British Colonial Secretary was directly implicated. The question has never been satisfactorily answered. The question is not whether Chamberlain knew about the preparations for rebellion – there was scarcely any secret about them – but whether he had 'guilty knowledge', that is, was a co- conspirator. The Boers had no doubt that he was guilty and that once more the British Government was determined to seize the Transvaal by hook or by crook.

Kruger behaved with both resolution and skill. He offered an amnesty to all rebels in Johannesburg except for the 'reform committee' of ringleaders. With some difficulty he resisted the demands of his commandos who wanted the leaders of the Raid to be executed then and there. Instead, Kruger handed Jameson and his officers over to the British Government, which tried them in London under the Foreign Enlistment Act. Jameson himself was sentenced to fifteen months imprisonment. Sixty-four Uitlander 'reformers' were tried in Pretoria for high treason. All pleaded guilty. Four were sentenced to death, and the remainder to lesser penalties; in the event all were permitted to ransom themselves.

Kruger was not going to make martyrs; indeed, he stood out himself both as martyr and hero. Afrikaners all over South Africa were for the moment united in sentiment against what they believed to be calculated aggression against their kith and kin. In the intensity of the moment criticism of Kruger's government was stilled among his own burghers, and there and elsewhere in South Africa Afrikaners joined in condemnation of a British action that appeared both criminal and unsuccessful. The hand of the Almighty had been stretched over his *Volk* and the unrighteous had been humbled in the dust. Naboth had defended his vineyard, David had once more vanquished Goliath.

The Jameson Raid polarized opinion, both in Britain and South Africa. Some of the super-heated emotion in Britain was the result of the 'Kruger telegram', in which Kaiser Wilhelm II congratulated Kruger on repelling the raiders without calling on the help of friendly powers, a message which had the effect of linking Germany and the Transvaal, in parts of popular opinion, as enemies of the British Empire. The Poet Laureate, Alfred Austin, produced verses that evoked a raucous approval of the raiders:

> There are girls in the gold-reef city,
>   There are mothers and children too!
> And they cry, 'Hurry up! for pity!'
>   So what can a brave man do?
> I suppose we were wrong, were madmen,
>   Still I think at the Judgement Day
> When God sifts the good from the bad men,
>   There'll be something more to say.
> We were wrong, but we aren't half sorry,
>   And, as one of the baffled band,
> I would rather have had that foray
>   Than the crushings of all the Rand.

More soberly, the High Commissioner at the Cape, Sir Hercules Robinson, warned Chamberlain that any British intervention on the side of the Uitlanders would have a disastrous effect on Afrikaner opinion:

> The feeling of the Dutch African inhabitants of the Cape Colony has undergone a complete change since Jameson's raid and they would now neither sympathize with nor support any forcible measures undertaken by Imperial Government to

secure redress of Uitlanders' grievances. The situation at present is this. Kruger refuses to discuss alleged grievances relating to certain internal matters and sooner than do so ... [he] would, I believe, if necessary face hostilities. We have now only the choice of making such a refusal a casus belli or contenting ourselves with the private suggestions as to the interests of British subjects which he states he is willing ... to consider in a friendly spirit. Before Her Majesty's Government come to a decision on this question I think it my duty to point out that in event of hostilities growing out of the Jameson raid the South African Republic will be openly assisted by the Orange Free State [and] by a large number of Dutch both in the Cape Colony and Natal.[9]

It was with this warning in mind that Chamberlain publicly disclaimed belligerent intentions towards the Transvaal in a speech that was prophetic. 'A war in South Africa', he said, 'would be one of the most serious wars that could possibly be waged. It would be in the nature of a civil war [and] ... it would leave behind the embers of a strife which I believe generations would hardly be long enough to extinguish.'[10]

The Raid and its aftermath produced a tension which affected the whole of South Africa. Kruger's Government now began to arm itself on a formidable scale. New forts were built in Pretoria, and a new one on the heights just north of Johannesburg dominated that town. Orders were placed in France for Creusot 155-mm siege guns (they were later to be known as 'Long Toms'), and in Germany for Krupp 75-mm field guns, reputedly the best in the world, and for Mauser rifles. To Kruger these armaments were defensive; the knowledge that the Boers possessed them might be a deterrent, and if that failed at least the commandos would be readier for war than they had proved themselves when dealing with Jameson. That episode had shown Kruger how deficient in military strength the republic was.

True, when the call came, the burghers had answered it in their fashion. As Joubert reported: 'When the telegram was received that Jameson had crossed the border I would not believe it possible, but I sent round the country calling the men to arms. Each man jumps on his pony and rides off. He does not wait ... but goes as he is.' Of course it was easy for the six thousand burghers who had mobilized to round up Jameson's six hundred. But what if a real army had invaded the country? What if the British government had supported Jameson? The facts that the Raid brought to light were a scandal. By law, every burgher had to provide himself with a rifle and ammunition. Of the 24,238 burghers liable to be commandeered, 9,996 were found to have no rifle; the rest had old rifles or new rifles of an old pattern. There was only enough ammunition to make war for a fortnight . . . The country, concluded Kruger, was 'practically defenceless' at the time of the raid; 'the burghers had neglected their sacred duty to arm themselves'.[11]

But what appeared to be common prudence to the Boers appeared as preparation for aggressive war in the eyes of the Uitlanders and those who sympathized with them. What were these armaments for if not to be used against the British? Weaponry on that scale was far in excess of anything that would be needed against any likely Native enemy. It was at this time that the story of the 'Pan-Afrikaner conspiracy' began to gain credence among the South African English. Roger Casement, the British consul in Lourenço Marques, gave his support to the conspiracy theory in a letter from the Rand Club in Johannesburg that was seen both by Lord Salisbury, the Prime Minister, and by Chamberlain:

> there seems such a large body of the public in England who will persist in regarding the Boer patriot as a simple peasant only desirous of governing himself and being left alone. He's nothing of the kind. He is scheming, plotting and planning night and day, back door and front door, how to become the undisputed master of South Africa as a whole.[12]

To those who believed in the existence of such a conspiracy, almost anything done by Kruger's Government could be regarded as part of a plot. Thus the new treaty of alliance between the Transvaal and the Orange Free State in 1897 could be regarded as preparing the way for aggression, even though it was probably more defensive, in intent, than the treaty of 1889 which it replaced, since it contained a clause providing for consultation between the two governments; this had been added at the request of President Steyn of the Orange Free State to provide him with a means of dissuading Kruger from rash or provocative actions. But if the treaty ever did become operative – that is, 'when the independence of one of the two States may be threatened or attacked, unless the State which should render the assistance can show the injustice of the cause of the other State' – the combined military force of the two republics would amount to 40,000 men, seven or eight times the size of the existing British garrison in the Cape and Natal.

The Raid had shattered the alliance that had been struck between Rhodes and the Afrikaner Bond in the Cape, which had seemed to offer a political future for moderate men working for Anglo-Afrikaner co-operation. One striking example was its effect on the career of a brilliant young Afrikaner, Jan Christiaan Smuts. He was born in the western Cape in 1870 and graduated in science and

PLATE 7. *J. C. Smuts, 10 June 1948* (Courtesy of Popperfoto).

literature at the Victoria College, Stellenbosch in 1891. A scholarship then took him to Christ's College, Cambridge, where his performance was phenomenal. He wrote both parts of the law tripos in 1894 and was placed first in the first-class of each; F. W. Maitland, the great constitutional lawyer, thought him to be the best pupil he had ever taught. Then, after a short period in Strasbourg reading German philosophy and having been called to the London bar from the Middle Temple, he returned to South Africa, taking with him the manuscript of a book that he had written in his spare time about Walt Whitman. He was impressed by the ideas of Cecil Rhodes, and became a disciple. Then came the Jameson Raid. Smuts felt himself to have been duped and humiliated, both in his faith in Rhodes and in the British sense of justice. He shook the dust of British South Africa off his feet and emigrated to the Transvaal where in 1898 he deployed his formidable talents in the service of President Kruger as State Attorney.

Smuts was the most conspicuous of many Cape Afrikaners who shared his sentiments of disillusion, although most of them stayed where they were. They, and those who had always been anti-British, now found themselves in political agreement; together they outnumbered the English colonists in the Cape Colony. Old enmities between the two white peoples were reawakened, and became sharper and more difficult to reconcile. Sympathy for the Transvaal created a bond between Afrikaners, and this in turn stimulated English chauvinism, each sentiment drawing strength from the other. In 1896 *Ons Land*, the official newspaper of the Afrikaner Bond, wrote

> Afrikanerdom has awakened to a sense of earnestness and consciousness which we have not observed since the heroic war for Liberty in 1881 . . . The partition wall has disappeared . . . a new glow illuminates our hearts; let us now lay the foundation stone of a real United South Africa on the soil of a pure and all-comprehending national sentiment.[13]

The failure of the Raid had not extinguished the aspirations of the Uitlanders and their supporters, but it had produced a change in strategy. The Transvaal Government was far too strong to be overthrown by private enterprise. If there was to be a change it would have to come through the direct intervention of the British Government. This was the objective of the Transvaal branch of the South African League, formed in 1896, which was partly a patriotic association and partly an Uitlander pressure group that looked to London rather than Pretoria for the redress of grievances. The parent branch of the League was in the eastern Cape; it had branches in Natal. The existence of this organization meant that any disturbances in the Transvaal might easily send vibrations throughout South Africa.

There were members of the South African League who made it their business to publicize every questionable action of the Transvaal Government and to attribute it not to ignorance, incompetence or just bad luck, but to a malignant spirit against the Uitlanders. It was true enough that the Boers did not love the strangers in their midst; they had brought wealth to the Transvaal, but at a price that many Boers thought was not worth paying. Kruger made no secret of his detestation of Johannesburg; he never visited it after 1890 when he had been insulted by some rowdies who had burnt the republican flag. He once began a speech at Krugersdorp, the small town on the west Rand which bore his name, with the words: 'Burghers, friends, thieves, murderers, newcomers, and others'.[14] The Raid had multiplied the requests that Kruger had received from his burghers, that the Government should take action against those whose activities threatened the peace of the republic. The result was two pieces of legislation, one which permitted the deportation of an alien who was considered by the President and his executive council to be 'a danger to the public peace and order', and a second which restricted the immigration of 'undesirable foreigners', mostly Indians. Chamberlain took the view that both laws violated the Convention of London. These were matters on which legal authorities were divided. The Colonial Office drew up two dispatches, eventually dated 6 March 1897, one rehearsing the republic's alleged breaches of the Convention, the other demanding the repeal or suspension of the immigration law. At the same time, on Chamberlain's urging, the British garrison in South Africa was reinforced to bring it up to 8,000 men and 24 field guns. He did not believe that they would have to fight; he told Lord Salisbury that, if the Boers were convinced that the British were in earnest 'I believe they will give way, as they have always done'.[15] In this instance he was right; in May 1897 the Volksraad repealed the immigration law and modified the expulsion law to apply only to those convicted in a court of law.

Chamberlain took another decision in 1897, which was to have consequences of the utmost importance for South Africa: the appointment of Sir Alfred Milner as High Commissioner and

Governor of the Cape. The appointment was welcomed by both major political parties in England. Milner was already an established public figure; he had been recognized at Oxford as a man of high promise, and he had turned promise into performance by his work as under-secretary in the Ministry of Finance in Cairo and as chairman of the Board of Inland Revenue in London. He was one of those public servants whom a later age would describe as 'the great and the good'. Jan Smuts was probably the only man in South Africa who matched Milner's academic record.

Milner had been sent to South Africa to keep the peace, which meant reassuring the South African English of Britain's determination not to abdicate her claims as the paramount power in South Africa and playing a waiting game in relations with the Transvaal. Time, it would seem, was on Britain's side; Kruger could not last for ever, and if he were succeeded by a reforming president there seemed no reason why Englishmen and Afrikaners could not live together as peacefully in the Transvaal as they did in the Orange Free State. Milner had hoped that Kruger would be defeated in his fourth campaign for the presidency. He greatly underestimated Kruger's appeal. If there was one thing that Kruger was known to stand for, it was the independence of the republic, and the great majority of his burghers were clearly of the opinion that this was no time for a change of regime.

The results of the election were announced on 10 February 1898: Kruger had 12,858 votes, against 3,750 for Schalk Burger, one of the younger of the Boer reform party, and 2,001 for Commandant-General Piet Joubert. Milner's hopes that the 'Transvaal oligarchy' would be destroyed by its own voters had come to nothing. It was then that he set himself the task of solving 'the Transvaal question' and solving it within his own term of office as High Commissioner. In Milner's mind a great deal more was at stake than the fortunes of the Uitlanders; the Transvaal, he reasoned, was the key to the maintenance of British supremacy in South Africa. Kruger had become a rival of the British Government for the respect, and it might be the loyalty, of Afrikaners in the Cape Colony and Natal. Kruger had become a symbol of 'Afrikanerdom'; his prestige, therefore, must be diminished, if not destroyed, and the Transvaal must come under British influence. There was no room in South Africa for rival nationalisms. In his own words, Milner was determined to 'break the dominion of Afrikanerdom'. His instructions from Chamberlain stood in the way; he had been told emphatically that the principal object of the British Government was to keep the peace in South Africa and that nothing but 'a most flagrant offence' on the part of Kruger would justify the use of force.

It was one of Milner's characteristics to think in terms of polar opposites. When, at Graaff-Reinet, the local branch of the Afrikaner Bond presented him with an address which affirmed its loyalty, he replied, 'Of course you are loyal. It would be monstrous if you were not', and then made it clear that his interpretation of loyalty excluded approval of President Kruger. He privately stigmatized the Prime Minister of Natal (an English South African) as 'disloyal' because he had congratulated Kruger on his re-election. Milner simplified the South African situation to Chamberlain by depicting it in the form of an irreconcilable alternative: there was no way out of the political troubles 'except reform in the Transvaal or war'.[16]

By reform, Milner meant the defeat of 'Krugerism', so that the Transvaal should cease to be an alternative to Britain for the loyalty of Afrikaners throughout South Africa. This would not come about without the intervention of the British Government. If Kruger were convinced that Britain was in earnest and would use armed force if necessary, he would probably give way, as he had done over the matter of the drifts and over the immigration law. This involved a high risk: if Britain threatened to use force, and then flinched, it would be she, and not Kruger, who would lose prestige. But then Milner prided himself on his invariable willingness to 'risk everything'.[17] His strategy required him to convince Chamberlain, and through him the British Government, that Kruger must be humbled. But if Kruger's Government kept within the terms of the London Convention, there was no justification for British intervention. Milner proposed, therefore, to go outside the Convention, to base his case on Britain's claims as the paramount power, and to argue that paramountcy was endangered by the condition of the Transvaal. This contention was put most flamboyantly in Milner's dispatch of 4 May 1899:

> The case for intervention is overwhelming . . . The spectacle of thousands of British subjects kept permanently in the position of helots, constantly chafing under outdoubted grievances, and calling vainly to Her Majesty's Government for redress, does steadily undermine the influence and reputation of Great Britain and the respect for the British Government within its own dominions. A certain section of the press, and not in the Transvaal only, preaches openly and constantly the doctrine

of a Republic embracing all South Africa, and supports it by menacing references to the armaments of the Transvaal, its alliance with the Orange Free State, and the active sympathy which in case of war it would receive from a section of Her Majesty's subjects . . . I can see nothing which will put a stop to this mischievous propaganda but some striking proof of the intention, if it is the intention, of Her Majesty's Government not to be ousted from its position in South Africa. And the best proof alike of its power and its justice would be to obtain for the Uitlanders in the Transvaal a fair share in the Government of the country which owes everything to their exertions.[18]

What this meant was that Kruger should be pressed to grant the franchise to the Uitlanders on easier terms. This was not a matter contained within the Convention, and for the British Government to make such demands on the Transvaal was to trespass on its autonomy. If Kruger conceded he would not only suffer an irretrievable loss of prestige but also would open the way to eventual Uitlander supremacy by way of the ballot box. If he prevaricated, the consequence might be war; but the evidence is that Chamberlain thought this to be highly unlikely, provided that the British attitude was sufficiently menacing. (Half a century later, the term 'brinkmanship' would be coined to describe diplomacy of this nature.) Lord Selborne, the Undersecretary of State for the Colonies, spoke for himself and for Chamberlain when he said that 'Kruger . . . never had yielded and never will yield till he feels the muzzle of the pistol on his forehead . . . [and] that the surest way to avoid war is to prepare openly for war'.[19] The difference between Chamberlain and Milner was that Chamberlain thought that a show of force would make the use of force unnecessary and would wring concessions out of Kruger, and Milner was convinced that war would be a lesser evil than some unsatisfactory compromise. Thus, when Kruger and Milner met in conference in Bloemfontein at the end of May, Milner refused to accept anything less than the enfranchisement of Uitlanders after five years residence in the Transvaal, to be applied retroactively. Kruger did not refuse outright, but wanted to know what he would get in return; he must, he said, have something that he could show to his burghers: 'I must tell them that something has been given in to me, if I give in to something.' It was precisely this saving of face that Milner was not prepared to permit. From Kruger's point of view Milner was offering him a choice between the peaceful or the violent surrender of his independence. ('It is all one', as an American commentator wrote, 'to have your Government captured by a troop of horse, or to have your privileges taken away by alien voters.'[20]) Milner broke off the conference, with nothing decided; a telegram from Chamberlain, urging him to prolong discussion, arrived too late.

This was not the end of the matter. The Transvaal Government was willing to enlarge the Uitlander franchise, but not on Milner's terms, and put forward a complicated proposal of its own that Chamberlain was willing to consider. This was the very sort of compromise that Milner was determined to avoid, and he headed off Chamberlain by asserting that experience showed that nothing was to be gained by discussing 'a multitude of complicated details' with Kruger. ('There was', wrote one of Milner's admirers, 'a gnarled magnificence in the old Transvaal President, but he saw only a snuffy, mendacious savage'.[21]) Instead, he persuaded Chamberlain to propose a joint inquiry into the offer by both British and Boer commissioners. (The same sort of proposal was to be made in July 1914 by Austria–Hungary to Servia; that, too, was meant to be rejected.)

Milner was right in believing that Kruger would not agree; it would be compromising the independence of his republic. He was, however, still prepared to bargain. This time the proposal came through Smuts; it amounted to an acceptance of the demands which Milner had made in Bloemfontein, but on three conditions: there would be no more interference by Britain into the internal affairs of the Transvaal; the claim to suzerainty would be dropped; and any further disputes would be settled by arbitration within South Africa.

The British Government accepted the principle of arbitration but effectively rejected the other two conditions, whereupon the Transvaal's proposal was withdrawn. On 8 September the British Cabinet decided to send a 'final offer' to the Transvaal – a five years franchise without conditions, or else the British Government would 'formulate their own proposals for a final settlement'. At the same time it was decided to reinforce the garrison in South Africa from 12,000 to 22,000 troops. This decision made war inevitable. The Transvaal Government expected a British ultimatum and here, it seemed, were the means of enforcement. It made military sense to fight before the British reinforcements arrived. In fact the Boers delayed for another month, largely because President Steyn was unwilling to take the burghers of the Orange Free State to war until the arrival of a British ultimatum gave evidence that the Boers were the victims of aggression and thus strengthened their cause in the eyes of the world.

In the end the Boers got the worst of both worlds. Most of the British troops arrived, and still there was no British ultimatum. At last, on 9 October, the Transvaal's ultimatum was delivered to the British Agent in Pretoria. It was a formidable document: its tone, and the crispness of its language, suggested the authorship of Jan Smuts. It accused the British of breaking the London Convention by taking up the Uitlanders' case and interfering in the internal affairs of the Transvaal. It required the British Government to agree to arbitration in the future 'on all points of mutual difference', to remove all troops stationed on the borders of the Transvaal, withdraw all troops that had landed in South Africa since 1 June, and divert from South Africa any troops on the high seas. Unless these demands were met within forty-eight hours, the Transvaal would 'with great regret be compelled to regard the action as a formal declaration of war.'[22] On 11 October the war began. If the Boers had waited a day or so longer they would have received a British ultimatum. As it was, they appeared technically as the aggressors; this for the moment damaged their case in Britain. Sir Edward Grey, a leading Liberal, said in Parliament: 'We are in the right in this war. It is a just war. It is a war which has been forced upon this country'; and Lord Salisbury, the Prime Minister, said that the Boers' audacious defiance had 'liberated us from the necessity of explaining to the people of England why we are at war'.[23]

When Milner broke up the Bloemfontein Conference, Kruger reproached him with the words: 'It is our country that you want.' A man who had dealt with Shepstone and Frere, seen his country invaded by Jameson and then had to rebut the claims of Chamberlain and Milner, might be forgiven if he thought that Britain was once more on the annexationist trail. There have been many people, at the time and long afterwards, who believed that British rhetoric concealed a crude desire to grab the Transvaal goldfields, as many Boers believed (again erroneously) that Britain had annexed the diamond fields because she lusted after their spoils. I have not read any argument that alters my view that Milner was the principal architect of the war[24] and that his motives were political and not economic. Witwatersrand gold would be bought and sold in London whatever government ruled in Pretoria. Milner did not much mind what sort of government that was, provided that it was not Krugerite and that it was 'loyal' in his own extended use of that word. As late as 23 August 1899, ten weeks after he had broken up the Bloemfontein Conference, he was talking about the the the future of the Transvaal 'either as a republic or a British Colony'.[25] Lord Salisbury meant what he said in declaring that Britain's only interests in the mines was that they should be worked under good government. 'But that is the limit of our interest. We seek no gold fields. We seek no territory.'[26]

If the war had begun with decisive British victories, it was not unreasonable to think that a peace party in the Transvaal might have offered terms that would have given the British the substance of what they wanted. In any case, the British Government had no quarrel with the Orange Free State. But the war began very badly for the British, and the defeats of 'Black Week' in December 1899 – the Stormberg, Magersfontein and Colenso – paradoxically made annexation of both republics inevitable. Predominant public opinion would have accepted no less. It was when it became clear that both republics were prepared to fight on, even after the capture of their capitals, that the British accepted the formula of 'unconditional surrender' proposed by Milner and borrowed from General Grant who had used it during the Vicksburg campaign during the American Civil War. For the sake of its own prestige, Britain could hardly afford to demand anything less. It was not clear then what the cost of that demand would be, nor that it would not be achieved in the end.

This was a preventive war. Milner was concerned not so much with what Kruger had done but with what the consequences might be if he remained as a symbol of anti-British Afrikanerdom. L. S. Amery, the correspondent of *The Times* in Cape Town and in Milner's confidence, wrote: 'What we are committed to is the stamping out of a national movement which we have allowed to grow up in the last twenty years'.[27] It was after the war had begun that Milner told Amery about his hopes for anglicization of Boer territory after the war:

> In the Transvaal certainly the Boers will be a rapidly dwindling minority. Johannesburg, Pretoria, Heidelberg, Standerton, Potchefstroom, Krugersdorp, Barberton, Klerksdorp, Pietersburg either are already or will in a year or two be English towns, and under an English government English farmers will settle everywhere within accessible reach by road or rail of the Johannesburg market.[28]

What chance had the republics of success? During the last weeks of peace Smuts had formulated a plan both of political warfare and military operations, based on the premise that the British Empire was a ramshackle structure dominating 'great countries largely inhabited by antagonistic peoples (Cape Colony, India, Egypt etc.)' and therefore more dependent 'upon prestige and moral intimidation' than military strength. Quick Boer victories would shake that prestige; so too would subversion among the antagonistic peoples. A first step to the latter end was the publication of a tract entitled *A Century of Wrong*, a passionate indictment of the British record in South Africa over the past century, which appealed to Afrikaners 'to act as Leonidas with his 300 at Thermopylae in the face of the vast hordes of Xerxes, and to ignore men like Milner, Rhodes and Chamberlain, and even the British Empire, and to commit your cause to the God of your fathers and the Justice which sometimes acts tardily but never sleeps or forgets'. Militarily, the Boers should seek to conquer Natal, where a victory was to be had for the taking if they struck before reinforcements arrived. Defeat in South Africa could breed subversion elsewhere, so that the British would not dare to withdraw troops from places such as India or Egypt. There was always the possibility, too, of foreign intervention. But all would depend on a prompt and successful Boer offensive.[29]

This was asking far too much of the Commandant-General of the Transvaal, Piet Joubert. Not only was his heart not in the war, but

PLATE 8. *General Joubert and his staff at Newcastle, Natal, 17 October 1899* (Courtesy of Popperfoto).

he was cautious, and unimaginatively conservative. Deneys Reitz, son of the State Secretary of the Transvaal and author of a fascinating account of his own experiences as a combatant, relates why Joubert had refused an offer from a Russian society to equip an ambulance for the Transvaal: 'You see, my boy, we Boers don't hold with these new fangled ideas; our herbal remedies (*bossie-middels*) are good enough'.[30]

A sustained offensive of the kind imagined by Smuts would have required a discipline which the Boer commandos, at the beginning of the war, did not possess. They prided themselves on the civilian nature of their fighting forces; the word 'burgher', or citizen, was preferred to 'soldier'. The British private soldier had joined the army of his own free will and thereafter he did as he was told; with the Boers it was the other way about. Every burgher between sixteen and sixty was required by law to join a commando; the age limits were not applied with any strictness and boys of twelve and greybeards of seventy were not uncommon. Having joined, the burgher did much as he liked. Reitz described the next stage of mobilization:

> Our military organization was a rough one. Each commando was divided into two or more field-cornetcies, and these again were sub-divided into corporalships. A field-cornetcy was supposed to contain 150 to 200 men, and a corporalship nominally consisted of 25, but there was no fixed rule about this, and a popular field-cornet or corporal might have twice as many men as an unpopular one, for a burgher could elect which officer he wished to serve under, and could even choose his own commando, although generally he would belong to one representing the town or district from which he came.[31]

There were no uniforms, although Reitz noted that so many officers serving over him wore black claw-hammer coats and semi top-hats trimmed with crêpe, that these garments virtually amounted to an unofficial insignia of rank. Some burghers carried parasols to shield them from the sun. Those who possessed them brought along their Native retainers to do the menial jobs. Howard Hillegas, an American newspaper correspondent, commented:

> To call the Boer forces an army was to add unwarranted elasticity to the word, for it has but one quality in common with such armed forces as Americans or Europeans are accustomed to call by that name. The Boer army fought with guns

and gunpowder, but it had no discipline, no drills, no forms, no standards, and not even a roll-call.[32]

One field-cornet of the Kroonstad commando insisted on holding a morning roll-call and a rifle inspection, but his men complained to higher authority and he was told to stop harassing them. The commandos of 1899 were a primitive democracy: there were frequent councils of war, at which every officer from corporal upwards could speak and vote. Discipline was lax. 'The burgher who had assisted in electing his field-cornet felt that that official owed him a certain amount of gratitude for having voted for him, and obeyed his orders or disobeyed them whenever he chose to do so.'[33] If the officers of a particular commando were thought to be too eager for dangerous operations, or just became unpopular, it was easy enough to take one's horse and rifle and find safer or more congenial company. 'There were hundreds of men in the Natal laagers who never engaged in one battle and never fired a shot in the first six months of the war.'[34] Burghers were entitled to ten days leave every two months, but during the early and static part of the war, when the Boers were engaged in siege warfare, it was common enough for families to visit the front lines, coming and going by ox-wagon.

Yet the commandos, primitive though they might appear, had certain advantages over their opponents. They were well mounted, and they (or their Native attendants) took excellent care of their horses. (British horsemastership was miserable; the War Office calculated that over 400,000 horses, donkeys, and mules were 'expended' during the war.)[35] A Boer horseman, with his equipment, probably weighed about 250 pounds, compared with 400 pounds per man for the British. Boer horses lasted longed and moved faster. Their officers had excellent maps, made by the Transvaal Government's survey department since 1897. (When General Buller moved up to the line of the Tugela River in Natal, he was dependent on a map torn from an atlas found in an Estcourt schoolroom.) The Mauser rifle was lighter and quicker to fire (its magazine being clip-loaded) than either the British Lee- Metford or Lee-Enfield. The Boers were superior in artillery. Their Krupp 75-mm field-guns outranged the British 15-pounders by a thousand yards and their gunners had been trained by German instructors.

It was easy to despise the Boers before one had met them in the field. Winston Churchill, aged twenty-four, who had thrust his way to the war as a correspondent for the London *Morning Post*, was taken prisoner in November 1899 while reconnoitring by armoured train in the direction of the siege of Ladysmith. He was afflicted with dismal forebodings during his first night as a captive. He had seen the Boers at close quarters for the first time. He was impressed by their self-assurance, their horses, their weapons, and the fierce tone of their evening psalm, 'more full of indignant war than love and mercy'. In this mood, he was inclined to think that the war was unjust, that the Boers were the better men, and that England would lose South Africa. His confidence returned when the sun rose next morning. (He was to be afflicted with forebodings of a similar dismal nature as prime minister; reflecting then on the defeats of 1941 and 1942, he doubted for a while whether the British soldier any longer possessed the same deadly resolution in battle as his enemies.)[36]

As it happened, by the time that Churchill was captured the danger to Natal was over. The Boers had lost their chance of a quick invasion by locking up large forces in unprofitable sieges. On 23 November Joubert was thrown from his horse and suffered injuries from which he never recovered. The subsequent council of war decided to remain on the defensive in Natal. More important, Joubert's authority was for the time being assumed by Louis Botha, then thirty-seven, who was to be recognized as among the most outstanding commanders on either side.

In military terms the war fell into three phases of unequal length. In the first of these, which lasted from October 1899 until the end of that year, the initiative lay with the Boers. They invaded Natal and the Cape Colony where they stirred up a small rebellion among the Afrikaner inhabitants and purported to annex British territory. In the second week of December ('Black Week' it was called in London) they won the victories of the Stormberg, Magersfontein and Colenso. These were damaging to British prestige – ten guns were lost at Colenso, the largest number since Yorktown during the War of American Independence – but none of them was decisive, and the Boers had already reached what Clausewitz would have called 'the culminating point of victory'. The British changed the command after Black Week. Buller was superseded as commander-in-chief. In his place came Field Marshal Lord Roberts, with Major-General Lord Kitchener as his chief of staff; the 1st XI was being put into the field. Their coming began the second phase. Two Boer armies were forced into surrender – that of General Cronje at Paardeberg and of General Pretorius in the Orange Free State. The besieged towns were freed, and a new verb, 'to maffick' entered the English language in consequence of the extraordinary scenes of mob jubilation in the London streets at the relief of Mafeking. Bloemfontein was captured and the Orange Free State annexed. There was then a pause for seven weeks caused, ominously enough, by a serious outbreak of typhoid fever among the British troops. Roberts then resumed his march to the north, occupied Johannesburg and Pretoria, and shepherded the Transvaal commandos eastwards down the railway line leading to Mozambique. President Kruger, a broken man, was persuaded by his advisers to sail for Holland by way of Lourenço Marques. Lord Roberts proclaimed the annexation of the Transvaal in September 1900. It seemed that the war was over.

Yet the third phase lasted for another twenty months, and it was in this period that real bitterness developed and things were done from which, in the words of William Plomer, 'an alp of unforgiveness grew'.

This phase is often referred to as one of guerrilla warfare, although the term is not strictly accurate: it refers to operations carried out by irregular forces not under government control. What now happened was that the remaining Boer commandos avoided pitched battles and reverted to their natural style of fighting – swift movements of bodies of mounted infantry, harassing communications and from time to time making sorties against detachments of British troops. The Boers had been dislodged from their capitals; but this was not a mortal blow to States that had never been highly centralized. The Boer Governments continued to exercise authority over those of their forces that remained in the field. The site of the Orange Free State Government was now wherever President Steyn happened to be. Authority in the Transvaal devolved upon Schalk Burger, the constitutionally-appointed vice-president, and was effectively shared with General Botha, now commandant-general. Although the republics had been formally annexed, the British had achieved only partial occupation.

The limits of British authority were swiftly made clear in the Orange Free State, now renamed the Orange River Colony. Those burghers who had surrendered were allowed to return to their farms on condition that they took what was called, oddly, the 'oath of neutrality', a promise to take no further part in the war. This read: 'I will not take up arms against the British Government during the present war, nor will I at any time furnish any member of the Republican forces with assistance of any kind, or with information as to the numbers, movements, or other details of the British forces that may come to my knowledge. I do further promise and swear to remain quietly at my home until the war is over.' Neither President Steyn nor, later, acting-President Burger recognized either the annexations or the right of their own people to contract out of the war.

The lack of effective occupation was shown by the British inability to protect those who had taken the oath and returned home. The Boers still in arms called these men the 'hands-uppers', sought them out on their farms and swept them back into the commandos. The 'hands-uppers' were often faced with a cruel dilemma, of being treated by the British as oath breakers or by their own people as deserters; and usually it was their own people who put the immediate alternative most compellingly. In August, Roberts warned that oath breakers would be punished by death, imprisonment or fine. In September he proclaimed that all burghers of the old Orange Free State, except those who had been continuously in arms since the war began, had now become British subjects, and that resistance would be regarded as rebellion. On 14 September he gave notice that he would take any means necessary to bring resistance to an end: 'The means which I am compelled to adopt are those which the customs of war prescribe as being applicable to such cases. They are ruinous to the country and entail endless suffering on the burghers and their families, and the longer this guerilla war continues, the more vigorously must they be enforced.'[37] This meant farm burning, and it was carried out with a casual and undiscriminating ruthlessness that soon acquired a momentum of its own. Neither Chamberlain nor Milner approved; but both could do little, under the conventions of the times, when confronted by the commander-in-chief's insistence that the measures he was taking were justified by 'military necessity'. Milner protested, without result, against a policy which would turn into desert what were intended to be British colonies and antagonize those who he hoped would become loyal British subjects. Captain March Phillipps, who served with one of the farm-burning columns, commented: 'There will be a Dutch South African conspiracy, but it will be one of our own making. We shall have our treatment of these people to thank for it. Be sure of this, that for every house up here that is destroyed, three or four in the south are slowly rousing to arms.'[38]

Farm burning created a new problem: what was to be done with the homeless? This was the beginning of what were called 'camps of refuge' by the army, but came to be known as concentration camps. They were intended to accommodate both those who had surrendered and their families, and those who had been interned against their will. Kitchener for a time enforced a differential issue of food for the two classes of inmates; a prison doctor gave his opinion that the diet prescribed for the internees was 'not consistent with the maintenance of health for any lengthened period'.[39]

Of all the actions ever done by the British in South Africa, none produced so much bitter and helpless anger as the concentration camps. According to Boer estimates 26,000 men, women and children died in the camps; British Blue Books gave a figure of 18,000. In addition there were between 7,000 and 12,000 deaths among Natives confined in separate camps. Most of the deaths were from pneumonia, measles, dysentery and enteric fever. There was an unregulated influx into the camps, which were at first managed by the army with unskilful improvisation. The growth of the camps was a direct consequence of the policy which Kitchener adopted in 1901, after he had succeeded Roberts as commander-in-chief, of 'clearing the country'. This was a tacit admission of military failure. Unable to bring the commandos to battle, Kitchener turned to what a later generation would call 'scorched earth'. The theatre of war was to be compressed by making large parts of it uninhabitable. Much of the activity of the British Army in the third phase of the war was taken up with the 'great drives'. This meant burning or blowing up farm houses, destroying dams, burning crops and killing or driving off livestock – several million horses, cattle and sheep. Later this was supplemented by the building of barbed wire fences totalling nearly 3,000 miles, with block houses every few hundred yards. The aim was to restrict Boer mobility; the wire would hardly restrain a determined column but at least it would hinder the Boers from taking with them their impedimenta without drawing fire from the miniature forts, each within rifle range of one another. Meanwhile, the drives continued. In the end this policy was bound to succeed. There could be no replacement for each fighting Boer killed or captured, while the British resources were boundless; but the price was high in effort, effectiveness and, in the end, in the reputation of Britain and its army. Lieutenant-Colonel Allenby commanded 1,500 men at the beginning of 1901, one of eight columns 'driving' the eastern Transvaal. His 'bag' at the end of three months was: 32 Boers killed and wounded; 36 captured; 154 surrendered; 5 guns; 118 wagons, 55 carts; 28,911 rounds of ammunition; 273 rifles; 904 horses; 87 mules; 483 trek oxen; 3,260 other cattle; and 12,380 sheep. He also brought in 400 women and children.[40] It was hard to rebut the accusation that the main effort of the British army was collecting non-combatants and livestock.

Protests against this policy began to be heard in Britain. The greatest publicity came after the visit of Emily Hobhouse. It was easy for her enemies (of which she made many) to dismiss Miss Hobhouse as a crank – a middle-aged spinster devoted to the espousal of unpopular causes. She had already tried in vain to convert Cornish miners in Minnesota to temperance; towards the end of her life she tried to raise money in England for the relief of victims of the British blockade of Germany during the Great War. In 1901 she made her way to South Africa on behalf of the Women and Children Distress Fund, a 'pro-Boer' charity. On her return she had a terrible story to tell. Members of the Government were non-committal, but she found a more sympathetic hearing from the Leader of the Opposition, Sir Henry Campbell-Bannerman. He listened for nearly two hours as she told him what she had seen:

> the wholesale burning of farms and villages, the deportations, the desperate condition of a burnt-out population brought in by hundreds in convoys, the people deprived of clothes, bedding, utensils and necessities, the semi-starvation in the camps, the fever-stricken children lying . . . upon the bare earth . . . the appalling mortality . . . he was deeply moved and now and again murmured sotto voce 'methods of barbarism, methods of barbarism'.[41]

Those were the words which Campbell-Bannerman used in a public speech that was publicized around the world. This was to bring the matter to the forefront of public controversy. Official investigations followed; their reports were written in less emotive language than Miss Hobhouse's but the substance of her charges could not be denied: at its peak, the death-rate in the camps was 430 per 1,000 inmates. But it was not until November 1901 that the camps were transferred from military to civilian control. Then the mortality rates dropped dramatically – from 344 per 1,000 in October 1901 to 20 per 1,000 in May 1902. But by then the damage was done. Many Boers had become convinced that the British Government was determined not only to annex their countries but also to extinguish them as a people. The concentration camps passed into the mythology of Afrikaner Nationalism.

Lord Kitchener was responsible for other matters which the Boers did not easily forgive. Both sides used Natives as non-combatant auxiliaries; Kitchener gave them rifles and used them as spies, scouts and garrisons of block houses. Kitchener eventually, after prodding from the War Office, gave the figure of armed Natives as 10,053. The Boers did not hesitate to shoot such armed non-Whites as they had captured. Captured Boers could, in return, be charged with murder. A deadly cycle of reprisals was beginning. In 1901, after Boer commandos had invaded the colony once more, there was a second, and this time more formidable, Cape rebellion. On Kitchener's orders, the death penalty began to be inflicted on rebels captured in the field; sometimes executions were carried out in the compulsory presence of the condemned man's neighbours. This practice was forbidden from London, but again not until it had passed into folk memory. In all, fifty-one executions were carried out. Kitchener asked permission to shoot the whole of a small commando of captured rebels; the War Office refused, but the commandant, Lotter, was executed by firing-squad after a court-martial had convicted him of two charges of treason, two of murdering Natives and one each of train-wrecking, marauding, and 'disgraceful conduct'. Lotter did not find a place in Boer mythology; it was otherwise with Gideon Scheepers, another leader of rebels, whose execution transformed him into a martyr. In 1948 an Afrikaner Nationalist government changed the name of a distinguished militia regiment to commemorate Scheepers, much to the indignation of many of the regiment's officers, some of whom resigned in protest.

But not all the executions were on the British side. The Boers court-martialled and shot those of their own countrymen whom they convicted of collaborating with the British, including members of 'Burgher Peace Committees' of Boer notables who were ready to try and convince the commandos that further resistance was hopeless. Moreover, the British were having ominous success in recruiting 'National Scouts', Boers prepared to serve against their own countrymen; many of these were former prisoners of war. In the Orange River Colony they were led by Piet de Wet, brother of Christiaan de Wet, the most celebrated of all the Free State generals. By the time the war ended there were 5,464 National Scouts in British service. Thomas Pakenham wrote in 1979: 'The fact that a fifth of the fighting Afrikaners at the end of the war fought on the side of the British was a secret that has remained hidden until today.'[42]

The opposite of a 'hands-upper', one who wished to give in, was a 'bitter-ender', one who was prepared to go on fighting indefinitely in the hope that the British would eventually tire of the war and restore Boer independence. This point of view was strongest among the commandos of the Orange Free State. It was the citizens of Bryce's model republic who had become most bitter, not only against the British but against those of their compatriots of the Transvaal who were beginning to talk of making peace while they still had military strength enough to insist on something less than unconditional surrender. Both Boer Governments were formally bound by a joint agreement of June 1901 that they would make no peace which did not restore their independence and grant amnesty to Colonial rebels. These were brave words. In fact, the outlook of the two former republics was very different. The Orange Free State had gone to war on a point of honour as a faithful ally of the Transvaal, and for that fidelity it had paid a high price. On it, the brunt of the war had fallen. Its territory had been devastated and had come under British rule. Yet, under whatever name, it could still expect that it would effectively remain a society of Afrikaners. But with every month that passed Milner's hand was tightening on the Transvaal. Milner had now assumed the responsibility of administering the former republics; his seat of government was in Johannesburg, the Witwatersrand had become a 'protected area' safeguarded by the military, and there reconstruction had already begun. The Uitlanders were beginning to return, not now as strangers but as British subjects in British territory. If this process went on much longer the Transvaalers might find themselves subjected to the full rigours to be expected after unconditional surrender – their leaders banished and their followers abandoned to the mercy of the conqueror in a land now dominated by Uitlanders and 'hands-uppers'.

It was the British, after some prodding from the Dutch Government, who made the first move towards negotiation. Peace making was a complicated and protracted business. Kitchener granted a safe conduct to acting-President Burger to enter the Orange River Colony in search of President Steyn. When he had been found, representatives of the two Boer governments met at Klerksdorp where for three days they wrangled over what terms they were prepared to accept. Eventually they asked for a meeting with Kitchener in Pretoria, where he had established his headquarters. There they met Milner as well. It was made clear to the Boers that the British regarded independence as out of the question; the Boers replied that they could not consider anything less without the authority of the 'people', by which they meant the representatives of the commandos still in the field.

Milner asked whether it was intended to consult the prisoners of war, and thereby lost a brisk argument with President Steyn who asked him what would happen if the prisoners of war decided that the war should continue and the fighting commandos that it should not. The debating point won by Steyn was important, for the British had now admitted that the 'People' comprised only those who were still fighting, and that the prisoners of war, the civilian 'hands-uppers' and *a fortiori* the National Scouts were not to count. On this basis the British granted a cease-fire to enable the Boer leaders to consult the representatives of the commandos.

Thus, on 15 May 1902, the Boer Assembly of the People – thirty from each republic – met at the small town of Vereeniging. There the division between the peace party of the Transvaal and the war party of the Orange Free State emerged once more; but as reports came in from each of the districts it was increasing clear that further resistance was becoming physically impossible and that those who thought otherwise were relying on faith rather than reason. General Botha, Commandant-General of the Transvaal, referred to the National Scouts: 'If things go on as at present, there will shortly be more Afrikaners fighting against us than for us.'[43] General de la Rey, of the Transvaal, who had recently won a notable victory over General Lord Methuen in the western Transvaal, said that his own commando could continue to fight, but that since he had heard reports from other districts he had come to the conclusion that the time had come to ask for terms. 'Fight to the bitter end, it is said. But has the bitter end not come?' This was a proposition which the Assembly was not yet prepared to accept. A proposal had been made by F. W. Reitz that the Assembly should offer terms of their own – an acceptance of a British protectorate over both republics which would entail no independent conduct of foreign policy and the cession by the Transvaal of the Witwatersrand gold fields. After three days, the Assembly passed two resolutions. The first empowered the two governments to accept peace on the basis of Reitz's proposals; the second appointed a commission of five who, if the British should reject the proposals, were empowered to negotiate and to submit the results to the Assembly for acceptance or rejection. The commission consisted of five generals – Botha, de la Rey, and Smuts from the Transvaal; de Wet and Hertzog from the Orange Free State. Two days later, this commission met Milner and Kitchener in Pretoria. It was made clear to the Boers that their own proposals were unacceptable, although the Boers insisted that they should be put to higher authority in London. More than once it appeared that the meetings would break up with nothing settled. After much wrangling Smuts and Hertzog – both lawyers in civilian life – joined Milner in drafting terms.

All this was very far from 'unconditional surrender', and the two Boer lawyers continued to press for further concessions. In the end the draft terms contained three clauses which were to be of critical importance in the future. The Dutch language was to be taught in schools 'where the parents of the children desire it', and was to be allowed in courts of law 'when necessary for the better and more effectual administration of justice'; representative government would be introduced 'as soon as circumstances permit'; and the question of granting the franchise to Natives would be postponed until after the introduction of self-government. When these terms were telegraphed to London for approval Frederick Graham, an assistant-secretary in the Colonial Office, commented that this meant that 'the Native will never have the franchise. No responsible government will give it to him.'[44]

The commission reported back to the Assembly of the People for what was to be three more days of debate. It had now become clear that the issue was no longer whether the war would continue but whether the Transvaal and Orange Free State delegations would stand together in defeat or would part in anger; with the possible exception of three or four delegates, the Transvaalers were in favour of accepting terms, no matter what their allies decided. General du Toit put it bluntly when he said that even if there were a majority vote for continued resistance the majority would have to yield to the minority, for those who were outvoted would fight no longer, and the 'bitter-enders', without their support, would be forced into piecemeal surrender. Botha disclosed the figures which he had learned in Pretoria were the extent of Boer losses – 3,800 killed in action or died of wounds, 31,600 taken prisoner, of whom 600 had died in captivity, and over 20,000 men, women and children dead in the concentration camps.

General Smuts intervened on the second day and made what was perhaps the most persuasive speech of his life. He was, he said, one of those who, as a member of the Government of the South African Republic 'provoked the war with England'. There was a danger that the question before them would be decided purely on military grounds; it was still possible to continue fighting because the Boer armies had not been beaten in the field.

> But it is as a nation, and not as an army, that we are met here, and it is therefore for the nation principally that we must

consult . . . One and all, we represent the Afrikaner nation, and not only those members of it who are now in the field but those who rest beneath the soil, and those yet unborn who shall succeed us. From the prisons, the camps, the grave, the *veld*, and from the womb of the future, that nation cries out to us to make a wise decision now . . . We must not sacrifice the nation itself on the altar of independence.[45]

At the end of the second day acting-President Burger told the Free Staters that if they wished to go on fighting they would have to do so alone. On that sombre note the Assembly adjourned. On the third day, after the two delegations had debated separately, the Assembly met for the last time, this time to vote on a resolution, drafted by Smuts and Hertzog, which amounted to an acceptance, under protest, of the British terms. This was a document for posterity; and it was so worded that the British appeared as suppliants and the Boers as not having finally abandoned claims to independence: 'This Assembly expresses its confidence that the conditions called into being by accepting the proposal of His Majesty's Government may soon be so improved that our Nation will attain the enjoyment of those privileges which it considers itself justly entitled to claim.' This resolution was carried by fifty-four votes to six, with three members from each delegation in the minority. For the third time a Boer delegation travelled to Kitchener's headquarters, this time for a formal ceremony of acceptance. The document which was signed by representatives of the two Boer Governments, and by Kitchener and Milner for the British Government, is usually referred to as the Treaty of Vereeniging after the venue of the Assembly of the People. The date was 31 May 1902.

Few people, in 1899, could have predicted the course of the war, or its cost. This was not one of the 'little wars' that had marked the formal extension of the British Empire over the past half-century. From first to last the British Empire put into the field 448,000 men. The direct cost to the British Government was £217,000,000. Deaths among British troops, from all causes, amounted to 22,000 men. This was a higher figure, as a proportion of troops engaged, than that suffered by Britain in the Second World War – 4.9 per thousand compared with 4.5. (The comparable figure for the war of 1914–18 was 4.9).[46] From 1900 onwards the morning strength of the British Army was never less than a quarter-of-a-million men. During the last part of the war it was demonstrated that a large articulated army could be effective only when facing another army of the same kind. British commanders found it very difficult to bring a Boer commando to battle against its will once the Boers had adopted the tactics of mobility. It was this difficulty which turned Roberts and Kitchener towards farm burning and 'clearing the country', with all their consequences. There was a contradiction between the political object of the war and the means by which the war was fought; the latter put the former out of reach. Milner had hoped to strike a mortal blow at Afrikaner nationalism; instead, the war intensified it. The war gave the Afrikaners throughout South Africa victims to mourn, injuries upon which to brood and an anguished nostalgia for the lost independence of the republics. Kruger in exile became a formidable tragic hero at the same time as Boer leadership passed into very different hands. Three of the Boers who negotiated the Treaty of Vereeniging were to become prime ministers of the Union of South Africa. In 1902, Botha was thirty-nine, Hertzog was thirty-six, Smuts was thirty-two. Only Smuts, and that with reservations, could have been called a Krugerite. One shrewd observer was quick to appreciate the change in the quality of Boer leadership. On 21 July 1902 John X. Merriman, a Cape politician, wrote to Bryce:

The old Boer – the so-called 'takhaar' [backwoodsman] – of whom Paul Kruger was the idol and the most prominent representative, has practically disappeared as a factor. He it was who by his impracticable attitude forced the progressive section into the attitude that led up to hostilities and brought on the suicidal ultimatum. When actual hostilities began he did not bear the brunt of the fighting. All or nearly all the prominent leaders were either progressive farmers like de la Rey, de Wet, Botha [and] Kemp or educated men from the towns like Steyn, Hertzog, Smuts and others. The soul of the fighting forces consisted of young men and progressive farmers, many of them well-to-do, in some cases rich men. The takhaar when he surrendered became a 'National Scout' in many cases. Now this has a very important bearing upon the future.[47]

6 HUMILIATION AND REVIVAL

Foreboding had become reality. In the past, Afrikaners had compiled catalogues of grievances against British rule, of which the South African Republic's tract, *A Century of Wrong*, had been the most eloquent and comprehensive. They now had to face hardships more crushing and charged with misery than they had ever imagined. The net of bereavement was cast very widely; the Afrikaners had become a people in mourning. In the old republics there was scarcely a man or a woman who had not suffered personally – parents, children, relatives or friends who were dead, farms destroyed, livelihoods lost, friendships broken. Afrikaner had fought against Afrikaner: this was the *broedertwis* intensified to the level of civil war and those who had resisted to the end, in person or in spirit, had to come to terms not only with their conquerors but also with their false brethren. The last words at Vereeniging had been spoken by acting-President Burger of the Transvaal: 'Let us pray to God to guide us and to direct us to keep our people together. We must also be inclined to forgive and forget when we meet our brothers. We may not cast off that portion of our people who were unfaithful.'[1] This was easier said than done. The National Scouts found themselves shunned to the extent that they were sometimes excluded from church services, so that some of them formed their own congregations.

The responsibility for reconstruction fell upon Milner's administration. It was a vast task that amounted to the resettlement of a whole people, in many cases without their co- operation and sometimes in the teeth of bitter resentment. The British Government had promised £3,000,000 at Vereeniging; in the end the cost was more than three times that figure. The Boers were not in the least grateful; why should they be?

The Afrikaners of the Cape had suffered less severely, but there too the war had brought its train of sorrow. There had been two rebellions with their aftermath of punitive retribution. Under martial law many Afrikaner colonists had been interned without trial. Some active rebels had been sentenced to death and there had been fifty executions. There would have been far more if Kitchener had had his way; his hand had been stayed by orders from London. But the deepest grievances of all had their roots in the concentration camps, and those multiplied with the years, passed on from generation to generation and accumulating an encrustation of legend. The facts were grim enough: there were 26,000 dead. The Boers came to believe that the British had made a deliberate effort to exterminate them as a people, and the accusation spread that the food in the camps had been contaminated with vitriol, ground glass and sometimes with fish-hooks.[2] Such welfare attempts as had been attempted were afterwards interpreted as evidence of British malevolence. After the camps had been turned over to civilian administration schools were set up and many children found themselves in a classroom for the first time in their lives. This was held to be part of Milner's policy of anglicization; the Boers were to suffer not only conquest and humiliation but also a loss of national identity, to be inflicted on the children of the coming generation. Milner would probably have done just that had it been within his power; he took as restrictive a view as he could of the provision of the Treaty of Vereeniging, which permitted the teaching of Dutch in schools.

> My view is that any school relying on aid from the State should not only teach English, but make English the medium of instruction in all but the elementary classes . . . I do not think that there is any class of man so likely to influence the future generation for good or evil, loyalty or the reverse, as the teachers . . . I believe really good historical teaching, which should include South African history from an honest and impartial point of view, and something of British history and the growth of the Empire, should be of immense use. We want a good text-book of this sort. At present I shrewdly suspect the 'studious youth' are brought up almost exclusively on Majuba, with a little Jameson Raid thrown in as a seasoning.[3]

When peace came Milner tried to promote the use of English in the former republics. An appeal had brought women volunteer teachers from England, Canada and Australia who were sent into the country districts. They had to face the hostility of both parents and pupils, and this particular experiment had to be written off as a failure. The most formidable competition to Milner's schools came from the movement for 'Christian national education', which had the full backing of the Dutch Reformed Churches and the enthusiastic support of Boer parents. Attendance at these schools could be regarded as a form of patriotic resistance. Ex- President's Steyn's pronouncement was quoted with much approval: 'The language of the conqueror in the mouth of the conquered is the language of the slave.' In the same vein Smuts wrote to Emily Hobhouse that Milner 'has dreamed a dream of a British South Africa – loyal with broken English, and happy with a broken heart.'[4]

Smuts might have added 'and in a broken country'. The Orange Free State had felt the full weight of Kitchener's hand. A government had been swept away and the fabric of the former rural society had been destroyed. G. B. Beak, who served as repatriation officer, gave a description of the gruesome conditions which he found when he took up his task.[5] In the village of Vrede there were only five houses that could be occupied; the remainder had been filled with the carcasses of sheep slaughtered and left to rot. Bothaville had been fired in a few hours; Lindley was 'literally razed to the ground in a day'. Heilbron had become a 'tenantless waste'; in Vredefort 'there was no living thing to be seen anywhere'. The tasks of repatriation were, first, to get prisoners and refugees back to where their farms had been; next, to provide rations to bridge the gap before the first crops could be harvested; and then to provide seeds, agricultural implements and animals. All this was made more difficult by the great drought which afflicted the country in 1903.

The return of prisoners of war was another laborious task since they had to be brought from places as distant as India, Ceylon, St Helena and Bermuda. Some of them were unwilling to return if they were required to take an oath of allegiance to the 'English king'; the first ship from St Helena, where there were more than 5,000 prisoners, found only 278 willing to embark. There were more than 150,000 Boers in the concentration camps and perhaps the same number of Natives. Beak noted that extreme depression characterized the first stages of repatriation; some were unwilling to leave the security of the camps.

Considering the scope of the enterprise the work of repatriation was carried out with consideration and efficiency, and by the end of 1902 most farmers were back on the land doing the best they could to rebuild their shattered homes and reconstruct their shattered ways of life. They were a divided people among whom there were sharp animosities. Life was particularly hard for the 'hands-uppers', those who were thought to have surrendered too easily, and still harder for the National Scouts who were no longer wanted by the British and were treated as lepers by their own countrymen. It was these men whom General Botha had in mind when he made his first pleas for reconciliation. What he was thinking of was the reuniting of Afrikanerdom, not of holding out the hand of friendship to the British. (He was not a reader of those English school stories in which there was nothing like a good fight for making enemies into chums.) When Botha talked of building a nation, as he did to the Wakkerstroom commando when ordering it to lay down its arms after the signing of the peace treaty, he was referring to the regeneration of a people in which adversity had exposed the weaker characters. They should be treated, Botha said, like blind sheep; a Boer remedy for this condition was a caustic solution dropped into the eyes. The faithless, therefore, must be admitted to the *Volk*, but after suitable penance and chastisement. The chastisement was sometimes real enough; General Christiaan de Wet assaulted his brother, a hands-upper, on the platform of Bloemfontein station. Nor were the bitter-enders yet willing to abandon the hope that somehow, at the thirteenth hour, all would come right. When Russia went to war with Japan in 1904 many of this persuasion were much encouraged by the thought that Britain would be involved, that the garrison in South Africa would have to be withdrawn to fight the Russians, and that the republics would then either be returned, or else could be taken back without difficulty. Milner had no hope of finding collaborators among the Boer leaders. He offered places on the new legislative council for the Transvaal to Botha, Smuts and de la Rey; and all three refused. Smuts's attitude may be deduced from his refusal to speak English to Joseph Chamberlain in South Africa and his insistence on the use of an interpreter.

It is doubtful whether Milner understood the Boers; it may be that he equated them too easily with the *fellahin* whom he had observed in Egypt. 'The average Boer', he wrote at the end of 1902, 'really is the most good-natured manageable creature in the world as long as he realizes that you have got the thick end of the stick.' He thought that their leaders were incorrigible, but his attitude to the rank and file was of not-unkindly contempt. He hoped that they would settle down once they were weaned from the malign influence of their leaders, while their children learnt the English language and English ways. If not, they must be made to realize that they would be ignored in the reconstruction of their country. This was the course which Milner had set for himself as early as 1900 when he had written to Chamberlain:

> I do not think the reconciliation of the two races hopeless, but the Dutch must be made to feel from the first that it is a question for them of a change of attitude or of political extinction. Either they must accept our flag and membership of the British Empire in good faith ... or we shall have to keep up a system of autocratic rule till their opposition to the new order of things is completely broken.[6]

John Buchan was at this time one of Milner's private secretaries and he too attempted an evaluation of the Boer character. It was, he thought, a tissue of contradictions. The Boer was religious, yet materialistic; he was without imagination, yet he had the coarse instincts of a poet; he was grasping, yet hospitable; he was just, yet he connived at corruption; he was a moral critic with lax sexual habits: in short he was a mixture of satyr, Puritan, and successful merchant. Buchan created the Boer character Peter Pienaar in his novels, *Greenmantle* and *Mr Standfast*, made him a collaborator of the British Empire and invested him with a posthumous Victoria Cross. Buchan, though displaying some of Milner's condescension, showed himself a better prophet: 'if they have real grievances to fight for, it is not inconceivable that the Dutch people might be organized into as solid a voting machine as the Irish peasantry under the control of the Land League and the Church.'[7]

A new phenomenon was appearing in the aftermath of the war – the urban, poor-white Afrikaner. The easy days of the 6,000-acre farm had gone for ever. One consequence of this was a reduction in the number of *bywoners* – squatters who paid their way either by their labour or by a proportion of their crops. Many of these now found it impossible to find accommodating landlords. Parasites without a host, they drifted to the towns, there to form not so much a proletariat as an under-class. Not all of them, though, were to sink into degeneracy, alcoholism and miscegenation; after the war there could be discerned the outlines of an Afrikaner class of artisans. The gold mines might, in Boer opinion, be the source of all the Transvaal's woes, but they provided good employment. Most of the original white underground workers had come from abroad. There were serious strikes in 1907; thereafter the Chamber of Mines ceased to encourage the recruiting from outside South Africa of white miners, who were disposed to bring with them ideas of syndicalism and to show themselves unduly susceptible to trade-union organizers. The British miners decreased in numbers after 1907; some returned home, others found work elsewhere. Their places were taken by Afrikaners. The mines operated a colour bar, so that Natives did most of the manual labour: none the less, it was a break with the past to see Afrikaners wearing the hard hat of the industrial worker.

'You lose', wrote Burke, 'the object in the attempt to attain it. What you fought for is not what you recover.' Milner's part in bringing on the war had been with the aim of extinguishing a rival Nationalism. It is doubtful whether that had ever been possible. There were Afrikaner Nationalists in the Cape Colony, as well as in the Boer republics, and there was no way by which they could be either extinguished or force-fed with imperial sentiments. The terms agreed at Vereeniging put limits to Milner's actions. In the short run, he could keep power out of Boer hands by continuing Crown Colony government. In the longer term, there was the promise of self-government, and that would mean the certainty of a Boer government in the Orange River Colony and the probability of one in the Transvaal, unless there were massive British immigration. Milner had hoped that once Krugerism had been overthrown British immigrants would flock in their thousands to the Witwatersrand. But that would not be enough to maintain British supremacy. A predominant influence must also be established in the rural areas, but judicious plantations of British settlers would not be possible in a wilderness. Therefore the rural areas of the Transvaal must be developed.

Milner's imagination ranged over the building of railways and telegraphs, the making of roads and irrigation works, the improvement of stock breeding and the application of science to agriculture. The financing of this would come from the 'overspill' of mining revenue.[8] But there was no overspill and there was no great influx of settlers. The mines were short of unskilled labour and unless more were found profitability would suffer. After trying without success to find labourers elsewhere – for in the nature of Transvaal custom they had to be non-White – Milner sanctioned the importation of indentured Chinese. Politically, this was a serious mistake. It evoked indignation from racially-conscious Afrikaners; that was to be expected and could be ignored. What could not be ignored was the cry of 'Chinese slavery' raised in Britain, nor the community of interest which the 'Chinese question' stimulated between the Boers and a section of the indigenous English. Self- government could not be postponed indefinitely and when it came it would have to include the Boers; that much had been promised at Vereeniging. But self-government, with the English divided, might well produce an electoral majority of Milner's opponents. It would be ironical if he were baulked by an Anglo–Boer combination.

With good reason, both Botha and Smuts who, with de la Rey, had been the Transvaal's principal advocates at Vereeniging, regarded Milner as their enemy. Milner may have mistaken this for an abhorrence of all things British and he may, therefore, have underestimated their pragmatism and their political skills. Milner, as his correspondence shows, was disposed to make generalizations about Boers which seemed to be based on his recollections of

PLATE 9. *Louis Botha* (Courtesy of South African Embassy, London).

President Kruger. He now found himself having to deal with the formidable combination of Botha and Smuts.

Louis Botha was born in Natal in 1862, the ninth in a family of thirteen children. His father, also named Louis, and his mother Salomina, formerly van Rooyen, were both the children of emigrant farmers – Voortrekkers – from the Cape Colony. In 1869 the family moved to the Orange Free State where young Louis grew up and assisted his father on the family farm. He had only the rudiments of formal education. He married Annie Emmet, a direct descendant of Robert Emmet, the distinguished Irish rebel executed in 1803. By the 1880s Botha was farming on his own account in the Transvaal. He was elected to the Volksraad in 1897 and was prominent as one of the small group of 'reformers' who opposed Kruger; he was one in the minority of seven who voted against the ultimatum in 1899. As field-cornet of his district he went with General Lucas Meyer's commando in the invasion of Natal and was appointed assistant-general when Meyer fell ill. When Piet Joubert, Commandant-General of the Transvaal forces, was injured, Botha was left in charge of the Boer defences north of the Tugela River; there he inflicted a signal defeat on General Buller at Colenso in December 1899. In the following February, after Joubert's death, he succeeded him as Commandant-General, a position which he held until the end of the war.

Compared with Smuts, Botha was a simple man, but he shared with Smuts a commanding willpower. Botha had shown, during the war, a remarkable capacity for winning the trust, and even the affection, of his burghers. There was a warmth in his personality which was different from the steely exterior of the man who was to become his principal political associate. Smuts had shown himself as a man of action when he had forcibly removed the gold reserve of the Transvaal from the National Bank shortly before Roberts's army entered Pretoria in June 1900. He then joined General de la Rey in the field and demonstrated a marked ability for command. In July 1901, when the Transvaal Government decided to send a commando into the Cape in an effort to provoke rebellion, it was Smuts, now a general, who was given the command. He failed to raise the Cape; but he led his commando on an extraordinary ride of eight months duration which took him through the British lines as far south as the neighbourhood of Port Elizabeth and then westwards almost to the Atlantic and northwards into Namaqualand. Deneys Reitz, the author of *Commando*, who rode with Smuts throughout that epic campaign, was fond in later years of relating how Smuts's exiguous baggage was captured by a British patrol: a British subaltern, examining Smuts's Greek Testament, was supposed to have remarked: 'What do you suppose this old Boer bastard is doing with Pitman's shorthand?' When the peace parleys began in 1902 Smuts was besieging the town of O'Kiep, from where Botha summoned him to come, under safe-conduct, to Vereeniging. There he had made a powerful speech to the effect that the only choice left was between making peace and inviting political extinction. Those, too, were Botha's views, and the debates at Vereeniging and in Pretoria marked the beginning of a political partnership and close friendship that were to last until Botha's death. Where Botha could move men's hearts, Smuts could appeal to their reason. Where Botha could charm, Smuts could overawe.

When Chamberlain visited South Africa Botha promised him that he would not form any political associations without Milner's knowledge. When Chinese labour became a public issue Botha wrote to Milner giving notice that, 'as times had changed', he intended to hold 'some meetings' of former burghers. The letter was signed by Botha but drafted by Smuts. (That was a typical example of their relationship.) These meetings were the prelude to the formation of Het Volk, 'the people', a political party in all but name. It was launched in the highly charged emotion that was aroused by the return of the dead body of President Kruger from Holland to its burial place in the Transvaal. The funeral train travelled slowly from Cape Town to Pretoria, its drivers under orders to halt wherever there was a gathering between stations or whenever a light was seen near the railway line by night. For a brief period the Afrikaner people became one in a solemn act of mourning, not only for a defeated hero but for a defeated cause.

From one aspect Het Volk resembled a commando in *laager*, this time not so much against the British as against Milnerism – by which was meant not only the anglicizing policy of the High Commissioner but also his unspoken alliance with the mining industry's magnates, now organized as the Progressive Association and looking remarkably like the old Reform Committee in the days of Jameson's raid. But those who inferred from this grouping of forces that the Transvaal had learnt nothing and forgotten nothing would have been in error. For this time it was the Uitlanders who were divided: the pro-Milnerite Progressives were opposed by the Transvaal Political Association, an English organization that pressed for immediate representative government and had small enthusiasm for the mining magnates. There was no chasm of principle between this association and Het Volk.

There was a discipline in Het Volk and an authority by its leadership over the mass of its members that resembled the commandos of 1902 rather than the ramshackle formations of 1899. Het Volk published at first neither manifesto nor statement of principles. In part, this reticence was to avoid giving Milner a chance to suppress it as subversive, in part because it did not need to because its aims were clear enough to all who joined it: the resurgence of Afrikanerdom. The first purpose, the key to all else, was the reunion of the *Volk*, hands-uppers and bitter-enders. Botha was the undisputed leader, and the emergence of Het Volk marks the success of his quiet but unceasing efforts to damp down the feuds and heal the breaches that the war had caused. His policy of inclusion extended even to the National Scouts; now, after penance and because it was convenient, they were to be regarded as part of 'the People' once more; the lost sheep, suitably chastened, might now return to the fold. Some of the recruiting committees which Het Volk sent into the country districts consisted, in equal numbers, of bitter-enders, National Scouts and former prisoners of war. This was the first of modern-style parties to make its appearance in the Transvaal. Branches were formed in all the old constituencies of the republic. Formal authority was concentrated in the head committee, which could discipline members and dissolve subordinate bodies if, in its opinion, they had fallen under 'detrimental or hostile influences'.

The President of the Transvaal Progressive Association was Sir George Farrar, who had been sentenced to death and then reprieved for his complicity in the Jameson raid. The Association was based less on a principle than on a fear of revived Afrikaner domination. It expressed confidence in Milner and was quite content to see the Transvaal remain under imperial protection, which meant indefinite Crown Colony government. It was a political party which disclaimed a desire for power, a sort of English laager. Abe Bailey, another of its leaders who had been a member of the Reform Committee, wrote in the *Transvaal Leader* of 8 February 1905: 'Despite their protestations, the policy of the Dutch party is not "South Africa for the South Africans" but South Africa for the Dutch and those who will subordinate themselves to their ideas.' R. Orpen said at a Progressive meeting:

It was not a question of want of trust in the Boers. He had the most implicit trust in the Boers and in their ability to run the government of this country according to their own ideas, but he also recognized them to be the most clever people in the world in politics. The Boer would be found as able with the vote as with the Mauser, as formidable with a portfolio as with a Long Tom.

The Progressives, in short, summoned up the spectre of the Pan-Afrikaner conspiracy.

The Transvaal Responsible Government Association was, like the Progressive Association, predominantly English but its directing body was drawn from commerce and the professions. It disliked the pretensions of the mining magnates, it was critical of Milner's administration and it particularly disliked the importation of Chinese labourers. The Chinese issue drew together the Afrikaners and many of the English, especially English miners, who combined anti-capitalist with anti-Asiatic prejudices. The sharpest difference between Progressives and Responsibles was their attitude to the Boers. The British Government, argued the Responsibles, had laid upon itself an obligation to trust the Boers when it had insisted on their taking the oath of allegiance in the Treaty of Vereeniging; they believed that the Boers would be loyal when they had 'attained their legitimate desires'. (A critic might have argued that the validity of this argument depended on the weight to be given to 'legitimate'.) The Boers cannot be trusted, said the Progressives, because they do not accept the British Empire. The Boers never will accept the British Empire, replied the Responsibles, until they are trusted. Thus the Responsibles stood for full and immediate self-government, and were prepared to run what risks there might be from the presence of a large Boer contingent in a future legislative assembly.

Divisions among the English did not end there. All along the Witwatersrand labour organizations appeared. Their politics were abrasive; many of their leaders preached a strident 'all-White' socialism with strong Australian overtones, which was hostile alike to Natives, Chinese, Indians and capitalists of all nationalities. They wanted self-government, and they wanted it at once. Here, then, were opportunities for electoral accommodation, if Het Volk were skilful enough to exploit them.

Meanwhile Milner had cobbled together a form of representative government which would give the sensations of autonomy without permitting the Boers to win a legislative majority. This was an admission of the failure of the whole 'grand design' which he had formulated for the creation of a British Transvaal. He hoped, forlornly, that racial animosities might not entirely dominate the first elections. The ties of language and religion would bind together the Afrikaners. (He might have added that they would also be bound together by their dislike of all that they believed that he stood for.)

> On the other hand [he continued] it would require some very potent and exceptional influence to unite the non-Dutch population in support of anything. Differing widely to begin with in origin and traditions – home-born British, South African British, and British from other Colonies, together with a large admixture of naturalized foreigners – they are further split up by numerous cross-divisions arising from business rivalry, from class antagonism or from local jealousies. Pretoria versus Johannesburg, Town versus Country, each of these antagonisms, and others which might be enumerated, tend to divide the Europeans of more recent advent, and would make co-operation between them, except in the actual presence of some grave catastrophe threatening them all, almost inconceivably difficult.[9]

Botha devoted himself to the intricacies of coalition building. In his tours of the country he played down racial antagonisms and said little of Afrikaner ambitions. But while he seemed to hold out the hand of reconciliation, this time to the 'moderate' Englishmen, some of his lieutenants seemed to be less propitiating. Smuts talked of a united South Africa from the Zambezi to the Cape, which reminded some of the old claim, last expressed in the closing words of *A Century of Wrong*, of 'Africa for the Afrikaner'. Ewald Esselen used an old and tried form of rhetoric when he told a meeting that they were not there to say to the British Government. 'You have killed my wife and you have slaughtered my cattle', but they were there to say that they would have not have the bastard form of government, neither fully representative nor fully autocratic, thought up by Lord Milner. General Beyers, a hero of the commandos, showed no disposition whatsoever towards reconciliation. At Pietersburg, in the northern Transvaal, he came out hot and strong against 'Kaffirs', compensation committees for war losses, Lord Milner, English school teachers, Johannesburg capitalists and veterinary surgeons. The Boers, he said, were being driven to despair, and after a reference to the 'rebellion' of Slagtersnek (now firmly established in Afrikaner mythology as resistance to the oppression of the conqueror), he hinted that there would be another war in South Africa 'if the Government does not treat us fairly'. Botha repudiated Beyers, but the reverberations of menace lingered on, especially when Beyers added to them a few days later at Louis Trichardt by saying that the Boers 'had fought for their rights but by divine will had been beaten. Now they would fight for their rights another way.'[10] This did not sound much like co-operation. Some of Het Volk's stump orators seemed bent on buttressing the fears of those who argued that it was folly to give the Boers a chance to win back through the ballot box what they had lost with their rifles.

By the time that Milner's scheme was accepted in London he had already lost faith in it. (It was called the 'Lyttelton constitution' after Chamberlain's successor as Colonial Secretary.) When its terms were published the Progressives announced that they were grateful, Het Volk that they were unacceptable and the Responsibles that they would see to it that they were unworkable. In April 1905 the Responsibles announced that they had made an electoral alliance with Het Volk against the day when real self-government arrived. There was agreement on the restriction of the franchise to Whites only; and that the government to be formed should impose the same control over Asiatics in the Transvaal, and the same restrictions on the entry of any more, that had existed in the old South African Republic. 'The Responsible Government Association claims, as the outcome of these negotiations, to have eliminated the racial question from the politics of the State.' Bold and revealing words!

So far as a colour bar in the franchise was concerned, the new alliance was pushing at an open door. The British Government had already accepted the Boer interpretation of the word 'Native' to include any non-White, including British Indians. The Association of Coloured Peoples of the Witwatersrand had already addressed a resolution of complaint to the High Commissioner. One official in London did suggest that the Letters Patent should be amended to enfranchise 'coloured British subjects, not natives of South Africa'. Milner objected on the grounds (which not everyone found convincing) that this would be unfair to the Cape Coloured peoples who had always been classed as Natives (a highly disputable assertion). However, it seemed that the only friends which the Lyttelton constitution had in the Transvaal were the Progressives, and by the end of 1905 even that had disappeared when their leaders warned Lord Selborne, Milner's successor, that their followers were now demanding responsible government. Before this development could be digested in London, the government had resigned, Sir Henry Campbell-Bannerman had formed a Liberal administration, and Britain was preparing for a general election.

This was the background against which Smuts went to England to put the case to the new Government for immediate self-government both for the Transvaal and the Orange River Colony. He took with him a memorandum on the subject, which read like an anthology of Liberal principles. He had an interview with Campbell-Bannerman, and claimed to have convinced him. 'That talk', Smuts said later, 'settled the future of South Africa.'[11] It was indeed on 8 February 1906, the day after he had seen Smuts, that Campbell-Bannerman carried his Cabinet with him on the issue of self-government, but it is likely that Smuts, in pardonable exhilaration, overestimated the result of his own intervention. The premise of his memorandum, that consent was likely to be a more enduring bond of union than coercion, was standard Liberal doctrine that Campbell-Bannerman had been preaching for years. It may be that the meeting of the two men had the greater effect upon Smuts, in that it it caused him to revise his opinion of British statesmen; in the person of Campbell-Bannerman, he saw the England of John Bright, which he had learnt to revere, rather than the England of Joseph Chamberlain, whose dust he had cast off from his feet. The meeting took him back to what Sir Keith Hancock called 'the sanguine years', when he had returned from Cambridge full of hope. From then onwards Smuts's attitude to Britain began to change from opposition to co-operation. It was a lasting change, and he was to become the greatest of all imperial collaborators – lieutenant-general and then field marshal in the British Army; member of the British War Cabinet in 1917; Rector of the University of St Andrews and Chancellor of the University of Cambridge; Companion of Honour and Officer of the Order of Merit; intimate friend of Winston Churchill and respectful subject and confidant of King George VI.

Emphatically the Liberal Government was not, as some of its detractors alleged, seeking to 'give the republics back to the Boers' (Milner called it 'the great betrayal'). Liberal policy aimed at the continuance of imperial predominance by other means. Churchill, once a prisoner of the Boers and now Under-Secretary of State for the Colonies, emphasized this in the House of Commons:

There is a profound difference . . . between the schools of thought which exist upon South African politics in this House. We think that British authority in South Africa has got to stand on two legs. Hon. Gentlemen opposite have laboured for ten years to make it stand on one. We on this side know that if British dominion is to endure in South Africa, it must endure with the assent of the Dutch. We think that the position of Agents and Ministers of the Crown in South Africa should be just as much above and remote from racial feuds as the position of the Crown in this country is above our party politics.[12]

The grant of self-government to the Transvaal and the Orange River Colony resulted in the return of Afrikaners to political power in both former republics. It also reawakened a subject that was to dominate South African politics for the next half-century: what should be the attitude of the Afrikaner towards the South African English at home and the British Empire abroad? At home, should he seek for co-operation and compromise, or should he seek for Afrikaner supremacy as the goal of politics? Was there any formula which could reconcile national independence with allegiance to the King–Emperor, or should the aim be a republic, if necessary in splendid isolation? All this was subsumed under what was called 'the racial question' and it was a matter for and about Whites, and Whites only. There was also the 'Native question' which was about all non-Whites, but on that there was a broad consensus everywhere but in the Cape, where there were divided opinions; elsewhere it was assumed that South Africa was and would remain a 'white man's country', and the 'Native question' was one of means: how could white supremacy be combined with just treatment of the non-Whites, according to the station in which God had seen fit to place them? It was a question that was regarded as chronic, not acute.

The first elections produced conclusive Afrikaner majorities. In the old Free State Orangia Unie, the analogue of Het Volk, won 30 out of 38 seats. The results in the Transvaal were more complex. There were 69 seats in the Legislative Assembly. The total electorate was 105,338; and of these 54,972 were on the Witwatersrand. Het Volk won 37 seats, a clear majority; the Progressives 21; the National Association (as the Responsibles had renamed themselves) 6; Labour 3; and Independents 2. The total votes cast were perhaps more revealing. Excluding ten constituencies where the Het Volk candidate was returned unopposed, the figures were:

Het Volk	24,123
Progressives	17,635

Independents	8,255
Nationalists	6,025
Labour	5,216

In all respects Het Volk had demonstrated the power of its appeal and the quality of its organization. The total turn-out was 67.5 per cent of the electorate. The average for the Witwatersrand was 65.1, for Pretoria 68 and for the rural districts 72.5 – that is, the higher the proportion of Afrikaners, the greater proportion of votes cast. Well might Smuts exclaim: 'We are in for ever!'[13]

Het Volk had fought the election in alliance with the Nationalists, and Botha was scrupulous in honouring the pact when he came to form his government: two of the six places went to Nationalists, both of them from the 'English section'. In the Orange River Colony, a purely Afrikaner ministry was formed by Abraham Fischer. Within six years of the war's end the 'imperial' party held office only in Natal. In the Cape, John X. Merriman had in 1908 formed a coalition ministry which included four members of the Afrikaner Bond in a Cabinet of seven. The British Government had now devolved responsibility for the political future of the Natives to white South Africans. The Government in London might justify this to its critics by claiming that the history of political participation was one of progression, that the Cape Colony had a colour-blind franchise and that political experience showed that a vote once given could hardly be withdrawn. Otherwise, they could regard the results of self- government with satisfaction, remembering Edmund Burke's dictum that magnanimity was not seldom the truest policy. The coalition ministry in the Transvaal was especially encouraging as a sign of reconciliation; Afrikaners, though they would never forget the war, might obey Kruger's injunction to take the best from the past and build the future on it. General Botha had welcomed the new dispensation with almost fulsome appreciation. The 'old population', he said, 'were actuated by motives of deep gratitude, because the King and the British Government and people had trusted the Transvaal people in a manner unequalled in history by the grant of a free Constitution. Was it possible for the Boers ever to forget such generosity?' Botha's subsequent conduct is evidence that he had experienced a change of heart and that he had now become a champion of conciliation between Afrikaner and Englishman.

That feeling was by no means shared by all his countrymen. Many Boers regarded self-government as no more than their right, and perhaps as a sign that God had not forgotten them. They had, by their own exertions and with the help of Providence, reached the upper slopes of Mount Pisgah. The Promised Land, when they reached it, would be governed on sound republican principles. The euphoria of General Botha, and the more reflective satisfaction of General Smuts, were not typical of all Boer opinion.

Discordance showed first showed itself in the Orange River Colony. It had been with difficulty that the bitter-enders among the Free Staters had been brought to agree to accept the terms presented to them at Vereeeniging. There were many there who were willing to join President Steyn and General de Wet in what Sir Keith Hancock called a Boer suicide pact. They had been overborne by their Transvaal allies; and they loved them none the better as a consequence. Conditions facing the two new governments were quite different. At least four-fifths of the white inhabitants of the Orange River Colony were Afrikaners. There was no English electorate worth bothering about and therefore no political reason for the politics of reconciliation which Het Volk had chosen. That, in itself, did not appeal to those who could not forget the sufferings of the war. Sentiment aside, there were other matters which they deplored in the educational policy of the new Transvaal Government. General Smuts, who had the education portfolio in a coalition ministry, could not afford to alienate the Transvaal English, most of whom did not speak Dutch and saw no reason why their children should be forced to learn it in state schools. In the Orange River Colony, General Hertzog insisted on strict equality between the two languages in schools. To Hertzog, the language question had a double significance: it was essential to preserve the culture of the Afrikaner; and if the English were to become, in spirit as well as presence, genuine South Africans, then they should show respect for the Afrikaner by speaking his language. Bilingualism was the test of sincerity. By contrast, it seemed that Botha and Smuts were too ready to succumb to the conqueror's embrace. The argument that strict language equality would be a vote loser in the Transvaal was of no interest to Hertzog whatsoever; English votes did not matter to the Orangia Unie.

James Barry Munnik Hertzog had been named after James Barry, the woman who lived as a man, had risen to become inspector-general of the medical department of the British Army and whose true sex was discovered only after her death in 1865, the year before Hertzog was born. He was the fifth son and eighth child in his family, which moved from the western Cape to the Kimberley diamond fields in 1872 and then to Jagersfontein in the Orange Free State. Hertzog took a general degree at Victoria College, Stellenbosch, and a law degree at the University of Amsterdam, practised for a time as an attorney in the Transvaal republic and then became a high court judge in the Orange Free State. Like Smuts he was a lawyer who discovered in himself unsuspected military abilities. He became a general, showed skill as a commander of artillery and led a commando on a notable raid into the Cape Colony in 1901. At the end of the war he was offered a chair of law in Holland but he chose instead to enter politics and was one of the founders of the Orangia Unie. He was now Attorney-General and Minister of Education in Fischer's government. There he became increasingly mistrustful of the policies of Botha and Smuts, which seemed to him not to be in the best interests either of the *Volk* or of his vision of South Africa.

But for the moment these dissensions were muffled by the discussions that led at last to the unification of South Africa. Earnest men and women had been talking about 'closer union' for the past fifty years; but while the two republics remained in being there was little chance that the descendants of the 'emigrant farmers' would choose to re-enter a British Empire from which they had been at such pains to escape. But now union had become possible, politically, and urgent, economically. Quarrels over customs revenues threatened to embitter relations among the several governments. There had been a brief Zulu rebellion in Natal, suppressed with a severity which had produced a crisis in the relations between the British and Natal governments. The Natal Cabinet had resigned *en bloc* after the Colonial Secretary had refused to sanction some executions of rebels. In the end Natal had its way, but there remained the fear that precipitate action by one colony, uncoordinated with others, might produce war with one or other of the tribes which would become its neighbours' business. In all the earlier talk about union it had been assumed that southern Africa would follow the example of Canada, and more lately of Australia, and form a federation. Instead, a unitary state emerged. The mastering mind behind this decision was that of General Smuts. He had seen, no less clearly than Milner, the pivotal position of the Transvaal. He would probably have agreed with Churchill's analysis, in the House of Commons on 31 July 1906, of the Transvaal as the nerve centre of South Africa:

It is the arena in which all questions of South African politics – social, moral, racial, and economic – are fought out; and this new country, so lately reclaimed from the wilderness, with a white population of less than 300,000 souls, already reproduces in perfect miniature all those dark, tangled, and conflicting problems usually to be found in populous and old-established European states.

It was because he saw the potentialities as well as the problems that Smuts wanted a unitary constitution in which the influence of the Transvaal would grow with its industrial development. His jubilant cry after the elections of 1907 – 'We are in for ever!' – gave some indication of how his mind was working. The future was in the Afrikaner's hands, provided that he was not divided against himself. Milner had been an enemy because he saw South Africa in exclusively English terms. But the experience of the Transvaal since the war, and of the Cape in which he had grown up, demonstrated how Englishman and Afrikaner could work together. (He may even have been surprised at how easily Englishmen could be influenced by his own cold reasoning.) Intellectually, Smuts stood above and apart from nearly all other South African politicians; he was a metropolitan among provincials. There was much that Smuts would come to agree with in the final speech which Milner made before he left South Africa for ever:

> The Dutch can never own a perfect allegiance merely to Great Britain. The British can never, without moral injury, accept allegiance to any body-politic which excludes their motherland. But British and Dutch alike could, without loss of dignity, without any sacrifice to their several traditions, unite in loyal devotion to an Empire–State, in which Great Britain and South Africa would be partners, and could work cordially together for the good of South Africa as a member of that greater whole. And so you see the true Imperialist is also the best South African.[14]

In the consolations of philosophy in which he indulged, Smuts was already seeking for combinations resulting in greater wholes. (He had long mediated upon the arguments which he eventually published as *Holism and Evolution*.) It is not preposterous to regard Smuts as the mirror-image of Milner, and sharing some of Rhodes's vision before it had been blurred by the Jameson Raid. In time to come, his fellow-Afrikaners would taunt Smuts as 'the handyman of the British Empire', and reproach him for working towards an empire-state in Africa.

7 THE RISE OF HERTZOG

The Act of Union of 1909 had been passed by the Parliament at Westminster but its terms were drawn up entirely in South Africa. Agreement had not been reached without acrimony, and there were times when it seemed that the national convention of representatives of the four colonies might break up among recriminations. Controversy over the franchise went to the heart of disagreement. The Cape delegates argued for the extension of their own system, restricted but colour-blind; the other three colonies were adamant that voting should be for Whites only. No one seriously suggested that there should be votes for women. In the end each of the new provinces retained its existing arrangements, which meant that 'Cape liberalism' would be confined to the Cape. Only Whites might sit in Parliament. The choice of a capital was another matter where tempers ran high. Eventually an expensive compromise was reached. Cape Town would be the seat of Parliament, Pretoria the seat of administration; this meant that there would be a cumbersome movement of ministers and civil servants over a thousand miles, twice every year at the beginning and ending of each parliamentary session. Bloemfontein, in the Orange Free State (as it was now renamed), was to be the judicial capital – that is, the seat of the Appellate Division of the Supreme Court. In the end there emerged a bicameral parliament: a House of Representatives of 121 members, elected for five years, to be increased to 150 as the white population grew; and a Senate of 40, eight from each province elected by proportional representation and eight nominated by the Governor–General, of whom four should have a 'thorough acquaintance . . . with the reasonable wants and wishes of the coloured races'.

The Union of South Africa, then, had a 'semi-controlled' constitution, which could be amended by a simple majority in each House,

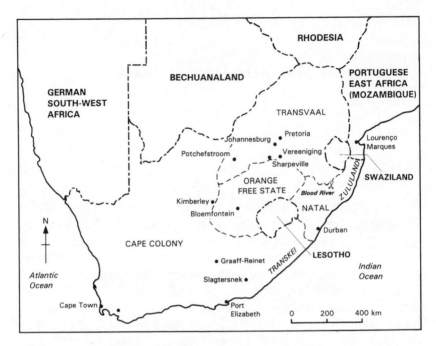

MAP 1. *The Union of South Africa, 1910.*

with the exception of 'entrenched clauses' safeguarding both the equality in all public matters of the English and Dutch languages and the maintenance of the voting rights of non-white men in what was now the Cape Province: to change either of these clauses required a two-thirds majority in a joint session of both Houses. It was the 'Westminister model' with local variations. The first governor-general was Viscount Gladstone, youngest son of the great Liberal politician.

General Botha was the first prime minister, at the head of what was called the South African Party ('Saps' to its opponents), which was a loose coalition embracing Het Volk, the Orangia Unie, and elements of the Afrikaner Bond of the Cape, supported by a substantial number of the 'moderate English'. The Unionist Party, predominantly English and imperialist in sentiment, formed the official opposition; its leader was Dr Jameson, whose re-emergence in Cape politics showed a remarkable personal rehabilitation from the odium of the Raid. At the first general election the S.A.P. had polled 52 per cent of the vote, and had a sufficient working majority with 68 out of 121 seats in the House of Representatives.

The era of good feelings that had ushered in the union did not last long. Beneath the surface, Afrikaners were divided in tone and teleology. Botha and Smuts were now among those who were prepared to regard the Boer republics, like the war that had extinguished them, as things of the past, a heroic memory but not a matter of political division. The future of the Afrikaner lay not in recalling the ghosts of the dead past but in working with Englishmen of goodwill as equal partners. This was what Botha meant by what he called 'conciliation': past quarrels should be forgiven, if not forgotten, and the Afrikaner should merge into the South African, the survival of his language and his traditions to be safeguarded by absorbtion into a society based on mutual respect and a common purpose.

Botha's policy of conciliation was not to the liking of all Afrikaners, especially in the Orange Free State and where rebellion had found support in the Cape. Below the level of high politics, racial resentment was unquenched. Botha and Smuts were thought to have become too anglicized, too careless of the traditions of the *Volk*, too ready to forget the past. It was remembered that Botha had spoken well of Dr Jameson, had unveiled a memorial to Cecil Rhodes, had worn knee-breeches at Buckingham Palace (stigmatized as the uniform of a lackey), had accepted an honorary major-generalship in the British Army and had presented the Cullinan diamond, the largest ever discovered, as a coronation gift to George V (he had received in exchange a handsome bill from the British Treasury for the diamond's cutting and setting). Smuts's laxity over language equality in the Transvaal was held against him. Many who had voted for the South African Party looked on the peace of Vereeniging as no more than a truce; the republics might be redeemed when, as seemed increasingly likely, Britain was involved in war in Europe. There may have been no anti-British conspiracy before the Anglo–Boer war, but there was the makings of one now. Men of this opinion would have liked to look for leadership to President Steyn, but he was ill and not to be coaxed back into active politics. But they found a voice, albeit one that was cautious and prone to ambiguities, in General Hertzog, now minister of justice. Botha would willingly have omitted Hertzog from his Cabinet; but Hertzog would not accept the judgeship that was dangled before him, and to leave him out against his will would be to jeopardize the Free State vote.

Hertzog denied that he was anti-English, and his future career was evidence that he meant what he said. The doctrines of cabinet solidarity or collective responsibility lay lightly upon his shoulders. His mind had some of the characteristics of a medieval schoolman. From within the Cabinet he openly challenged 'conciliation'; he did not, he said, know what it meant. There followed a battle of words, beneath which two sets of principles were in conflict. The way in which Hertzog habitually expressed himself and his insistence on 'South Africa first', rang menacingly in the ears of those of the English who were sometimes more imperial than the King. Hertzog advocated what he called a 'two-stream policy', expressed in a cloudiness of language that was his oratorical trademark. He was prone to a nervous tension that sometimes led him on the platform to say things that he would later qualify or painstakingly explain away. Thus he told Botha that he was opposed not to conciliation but to the cry for conciliation, which often seemed to him to be humbug since it required the Afrikaner to do all the conciliating. In the South Africa to which Hertzog declared himself to be committed there were two essential attributes – the equality of the two white races and the independence of the State. As it was, neither had yet been achieved, the Afrikaner was on the defensive, and if he appeared to be aggressive it was merely because he was determined to defend his right to equality with the Englishman, neither more nor less. Neither equality nor sovereign independence could be achieved by the subservience which he criticized in the general outlook of General Botha. The language and culture of the Afrikaner were in danger of being swamped by the English language and way of life. The Englishman did not have to worry about the preservation either of his language or of his 'culture', which he accepted as unconsciously as the air which he breathed: one was what he said and the other was what he did. The threat to either from an Afrikans competitor would have seemed to him to be preposterous. The Afrikaner enjoyed no such certainty. His own language was still in the making, for Afrikaans had not yet been delivered from the womb of High Dutch.

As he surveyed the South African scene it seemed evident that the Afrikaner was in a position of inferiority in all fields except the political. Englishmen, sometimes in alliance with Jewish newcomers, dominated industry, commerce and the professions. There was always the danger from 'Hoggenheimer' the plutocrat, a creature beginning to appear in the Afrikaans press as a caricature of the cosmopolitan capitalist without attachment to the country except as a place where he could grow rich, usually on the gold of the Witwatersrand at the expense of the honest patriot.[1] The Englishman in South Africa was a man of divided loyalties, all too often speaking of England as 'home', refusing to learn the Afrikaner's language, and treating him and his traditions with condescension or contempt. If the Afrikaner were to preserve his distinctive identity he must become linguistically and culturally self-sufficient, and this required some form of insulation from the distorting effects of Englishness. In the domain of politics the two races must perforce be jumbled together; but there was no reason why the Afrikaner and the Englishman should be at cross-purposes provided that the Englishman put South Africa first – that is, above the sentimental ties of 'home' or empire – and provided that he accepted the Afrikaner as an equal. But Hertzog's metaphysics took him beyond the world of politics. The Englishman's cultural heritage was world-wide, and it was not something which the Afrikaner was at present able to share without

PLATE 10. *J. B. M. Hertzog* (Courtesy of the South African High Commission).

compromising his own integrity. Hertzog therefore advocated what he called the 'two-stream' policy. 'The national life of South Africa flows in two streams of culture – an English and an Afrikaans; they will flow side by side until a historical destiny will in the distant future possibly cause them to merge.' Meanwhile he could not regard the monarchical principle in the Act of Union as representing South Africa's final destiny.

> Personally I have always been and will always remain true to the Treaty of Vereeniging; nevertheless I have the right to say that I regard the republican form of government as the best form of government for South Africa. Every nation has in course of time gained its freedom, and whether it takes a hundred years, or a thousand years, South Africa shall get its freedom.[2]

The implication was clear; as long as South Africa remained under the Crown, it was unfree and its present condition was transitional. Thus there was a division between Hertzog and Englishmen who felt no less free because they were the titular subjects of a monarch, and another division between him and Afrikaners such as Botha and Smuts who did not define 'South Africa' in Hertzog's narrow terms.

In the circumstances of the time, Hertzog's attitude put him at the cutting edge of domestic politics. What was important was not only what he said but the mood that he evoked. Alone among politicians, it seemed, he said things that many Afrikaners had long been waiting to hear from someone in authority. He stood for a nationalism that other Afrikaners seemed to have abandoned. He could claim not to be a racialist (as that word was understood in the context of local politics), but his definition of South Africa and South Africans was one that seemed to exclude most of the English section. Lest this point be unclear, he referred to Sir Thomas Smartt, Jameson's successor as Leader of the Opposition, and others like him, as 'foreign fortune-seekers', thus inferring that they were in the country only for what they could get out of it; by Hertzog's tests, they were not South Africans.

All this was deeply embarrassing to General Botha. If he dropped Hertzog from his Cabinet he would alienate the Orange Free State; if he kept him he put at risk his own policy of 'conciliation', especially among the English who controlled the mining, industrial and commercial assets of the country, at a time when South Africa's development needed capital from abroad and especially from

Britain. Hertzog's speeches would do nothing whatsoever to reassure potential investors. In effect, Hertzog dared Botha to dismiss him and to state publicly his reasons for doing so. What Hertzog said that he wanted was South Africa for those who put South Africa first. What was wrong with that? Did Botha, then, put South Africa second? Botha seemed faced with a choice between antagonizing the Orange Free State and abandoning 'conciliation'. The matter came to a head when Hertzog, in a speech at the hamlet of De Wildt on 7 December 1912, said: 'I am not one of those who always talk of conciliation and loyalty: they are idle words which deceive no one. I have always said that I do not know what conciliation means.' Botha was brought to bay. Hertzog would not resign, and Botha then took advantage of the British constitutional convention that the resignation of a prime minister entailed the resignation of his entire cabinet. Botha offered his resignation to the Governor-General who accepted it and then, after a very brief interval, invited Botha to form another government, from which both Hertzog and the most vocal of his critics, Sir George Leuchars of Natal, were excluded. The price that Botha paid was rather more than simply the loss of the Orange Free State (where the Party congress gave Hertzog a vote of confidence by 47 votes to 1). At the national congress of the South African Party in Cape Town, a vote of no confidence in Botha's leadership was supported by 90 votes out of 221. Hertzog and his former comrade-in-arms, General de Wet, walked out of the congress and a few months later they and other dissidents formed the National Party, with Hertzog as leader. For the moment Hertzog could find support from only five members of parliament; but Botha now had a formal party of opposition on his right as well as his left.

In May 1913 a dispute between management and labour in the mining industry developed into a major crisis in which 19,000 white miners were on strike by July. More was at issue than working conditions. There were anarcho–syndicalists among the miners' leaders, and the Chamber of Mines had been looking for a chance to break their power, even at the price of confrontation. Violence developed; the strikers burnt the Johannesburg station and the offices of the Johannesburg *Star*, the newspaper which they regarded as the mine owners' mouthpiece, and made themselves masters of the Johannesburg streets. With no effective armed force at their immediate disposal Botha and Smuts risked their reputations, and perhaps their lives, in parleys with the strike leaders, in which they conceded most of the strikers' demands.

The events of 1913 proved to be merely the prelude to more serious industrial troubles, which began in the Natal coal mines, spread to the nationalized railways and once more to the Witwatersrand gold mines, and culminated in the proclamation of a general strike by the Transvaal Federation of Trades. This was treated as a challenge to its authority by the Government. Smuts as Minister of Defence (he was also Minister of Mines and, since Hertzog's departure, Justice as well) had now completed the organization of the South African Defence Force, and this was used against the strikers in overpowering strength. If the strikers' leaders really believed that they could make common cause with Afrikaner opponents of the Government they were disillusioned when Active Citizen Force commandos under General de la Rey and General Beyers entered Johannesburg, surrounded the Trades Hall, and threatened to blow it to pieces with artillery fire if it did not surrender. Smuts then deported nine of the strikers' leaders without any legal authority; effectively the Minister of Justice had conspired against the courts and his own commissioner of police. He covered himself by an indemnity act passed through Parliament; but he had now made himself the enemy of the predominantly English industrial workers of the Witwatersrand.

There was another quarrel that was to have bleak consequences for Smuts and for South Africa thirty years later. This time it was with representatives of the Government of India, and it concerned discrimination in the treatment of Indians in South Africa. This was an old story whose origins went back before the Act of Union. The Indians had, however, discovered a champion of genius in Mohandas Karamchad Gandhi, a young barrister newly called to the bar in London, who had been invited in 1893 to act for two Indians who were involved in litigation in the Transvaal Republic. Sir Keith Hancock has described Gandhi's reception:

On the day of his disembarkation at Durban he visited a magistrate's court and was ordered to take off his turban; rather than submit to this affront he left the court and saw himself next day advertised in the newspapers as 'an unwelcome visitor'. On his journey from Durban to Pretoria (in those days it was by rail and road) he was pushed about by the ticket-collector on the train and pushed about again by the driver of the coach. In Pretoria he was pushed from the pavement into the gutter. His white tormentors, if only they had known it, were pushing him into politics, with consequences incalculable for the history of South Africa, of India, and the world.[3]

Smuts and Gandhi began their disputes when Smuts was Colonial Secretary of the Transvaal and continued them after the Act of Union. They were well matched; his enemies did not call Smuts 'Slim Jannie' for nothing. ('Slim' means 'crafty', with a touch of slipperiness.) Gandhi began to use in South Africa the tactics of passive resistance called 'Satyagraha' which he was to develop against the Raj in India, whither he returned in 1914. 'The saint has left our shores', Smuts then wrote, 'I sincerely hope for ever'. Gandhi took with him a first-hand experience of Indian disabilities in South Africa and an abiding impression that at least on one occasion Smuts had double-crossed him.

The outbreak of the Great War in 1914 produced new divisions among Afrikaners and led to a surge of support for Hertzog's National Party. The South African Government had not been consulted before the British ultimatum was presented to Germany, and there were many who argued that South Africans were being dragged into a war in which they had no interest against a nation that had done them no harm. The Unionist Party strongly supported Britain. Hertzog, who knew his constitutional law, did not deny that the King's declaration of war on Germany bound the whole British Empire, of which South Africa was a dominion; but he argued that the extent of each dominion's contribution was a matter for its own decision, in which the South African Government should be guided strictly by what was in the interests of South Africa, not the Empire. The matter of South African participation became critical when the British Government asked South Africa to capture the wireless station at Windhoek in German South-West Africa.

The outbreak of war had seemed to some of the intransigents that Britain's preoccupation in Europe was the Afrikaner's opportunity. Botha's decision to send troops into German territory produced outrage from Nationalists and may have encouraged some to remember the armed protests of republican days. But they were now dealing with a resolute government which would regard armed protests as what they were in law – rebellion. The war divided the former leaders of the Boer commandos. General C. F. Beyers, who had distinguished himself in the Transvaal, was now in command of the Active Citizen Force and Beyers himself, like many of his officers, was an unreconciled republican. The South African

Defence Force was principally Smuts's creation under the Defence
Act of 1912. It consisted of a small cadre army, with organized
around it what was called the Active Citizen Force, a form of
territorial army. It had been called into action in 1914 to put down
the general strike on the Rand, and it had then obeyed its orders
without question. What would it do now, especially in the rural
districts where Afrikaners were in the overwhelming majority?
Much would depend on personal leadership. General de Wet, the
hero of the Orange Free State, was of the same mind as Beyers. So,
too, was General S. G. ('Manie') Maritz, in command of the military district which bordered upon South-West Africa. Neither
Beyers nor Maritz had the prestige of de Wet, and among Transvaalers the prestige of General J. H. de la Rey stood very high
indeed.

De la Rey was remembered as a military leader of legendary
prowess. His siting of the Boer trenches at the victory of Magersfontein in 'Black Week' – well in front of a line of hills – would have
won the approbation of Clausewitz. In March 1902 his commando
had won the last victory of the war at Tweebosch in the western
Transvaal when he routed General Methuen's forces and captured
the general himself, along with his wagon train. At Vereeniging he
had supported Botha in arguing that the bitter end had come at last.
He was now a Senator. With de la Rey in rebellion, Transvaalers
would be faced with a bitter personal choice between him and
Botha, two heroes of the *Volk* now in different camps. De la Rey
combined military skill and business acumen with a certain simple-
ness of mind. He was deeply superstitious. During the Boer War he
had been under the influence of his private soothsayer–prophet,
known as 'van Rensburg the seer', whose occult powers, de la Rey
believed, enabled him to dream what the British forces were going
to do next. (Others, less credulous than de la Rey, thought that van
Rensburg had a private intelligence service based on Native infor-
mers.) Now van Rensburg claimed to have dreamt of a fight to the
death between two bulls in which the grey one had killed the red
one; and from this he inferred that Germany would vanquish Great
Britain. It is said that this dream–prophecy greatly disturbed de la
Rey. Certainly his behaviour was erratic. Within a few days after
the declaration of war he ordered his commando in the military
district   of Lichtenburg to assemble, mounted and armed, on 15
August. What was the purpose of this, and what opponent did de
la Rey have in mind? It is possible that in his confusion he was
toying with the idea of an armed protest. Botha and Smuts invited

de la Rey to meet them in Pretoria, apparently with success, for the assembly in his district ended by passing a vote of confidence in the Government.

Faced with divided opinions, not only among the public but in the Cabinet, General Botha thought it prudent to obtain the authority of Parliament for the expedition against German South-West Africa, and a special session was called in September. There, Hertzog led the opposition. He did not deny that the Union of South Africa was committed, by the King's declaration of war, to legal belligerency, but he seemed to believe that it would be possible to go no further and to adopt what amounted to political and military neutrality. He had, he said, every sympathy with Belgium, overrun by German troops, but he was not willing to condemn Germany for unjust aggression, 'as it might be shown afterwards that it was no such thing'. (Hertzog was to repeat this argument, this time with reference to Poland, twenty-five years later.) He ended with a warning: 'The Government would very speedily find that they had to deal with a population which felt that something was being done which ought not to be done.'

However cumbersomely expressed, Hertzog's warning was accurate enough if the word 'population' was confined to Nationalist Afrikaners. The Government won handsomely enough in the House of Assembly by 92 votes to 12. Outside Parliament, Nationalists called protest meetings, matched by counter-meetings of Botha's supporters. To most of the English it was enough that Britain was at war; Hertzog would have said that this showed that they were not South Africans in spirit. General Beyers resigned his commission. On 15 September, with de la Rey at his side, he set out by car for the western Transvaal. It was not clear what they intended to do; Beyers said afterwards that he had merely proposed to speak against the war at some public meetings. However, he seemed to expect that Government agents would stop him, which is why he drove through a road block. Had he pulled up, he would have been perfectly safe, for the road block had nothing to do with him or de la Rey but had been set up by the police in operations against a notorious band of urban brigands known as the Foster Gang. As it was, shots were fired after the car; a bullet richocheted from the surface of the road and killed de la Rey instantly. It was a freakish and unworthy death of a hero. A letter from his widow to Smuts expressed all the agonies of mind that were afflicting some Afrikaners. 'Ah, in the last bitter struggle in our land we were as brothers, although there were also Afrikaners who went against us . . . Now it seems to me as if I stand in the midst of the two parties, the one is as precious to me as the other and as yet I see light on no side.'[4]

Rebellion began on 9 October when General Maritz went over to the Germans and handed over part of his commando as prisoners of war. He made his intentions clear enough in a wild manifesto,

PLATE 11. *A cartoon of C. R. de Wet, from Vanity Fair 1902* (Courtesy of Vanity Fair).

issued on 16 December, the holy anniversary of the battle of Blood River:

> The former South African Republic and Orange Free State as well as the Cape Province and Natal are proclaimed free from British control and independent, and all white inhabitants of the mentioned areas, of whatever nationality, are hereby called upon to take their weapons in their hands and realize the long-cherished ideal of a Free and Independent South Africa.[5]

De Wet and Beyers both rebelled, at the head of forces of substantial size. Botha tried at first to resolve matters by negotiation; the English thought that this was a weak-kneed condoning of the actions of those who were waging war against the King in his own dominions. At last Botha acted decisively. He was determined to use, as far as he could, only Afrikaner troops; he had no wish to re-enact the conflict of Briton versus Boer. The legendary mounted tactics of de Wet were of little use in open country when he was opposed by reconnaissance aircraft directing motorized troops; after a defeat at Mushroom Valley he was rounded up as he was trying to make his way to German territory by way of Bechuanaland. Beyers was drowned after his horse was shot under him as he was trying to escape across the flooded Vaal River. The official figures were that 124 rebels had been killed in action, 229 wounded and 5400 captured. The question was, what was to be done with the survivors? De Wet was tried for high treason and sentenced to six years imprisonment and a fine of £2,000. Special courts were set up to try the lesser offenders who were given sentences of fine and imprisonment. All the rank and file were out of prison by the end of 1915; none of the leaders served more than two years in gaol. A new Afrikaner society emerged, Helpmekaar (mutual help) to pay the rebels' fines through public subscription. It was enthusiastically supported.

Militarily, the rebellion had been of little account; politically, Botha and Smuts paid a heavy price. The lightness of the sentences counted for little among those who thought that the rebels had done no wrong. Whatever sympathy the Government might have gained was outweighed by the one conspicuous exception to the policy of clemency. Lieutenant Joseph (Jopie) Fourie, a professional soldier, had not resigned his commission before he rebelled; he was also, it was alleged, responsible for the death of loyal men who had been fired on under a flag of truce. He was condemned to death by court-martial and executed by firing squad. Smuts, Minister both of Defence and Justice, refused to recommend a reprieve.

The Nationalists had their martyr. De la Rey was not a serious candidate: it could not plausibly be argued by reasonable men that he had been murdered, though there were plenty of unreasonable men to believe just that. Beyers could be seen as a victim of conscience who had died without firing a shot in anger, symbolically uniting Transvalers and Free Staters by dying in the river that divided them.[6] But no one in particular could be marked out as directly responsible for Beyers's death. Fourie was regarded as different, and the odium fell upon Smuts; until the end of his life there were those of his enemies who regarded him as a murderer, bearing the mark of Cain. Fourie joined the growing pantheon of Afrikaner martyrs. One account of his life and death compared his wounds with those of Christ.

> Along with the victims of Slagter's Nek and the other tragic heroes of Afrikaner legend he became the symbol of the piety and the sacrifice, the exultation and defiance of his people. Marvellous and significant things were told about him: he had been captured on Dingaan's Day and shot on a Sunday; he prayed that the cup might pass from him but when the moment came he offered his breast to the bullets with a serene faith in his God and his people; if he allowed himself to be blindfolded, it was only to make easier the task of his executioners; he died singing a psalm.[7]

The rebellion and its aftermath brought to the surface deep currents of resentment, and often of hatred, among the Afrikaner people. But, and this was one of the curiosities of the South African condition, these sentiments were seldom directed at individuals among the English. The full fury of the Nationalists was directed at men like Botha and Smuts, and Afrikaners who supported them. Whatever extreme Nationalists might think of the leaders of the South African Party, no one could impugn their gallantry or their services to the republics during the war. Now they had ordered Afrikaner to fire upon Afrikaner, and the memory of their previous patriotism could be expunged; they had become traitors to the People, *volksvyande*. National myths require villains as well as heroes, Benedict Arnolds as well as George Washingtons. Botha and Smuts were now outcasts from the bosom of nationalism.

Of course not all Afrikaners were nationalists, and for every zealot there was someone else sunk deep in apathy; the lower down the scale of living he was, the more listless he was likely to be. But the call of the blood had its effect and the rebellion had kindled old flames. This was the heroic period of Afrikaans prose and poetry, the fruit of the second language movement stimulated both by the war and by the policy of anglicization that Milner had tried and failed to achieve. Gustav Preller was beginning to chronicle the saga of the Voortrekkers, with ebullient imagination. The rough dress which the Voortrekkers had worn because they had nothing else was now elevated into a national costume. Voortrekker pastimes were invented, like *jukskei*, a pitching game, and blameless dances that, some said, bore a revealing resemblance to Swedish calisthenics. But no one could mock the literary merits of 'Totius', son of S. J. du Toit of the first language movement, or Eugene Marais, or Jan Celliers or C. Louis Leipoldt. Few Afrikaner children, at the secondary-school level, were ignorant of the experience of wartime suffering that produced poems of the quality of 'Dis Al', or 'Winternag'. One of Hertzog's two streams was beginning to flow, even though the English still seemed to be culturally dependent on importations from Britain. The Helpmekaar movement had prospered at a time of high emotion; the money left over after the rebels' fines had been paid went to the encouragement of Afrikaans cultural associations and sometimes to the Afrikaans press. A vehement nationalism was to be found in many Afrikaans schools and churches, where predikant found himself divided against predikant, and dissident congregations split off from their parent bodies. The students of the university college at Stellenbosch repudiated Smuts where he had once been regarded (with justice) as the most brilliant graduate of them all.

There was a general election in October 1915. The issue, underneath the rhetoric, was clear enough – to support the war or not to support the war. It was fought with far more than the usual bitterness, not all of it engendered by nationalist sentiment: Smuts was nearly lynched in a working-class suburb of Johannesburg, at a meeting broken up by left-wing members of the predominantly English Labour Party who had not forgotten his actions in the general strike of 1914. The results could give encouragement only to the Nationalists, who had won 26 seats out of 130, in this their first general election. The S.A.P. was down to 54, and had lost its absolute majority. That did not matter while politics were dominated by the war, since on that issue they could count on the 40 Unionist members. In round figures, and taking no account of uncontested seats, there were 94,000 votes for the S.A.P., 74,000 for the Nationalists and 50,000 for the Unionists. Labour had 24,000 votes, half of them on the Witwatersrand, and won 4 seats. The S.A.P. did not win a single seat in the Orange Free State, Hertzog country. The ominous facts were that the Nationalists had polled 30 per cent of the vote, compared with 36 per cent for the S.A.P., and had made significant gains in the rural areas both of the Cape and the Transvaal, once considered to be solid for Botha.

A new personality had emerged among the Nationalists. This was Dr Daniel François Malan, one of Smuts's neighbours when both were children in the western Cape and, bizarrely enough, one of Smuts's pupils in the local Sunday school in the 1880s. Malan was born in 1874, four years after Smuts; he was the son of a Cape wine-farmer of Huguenot descent. Like Smuts he was not a typical sport-loving young Afrikaner; but there the resemblance ended. At

PLATE 12. *D. F. Malan* (Courtesy of the South African High Commission).

Stellenbosch, where he took his first degree, he was not regarded as a devoted scholar but he busied himself with social questions 'upon which he could bring to bear a kind of idealistic discontent', in the words of his biographer in the *Dictionary of National Biography*.[8] From Stellenbosch he went to the University of Utrecht where he took a doctorate in divinity with a thesis on the idealism of Berkeley. Back in South Africa he started as a schoolteacher but soon exchanged the classroom for the pulpit as a predikant of the Dutch Reformed Church. He was a puritan of high moral courage, although his sermons on the virtues of temperance, if not of total abstention from alcohol, drew little approval in a wine-growing district. He was active in the second language movement for the development and refinement of Afrikaans. He joined the National Party as soon as it was formed, and presided over its first congress in the Cape, where he became party leader. (The party was federal in its organization, with separate leaders in three of the four provinces; there was as yet no branch in Natal.) He became editor when the Party decided to establish its own daily newspaper in Cape Town, *Die Burger*, which under Malan became the most eloquent, and the best informed, of all Nationalist publications. He did not win a seat in Parliament until 1919; but by then he had for long been one of the most controversial public figures in the country. His owl-like figure, with its habitually unsmiling countenance, became the embodiment of those stern and unbending Afrikaners who would be satisfied with nothing less than political domination in an Afrikaner republic which had seceded from the British Empire.

There was nothing in Malan's speeches or writings comparable to Hertzog's convoluted statements about two streams of culture and the possible future melding of the two white races. One stream was good enough for Malan, provided it was Afrikaans. When Malan spoke of unity, which he frequently did, he meant the unity of Afrikaners. In some sense the position of the Nationalists resembled that of Het Volk in its early days, when there were National Scouts and hands-uppers and other deviants to be chastised and then readmitted to the *Volk*. Now there were other Afrikaners to be converted into the ways of righteousness, those who had followed Botha and then been betrayed by him with assistance from Smuts, his evil genius. Malan's editorials breathed the fervour of the most unforgiving of Old Testament denunciators: woe to false brethen and misleaders of the People! There could be no compromise with the English; the war had shown where their true sentiments lay. In 1919 he made his way to England with a delegation of Nationalists to plead that the principles of self-determination should be applied to South Africa; he could hardly have been surprised when the delegation was given a brusque refusal. But he was treading in the footsteps of Paul Kruger, who had likewise made the pilgrimage to England to plead for the independence of his country and had likewise been denied.

The capture of South-West Africa was South Africa's most notable contribution to the Allied war effort. In a divided country there could be no compulsory military service, but a South African brigade of volunteers served on the western front in Europe, where it suffered heavy casualties during the battle of the Somme; the South African defence of Delville Wood held for a time the same significance among returned soldiers as Gallipoli did for Australians and New Zealanders. What distinguished South Africa from the other parts of the Empire was the singular influence of General Smuts in London, during the war and at the making of the Treaty of Versailles. At the Imperial Conference of 1917 he was responsible for the drafting and introduction of a resolution, that was to have great significance for the future, concerning the 'readjustment of the constitutional relations of the component parts of the Empire'. The themes were self-government, a voice for each of the Dominions in foreign relations and continuous consultation. This meant the rejection of imperial federation in favour of a loose association of what were effectively independent states, linked by a common allegiance to the Crown. In this may be seen the outlines of the formula drafted by Lord Balfour in 1926 and the Statute of Westminster in 1931. What this meant was that Britain could not assume that the Dominions would necessarily take part in any future wars in which Great Britain might be engaged.

To any but the most dogmatic of republicans, South Africa's independent status seemed to be recognized by the signature of her representatives to the Treaty of Versailles, though both of them, Botha and Smuts, had great reservations about the wisdom of the terms. Smuts's attitude was highly ambivalent. He thought parts of the treaty to be unwise, and he certainly encouraged J. M. Keynes to write his devastating polemic, *The Economic Consequences of the Peace*. But he also played a part in the decision to include the cost of Allied war pensions in German reparations. He put into circulation the word 'appeasement' (by which he meant concession from strength) and he was instrumental in drafting the system of mandates by which South Africa retained the administration of what was German South-West Africa. He was unhappy about the future of the world but pleased with South Africa's newly acquired international status. He could, with pardonable exhilaration, write to his wife from Paris:

> While the Nats. make a noise about our independence we have obtained this – that South Africa takes her place at the Peace Conference among the nations of the world. This is the second time that I appear at a Peace Conference – but how different is the situation in Paris from that of Vereeniging in 1902! There we had to drink the cup to the bitter lees; here South Africa is a victor among the great nations! I am thankful that it has been granted to me to do my part in the great work and to help lead my people out of the painful past into the triumphant present.[9]

Large numbers of his own people were not in the least grateful. In 1919 Smuts became Prime Minister on Botha's death. In the general election of 1920 the Nationalists pulled ahead of the South African Party, both in seats won and votes cast. The Nationalists had 44 seats and 101,000 votes; the South African Party 41 seats and 90,000 votes; the Unionists 25 seats and 46,000 votes; and Labour 21 seats and 40,000 votes.

No Unionist was likely to vote against Smuts to put Hertzog into power; but the attitude of the Labour Party was far from certain. There was much discussion of reunion, especially between the semi-contiguous wings of the South African Party and the Nationalists, but the stumbling block was the Nationalists' attitude to the Empire and their insistence that secession remain an open question. Smuts then turned to the Unionists and without great difficulty persuaded them to dissolve themselves and merge in the South African Party. Effectively he had absorbed most of the old 'imperialist' part of the South African English. The results were immediate. In the general election which he called in February 1921 the Nationalists slightly improved their position – 45 seats and 105,000 votes – but they were decisively defeated by the newly enlarged South African Party – 79 seats and 140,000 votes. Their gains were, however, at the expense of Labour, which slipped to 28,000 votes and 9 seats.

The most serious crisis which Smuts's Government faced was yet another revolt on the Rand, this time with some Communist undertones but curious variations; the strange slogan appeared: 'Workers of the world, unite and fight for a white South Africa'. The strike had been touched off by an attempt by the Chamber of Mines to cut costs by diluting expensive white by cheaper black labour. The novelty in these industrial troubles was the organization of strikers into what they called 'commandos' of their own. Both the Nationalist and Labour Parties supported the strikers' cause; not only could it be portrayed as 'anti- capitalist' (which meant, in Nationalist terminology, hostility to the mine magnates) but as safeguarding the standards of living of white workers. The Government, by contrast, seemed to be on the side of the mine-owners, whose recalcitrance in refusing to negotiate without a return to work was held by the strike committee to justify demands for a general strike. Smuts declared martial law, and there were several days of fighting between troops and the strikers' 'commandos' before the insurrection was defeated. This time strikers accused of murder were tried by a special court set up under Act of Parliament, which passed sentences of death upon eighteen of the accused, four of whom were hanged.

The Rand rebellion, as it was called, had its main political repercussion in the conclusion of an electoral pact between the Nationalists and the Labour Party (predominantly English, and vehemently colour-conscious). They shared a common aversion towards Smuts, who could be portrayed both as a man of blood and as a tool of the mining magnates. The pact involved compromises on both sides; the Nationalists would undertake not to press for secession in the immediate future, the Labour Party to tone down any socialist doctrines which its members might hold.

Smuts went to the country in 1924, after the loss of a by-election in what had seemed a safe seat. This time Hertzog had behind him not only the Labour Party but a Cave of Adullam of the generally discontented. The general election of 1924 was perhaps the only one in the history of the Union of South Africa in which class conflict played any significant part – especially on the Witwatersrand where Labour candidates linked together both class and colour in an appeal to safeguard 'civilized labour' against capitalist machinations and the 'black peril' These tactics were enough to win Labour 18 seats in all. The election was a disaster for the South African Party, which lost 19 seats, both to Labour on the Witwatersrand and the Nationalists in the rural areas, bringing them down to 53. The Nationalists had 63 seats, or 81 in alliance with Labour, a clear   majority in a House of 135. Hertzog's Cabinet included two English representatives of the Labour Party, Colonel Frederic Hugh Page Creswell, leader of the party and Thomas Boydell; both were 'prison-graduates' of the general strike of 1914.

There was an eerie similarity between Hertzog's pact with Labour and the alliance which Botha had made, back in colonial days, between Het Volk and the English Responsible Government association; the mining interest had been catalysts in each. This time alliance between Nationalists and Labour resulted in an extension of the industrial colour bar to protect skilled and unskilled white workers by reserving certain jobs for Whites only.

Thus, after consolidating the position of skilled white workers, mostly English, and enacting measures to ameliorate the plight of poor Whites, mostly Afrikaner, the Government could turn its attention to the status of South Africa, within the Empire and in domestic matters. So far as the Empire was concerned Hertzog found little to displease him. When he went to London for the Imperial Conference in 1926 he found that the winds of appeasement, so far as the susceptibilities of the Dominions went, blew fresh and clean through Whitehall and Westminster. There was not much that Hertzog said or did at this conference that could not equally have come from Smuts; and he found support from the Canadians who, likewise, had a divided electorate at their backs. The vexed question of the indivisibility of the Crown was tacitly avoided; later, theory would tiptoe gingerly behind practice on this issue. Hertzog declared himself satisfied, for the time being at least, with the formula which emerged from the mind of Lord Balfour, heavy with the British genius for ambiguity. Great Britain and the Dominions were described as 'autonomous communities within the British Empire, equal in status, in no way subordinate to one another in any aspect of their domestic or external affairs, though united by a common allegiance to the Crown and freely associated as members of the British Commonwealth of Nations'. There was little but felicity of language to distinguish this from the resolution which Smuts had proposed in 1917. Hertzog's deductions from Balfour's formula were for domestic consumption only. 'Free association', he insisted entailed the right of disassociation, although as a practical matter South Africa had no intention of implementing that right, at least not for the time being. Thus reassured, he could turn the attention of his Government from the external to the internal attributes of sovereignty. The front-running there was done by Dr Malan, his Minister of the Interior, Public Health and Education. The issue of a national flag was to convulse the country.

The 'flag debates', in and out of Parliament, produced angry exchanges in which imperialism, republicanism, anti-British and anti-Nationalist feelings were all bought to the surface in boiling emotions. As early as 1921, when he was still leader of the opposition, Hertzog had awakened the slumbering genie of imperialism when he said that he hoped that the armed forces would soon have a truly South African flag. The Union Jack, he said, was 'merely a piece of cloth', meaning that it awakened no patriotic sentiments among Afrikaners; once South Africa had its own flag it would lead to 'better feelings' among the white groups.[10] This was an early indication of Hertzog's propensity to ask the English to make gestures of accommodation towards the deeply held sentiments of their fellow-citizens. Critics of Hertzog pointed out that gestures tended to be demanded of one section only of the population. In 1925 a resolution against titles granted by the Crown was carried in the House of Assembly, moved by Arthur Barlow, a Labour member with strong anti-establishment convictions. A select committee was appointed to consider whether Afrikaans, rather than Dutch, should be the co-equal language of record in Parliament. (Hansard was regularly printed in English and Dutch.)

It was the Nationality and Flag Bill, introduced by Dr Malan as Minister of the Interior, that produced reactions of fury. The Bill was introduced, withdrawn, then introduced again. Malan did not mince his words. Any national flag, he said, which included the Union Jack would not be acceptable 'to a large, perhaps to the larger section of the community'. He offered what he described as a double concession. The Nationalists were prepared to give up the old republican colours; even though they were the party of secession from the Empire, they were prepared to fly its flag on specified occasions.[11] Hertzog added that if the Union Jack were included in the design of the national flag, the flag would stand not for independence but for subservience. Later he went back into history to describe the Union Jack as an 'intruder' which had pushed out the original and older flag of Dutch South Africa in all four provinces, each time with violence.[12]

It ended with compromise, even though in the meantime Natal had threatened to secede from the Union. There would be a flag of blue, white and orange horizontal stripes in equal proportions, with the Union Jack, and the flags of the Transvaal and Orange Free State in miniature, at the centre. The Union Jack was to be flown at the same time on ceremonial occasions and on public buildings; thus there were two flags, symbols of divided sentiment. There were devoted republicans who referred to the Union Jack, as represented in the South African flag, as a scab that would fall off, as in nature. Hertzog, true to the pact with Labour, refused to allow the Nationalist Party to declare itself avowedly republican, even though he added that 99 per cent of the party's members were republicans at heart.

The general election of 1929 saw the Nationalists increase their strength in the House of Assembly to 78 seats; the South African Party had recovered somewhat, to 61 seats, largely at the expense of a divided Labour Party which lost ten seats to bring its numbers down to eight.

A neutral observer in 1929 would have been justified in remarking that the outstanding characteristic of high politics in South Africa since Hertzog broke with Botha had been the steady growth of a solid Afrikaner Nationalist front. True enough, not all Afrikaners were nationalists; Smuts still had a large personal following. But it would be equally true that all nationalists, with insignificant exceptions, were Afrikaners. It would seem, too, that Smuts's cry of 1907, 'We are in for ever!', could now be repeated by Hertzog, this time to Smuts's detriment. However, the surface of politics was to be agitated, and then transformed, by the onset of the Great Depression that followed the collapse of the American stock market in 1929.

8 DIVISION AND REUNION

The great depression that followed the Wall Street crash of 1929 entailed the contraction of the South African economy and had as its corollary a disintegrating effect on party politics. The hardships, were exacerbated by the obstinacy with which General Hertzog's Government clung to the gold standard long after the British Government had been forced to abandon it. Part of this policy had its root in the conventional wisdom of the orthodox economists; but there was also a political slant, an assertion that South Africa was independent of Britain not only politically but financially as well; the results were especially damaging to primary producers of all kinds. One example will stand for many. South Africa's principal competitor in the export of wool was Australia, which had devalued early in 1931. This meant that by the end of 1931, £100 sterling bought 125 Australian pounds, but only between 70 and 75 South African pounds.[1] N. C. Havenga, Minister of Finance, combined impeccable nationalist sentiments with financial orthodoxy, but his attempts to balance the budget by protective duties and export bounties did not deter currency speculators from targeting the over-valued South African pound as a source of windfall profits and buying heavily on the London market, thus adding to the appreciation of the South African currency and to the general distress.

And, since it is possible to lose money in any language, the racial issue became for the moment less interesting than the ledgers of commerce or the state of the Stock Exchange. At this conjuncture of affairs, Mr Tielman Roos, whom everyone in politics had supposed to be desiccating respectably in the dignified *penetralia* of the Appeal Court, emerged upon the anxious gaze of the public, tacking hither and thither in a fever of infectious energy. While other statesmen eddied furiously in circles, Mr Roos floated triumphantly before the breeze, in a manner which claimed, and obtained, a considerable share of public attention. Sounding the tocsin . . . he proclaimed the downfall of the Golden Calf with an eloquence which would have done credit to the Old Testament. Nor, when General Hertzog gave ear to his calling, and linked himself once more to sterling (in despite of Self-Determination) was Mr Roos' prophetic ardour much abated. From being a voice in the wilderness, he became the conductor of a semi-chorus of fifteen Members of Parliament. He enjoyed the position. He intended that his semi-chorus should be heard, and to advantage. For after all, the Government's majority was only 16.[2]

Tielman Roos, who had emerged so dramatically from the wings of politics to occupy the centre stage, had been one of Hertzog's earliest and most ardent supporters and was the first leader of the National Party in the Transvaal; he belonged in the numerous company of those whose followers have called them 'the Lion of the North'. He possessed little of Hertzog's ambiguous circumspection. He believed in republicanism and in secession from the British Empire and said so, loudly. He was elected to Parliament in 1915. His reputation had suffered among the more sombre Nationalists after he had remarked 'I regard politics as a game'. In 1924, in Hertzog's first ministry, he had been Minister of Justice and Deputy Prime Minister. He had resigned from both Cabinet and Parliament in 1929 after his health had begun to fail, and had become a judge of appeal. Politically he had seemed to be an exhausted volcano; instead, he had suddenly erupted, with spectacular results: South Africa left the gold standard at the end of 1932. But Roos, revivified by triumph and exhilarated by the support which he had evoked from all points of the political compass during his foray into the world of high finance, now had ambitions on the premiership itself. He turned first to Smuts, to whom he offered the support of his fifteen MPs but his price was too high – equal representation of Roosites and Smutsites in a cabinet of ten, with Smuts as deputy prime minister under Roos – and Smuts declined. But by now the whole political atmosphere had become so charged with the expectations of change that there was no going back to the old disposition of parties; what the electorate seemed to want was the formation of a coalition government and reconciliation between

Afrikaner and Englishman. That much Roos had accomplished. There was, however, no place for him in the new arrangements. Early in 1933 Hertzog and Smuts came to an accommodation which was then approved by the parliamentary caucus of each of their parties. It amounted to a diarchy under the forms of parliamentary government. Hertzog remained as prime minister and Smuts became deputy prime minister. Each of them was to nominate half of the new cabinet.

The 'racial question' was not so easily to be swept from the stage by the appearance of a *deus ex machina*. The terms of coalition were such that the Smutsites accepted the legislation of Hertzog's Government, and the Hertzogites (whatever their private opinions might be) agreed that republicanism and secession should be dropped from the political agenda. This was regarded as heresy by that section of the Nationalists which had already begun to believe that Hertzog had been too easily beguiled by bland assurances of the equality of the Dominions with Great Britain within the British Empire, as contained in the definition of Lord Balfour in 1926 and reinforced in the Statute of Westminster in 1931. Nationalists of this way of thinking had no wish for equality with Great Britain; they wished to be rid of the British connection altogether. They now looked to Dr D. F. Malan rather than Hertzog. For the moment, they were prepared to accept coalition, purely on tactical grounds: part of the understanding was that in the forthcoming general election sitting 'coalitionists' should not be opposed. In hindsight, it would have been prudent for Hertzog to have insisted that his internal opponents could not claim the protection of the coalition umbrella. To have done so, however, would not have been in accord with the general euphoria; such was the atmosphere of goodwill that Smuts journeyed to Malan's constituency to speak in his support. The election results fully bore out the tactical acumen of the irreconcilables: the coalitionists had 138 seats in a House of 150. Once they were back in Parliament the Malanites felt themselves secure enough to go into open rebellion. In December 1933 they formed their own party which they called *die Gesuiwerde Nasionale Party* – the Purified National Party: the name itself was a rebuke to former comrades who were now to be regarded as false brethren. Malan had done to Hertzog in 1933 what Hertzog had done to Botha in 1913. The Gesuiwerdes had 19 MPs, and Malan formally became Leader of the Opposition. For the moment such strength as the new party had was concentrated in the Cape; there was only one Member of Parliament from the Transvaal, J. G. Strijdom.

The next logical stage for the coalition parties was fusion. This was not achieved easily. Some difficulties were concealed by semantics, some side-stepped by agreements to differ or by indulgences granted to tender consciences. By the middle of 1934 Hertzog and Smuts had agreed on the 'programme of principles' of what was now to be called the United South African National Party.

Its object is the development of a predominant sense of South African national unity, based on the equality of the Afrikaans-speaking and English-speaking sections of the community, coupled with the recognition and appreciation by either section of the distinctive cultural inheritance of the other.

Under 'Native policy' it was laid down that matters of political representation should be 'left to the free exercise of the discretion of individual members representing the party in Parliament'; this was a gesture to the left, towards the liberal wing now represented most eloquently by the young J. H. Hofmeyr, a former infant prodigy whose academic qualifications rivalled those of Smuts himself. The gesture to the left was accompanied by one to the right, on the matters of republicanism and secession, which were referred to in opaque language:

While the Party stands for the maintenance of the present constitutional position, no one will be denied the right to express his individual opinion about or advocate his honest convictions in connection with any change in our form of government.

There was one clause in the programme which was uncomfortably reminiscent of the presumptuousness of Robespierre's declaration in 1794 that the French people recognized the existence of a Supreme Being: 'The recognition of the Natives as a permanent portion of the population of South Africa under the Christian trusteeship of the European race is accepted as a fundamental principle.'

The concessions made to republican consciences were too much for the extreme right wing of the South African Party in Parliament, seven in number, which seceded to form the Dominion Party, almost exclusively English and devoutly imperialist, under the leadership of Colonel C. F. Stallard. Both Hertzog and Smuts, therefore, had lost the extremists of their respective parties, those who, without grotesque exaggeration, might be regarded as analogues of Kruger and Milner – or perhaps of Sinn Fein and Ulster Unionists.

From Hertzog's point of view, the creation of the United Party (as it came to be called) was the justification of all that he had stood

for since he had first broken with Botha over the realities underlying his slogan of 'South Africa first'. The place of the English in
the future was now settled; apart from Colonel Stallard and the
lunatic fringe in Natal, from whom nothing more enlightened was
to be expected now than it had been twenty years earlier, the
equality of the two white races was no longer in dispute. Nearly
twenty years earlier he had recognized that 'before you can get the
English to say "d", you have first to teach them to say "a", "b" and
"c".'[3] The process of education had been tedious, but it had been
successful in the end. South Africa now had its own flag; Afrikaans
had been elevated to the status of an official language, and the
evidence seemed to show that bilingualism was on the increase
among the English.[4] The differences which remained seemed to be
those on which there was no longer mortal disagreement: that
South Africa should remain a 'white man's country', which meant
a 'civilized labour' policy, and that something should be done about
safeguarding the proper interests of the Natives. He had already
tried to remove the Natives of the Cape Province from the common
voters' roll but had failed to gain the requisite two-thirds' majority
stipulated in the Act of Union. Fusion, surely, would take care of
that; it was the price which the United Party had agreed to pay for
reconciliation. Above all, it was now a matter of law that South
Africa was a sovereign independent state.

On this, one may ask whether it was the South African English,
the British Government or General Hertzog himself whose attitude
had changed. He had returned from the Imperial Conference of
1926 immensely reassured that Great Britain no longer had imperial designs on South Africa, could no longer drag her, willy-nilly,
into wars not of her own choosing, and neither could nor would
prevent her from seceding from the Empire if ever she should
choose to take that final step. That reassurance had been written
into the statute book of the United Kingdom by the Statute of
Westminster, 1931. In a speech at Potchefstroom in May 1933 he
uttered what amounted to a *nunc dimittis*:

> The struggle was brought to an end by the passing of the
> Statute of Westminster, because thereby South Africa was
> recognized by Statute as a free and sovereign nation. As to the
> equality of the languages in practice, that has been applied by
> the National Party ever since 1924, and as it has been accepted
> by the South African Party as a basic principle of co-operation,

the struggle has been finally decided. The two main points at issue since 1913 have therefore been disposed of.[5]

On reflection, Hertzog came to the conclusion that the Statute of Westminster was almost the last word, but not quite. For that was an Act of the Imperial Parliament, and as a constitutional lawyer Hertzog was aware that one of the attributes of parliamentary sovereignty was that no parliament could bind its successor. Moreover, there was something lacking in South Africa's own sovereign status if that depended legally on an Act of another sovereign state. Hertzog believed in something which, borrowing from the Greek, he called 'autochthony' – something sprung from the soil. Therefore the British Act of Union of 1909 was re-enacted as the Status of the Union Act of 1934 and supplemented by the Status and Seals Act which provided for a South African Great Seal and placed it in the keeping of the Prime Minister for use, at his advice, by the Governor-General.

In 1936 the long argument among Whites over the Native franchise in the Cape Province came to an end with the passing of the Natives Parliamentary Representation Bill, which removed Natives from the common voters' roll in the Cape Province but permitted them instead to elect three white members of the House of Assembly. This was the first major change in the compromise reached in the Act of Union. The objections to it were moral rather than legal; it was passed in accordance with the procedure laid down in the constitution, and it received more than the required two-thirds' majority in a joint sitting of both Houses; the third reading was passed by 169 to 11, in a division in which members of the United Party voted as individuals, with the whips off. The most notable speech in opposition was made by a cabinet minister, J. H. Hofmeyr.

Jan Hendrik Hofmeyr was the nephew of that other Hofmeyr, also Jan Hendrik (1845–1909), who had been the *éminence grise* of the Afrikaner Bond in the Cape Colony. The younger Hofmeyr was born in Cape Town in 1894 and had an academic career of unalloyed brilliance. After having taken the matriculation examination at the age of twelve (the normal age was seventeen) with the utmost distinction, he had graduated from the University of the Cape of Good Hope at the age of fifteen with an honours degree in classics, to which he added an honours degree in mathematics a year later. He was awarded a Rhodes Scholarship in 1910, when he was sixteen. He was adjudged too young to go to Oxford at once, and he spent the intervening period in writing a biography of his uncle. He took a double first from Balliol College in classical honour moderations (1914) and Literae Humaniores (1916). By the age of twenty-two he was professor of classics at what was to become the University of the Witwatersrand in Johannesburg; two years later he was appointed as its principal. There he suffered the first setback to his career. His widowed mother, a woman of determined opinions, had accompanied him to Oxford, and now she was with him in Johannesburg. It was probably through her influence that he became embroiled in a serious dispute with the academic senate of the university, after he had demanded the resignation of a professor who had been involved in a divorce case. The senate held that the private life of one of its members, where there was no public scandal, was none of the Principal's business; and it took the extreme step of refusing to meet under his chairmanship. He was rescued by Smuts, then Prime Minister, who appointed him as Administrator of the Transvaal at the astonishingly early age of thirty. In 1929, at the end of his term of office, he joined the South African Party and was elected to the House of Assembly for a Johannesburg seat.

Hofmeyr was a man of whom stories were told, not always to his advantage. It was said that he had asked for a tin of condensed milk as a present to mark his matriculation triumph, and that a neighbour who had called to congratulate him found him playing under the table with his cat. There were many of his colleagues who found the constant presence of his mother to be a burden on friendship. (Hofmeyr had no wish to rid himself of her influence, and he never did so; she outlived him.) He was a fanatical cricketer, a game at which he showed no competence whatsoever; the heart attack which killed him in 1948 struck him while he was attempting to go out to bat in a charity match. He was an outstanding speaker in either English or Afrikaans, and his gifts as an administrator were legendary. He was a devout Christian, and he was one of the small contingent in the South African Parliament who could be described as liberals in the European sense of that word. He was an original member of the coalition cabinet; in 1936 he was Minister of Mines, Education, and Labour and Social Welfare.

Hertzog had commended his Bill on Native representation as a measure to preserve 'white civilization' through the unity of the white races; the alternative might be a division of Whites into rival camps, one standing alone and the other having 'millions of Natives' behind it. Christian principles, he said, stood high, but self-preservation stood higher still, 'because it was the only way in which humanity, and Christianity itself, could be defended'. Hofmeyr challenged Hertzog's assumptions at their root. The Bill, he said, would have consequences which would run in the opposite direction to its intentions. The educated black man would be thrust back upon his own people, but in hostility and disgruntlement, there to become a leader in disaffection and revolt. As to the Christian principle of self-determination, he said, he was reminded 'of the eternal paradox that whosoever will save his life shall lose it'. Hofmeyr's was a voice in the wilderness, and he recognized this by not making his opposition to the Bill a matter of resignation.

Malan commanded only a small faction in Parliament, but his weakness there understated the increasing consolidation of nationalist influence outside the parliamentary arena. Hertzog might have satisfied himself that the way forward lay in co-operation between Afrikaner and Englishman; there were plenty of Afrikaners who would not be satisfied with anything less than a republic, and one that was 'purified' – cleansed of 'unnational elements' – by which they now meant not only the English but the bulk of the Hertzogites as well. Nationalists of this persuasion were looking beyond their immediate electoral prospects. They were equipping themselves with an economic base, they were developing an ideology and they were permeating established institutions as well as creating new ones for Afrikaners only.

In June 1918 a group of young Afrikaners met in a suburb of Johannesburg and founded an organization which was first called Young South Africa but swiftly changed its name to the Afrikaner Broederbond (League of Brothers). The first executive committee consisted of H. J. Klopper (chairman), Willem Nicol (vice-chairman), D. H. C. du Plessis, J. Combrink, H. le R. Jooste, J. E. Reeler and L. J. Erasmus.[6] Their first aims seem to have been innocuously modest, albeit somewhat priggish: to help each other, as opportunity offered, in their various callings and to 'propagate the Afrikaans language and bring together serious-minded young Afrikaners in Johannesburg and along the Reef'[7], but their ambitions swiftly spread beyond the bounds of these pious and limited objectives. In 1921 the Broederbond decided to become a secret society. It was to become a force in Afrikaner nationalism, and for a time perhaps the most powerful force.

The Broeders, to judge by their later success, were men of intellect, imagination, narrow intensity of purpose and unswerving ambition. They recruited new members with extreme care. In time they established a network of cells which linked them with members of the National Party, selected ministers of the Dutch Reformed Churches, the teaching profession at all levels, the public service, the armed forces, the police – in short, with every activity which might be used to promote the aims of an exclusive and vehement nationalism. Its faith in Hertzog was shaken when he returned from the Imperial Conference in 1926 and seemed to have faltered in his commitment to republicanism. Hertzog's son, Albert, was an energetic member; this may have been one reason why General Hertzog did not take the Broederbond seriously until it was too late. In the 1930s the Broederbond began to move into the economic field; characteristically, it chose to do this behind the shelter of the Federation of Afrikaans Cultural Societies (*Federasie van Afrikaanse Kultuurverenigings*, usually referred to as F. A. K.). The name was indicative: a typical Broeder would not have regarded politics as a discrete activity, merely one aspect of a working life. It was one of the props of Afrikanerdom, along with the Afrikaner's religion, his language and his culture. Moreover, the Broeder's life was that of constant vigilance in a world populated by abstract enemies – liberalism, universalism, tolerance, pluralism, 'sickly humanism', imperialism, atheism, communism, Judaism, monarchism: the list seemed endless. Had more been known about the Broeders it would have been easy for those more gifted with a sense of humour to have ridiculed such aims as 'the establishment of a healthy and progressive unanimity among all Afrikaners who strive for the welfare of the Afrikaner nation'; it would have been easy and it would have been profoundly mistaken, for these men were in deadly earnest. 'Brothers, our solution for South Africa's maladies is that the Afrikaner Broederbond shall rule South Africa.'[8]

By the 1930s the intellectual leadership of the Broederbond had moved to Potchefstroom University. This was no haunt of cloistered virtue: intellectual activity was linked to practice. Economic institutions were either founded or brought under Broederbond influence – banking, insurance, investment, to name only three. Its exclusiveness could be seen in its creation of purely Afrikaans equivalents of such organizations as the Boy Scouts, the National Union of South African Students, St John Ambulance and the South African Automobile Association. It was considered particularly important to form specifically Afrikaans trade unions, to protect Afrikaners from the perils of class- consciousness and to promote instead a sense of nationalist unity. Henning Klopper successfully

organized an Afrikaner railwaymen's union, and there were determined and ultimately successful efforts to control the mineworkers'
union. One notable, and much-publicized, failure was the attempt
to wean Afrikaner women away from the Garment Workers'
Union, an organization under the control of a cheerful Marxist
named Solly Sachs, which ignored the colour line. Earnest university students were enjoined to boycott traders who failed to treat
Afrikaans with proper respect:

> Never shop where you are not served in Afrikaans, and where
> Afrikaans is not accorded its rightful place on notices and
> signboards – and tell the trader why. Pay no accounts which
> have not been issued in Afrikaans and patronize no firm that
> does not advertise in Afrikaans newspapers and magazines.[9]

This was one indication of a shift in emphasis. It was no longer
capitalism that was the enemy, but 'foreign' capitalism. The
Broederbond was well on its way to becoming a network of capitalist enterprises. The change of emphasis was a recognition of the
urbanization of the Afrikaner, and with it the menacing increase of
the 'poor Whites'.

The 'poor White question' was nothing new; it had been discussed
at congresses of the Afrikander Bond in the 1890s. Part of the
'civilized labour' policy of Hertzog's government had been to find
some form of sheltered employment for poor Whites. Ironically
enough, 'civilized labour' sometimes involved reserving some kinds
of manual labour on the state-owned railways for Whites only. The
matter of urban poverty had been a continual concern of the Dutch
Reformed Churches, and they had encouraged the comprehensive
survey made by the Carnegie Commission which published its
report, in five volumes, in 1932. The findings were horrifying.

The Commission's definition of a poor White was 'a person who
has become dependent to such an extent, whether from mental,
moral, economic or physical causes, that he is unfit, without help
from others, to find proper means of livelihood for himself or to
procure it directly or indirectly for his children'.[10] It found that 17.5
per cent of families with children at school fell into this category;
by extrapolation, this meant 300,000 out of the 1,800,000 Whites
in South Africa.[11]

The Commission travelled along some familiar routes into the
past to explain why so many Whites had degenerated. Generally
speaking, it could be ascribed to inadequate responses to economic
change; it cited poor education, which inhibited the acquisition of

skills, and – a matter of resentment to Afrikaners – the importance of a knowledge of English for urban employment. In rural districts the Commission pointed to the clinging to overcrowded farms. 'This is a clear symptom of a type of mentality that is marked by narrowness of outlook, by lack of enterprise, and by a dread of the strange world beyond the farm.' Other contributing factors were a high birth-rate, insanitary habits, inadequate diet and the prevalence of chronic illnesses such as malaria. Ignorance was superimposed upon poverty. Part of the class of poor Whites was

> characterized by one or more of such qualities as improvidence and irresponsibility, untruthfulness and lack of a sense of duty, a feeling of inferiority and lack of self-respect, ignorance and credulity, a lack of industry and ambition, and unsettledness of mode of life ... The great majority of the poor whites are still imbued with the conviction of their superiority over the non-Europeans.[12]

These characteristics were shared by at least one other group, and the Commission found that some of the English 1820 Settlers of the eastern Cape Province had fared no better, and that 'the same forms of poverty and backwardness are today met with among many of their descendants'. But the overwhelming majority of poor Whites were Afrikaners. Moreover, the Commission was critical of the mystique that endowed the Voortrekkers with haloes of romantic glory. Among them, there were those in whom the spirit of independence had 'degenerated into self-righteousness, contentiousness and contrariness – traits which, particularly in the Transvaal, so often marred our history. Along with fine personal virtues, we find a striking lack of social qualities'. Moreover, many of the frontiersmen were 'mentally and morally weak'.[13]

One consequence which was especially unwelcome to Nationalists who had never ceased to desire the unity of the *Volk* was the growth of a secular squalor beyond the reach of religious admonishment. 'The surveillance of the Church which, as a rule, exerts a considerable influence in moral matters in rural areas, is apt to lose much of its force in the cities.'[14]

The grim prospect had to be faced that the poor White might be lost altogether to the community of 'right-thinking Afrikaners', that his 'national identity' might be lost in the slums of the cities, where racial segregation broke down, and the poor of many races might live, literally, cheek by jowl. Here was a new battleground for the survival of the *Volk*. The poverty- stricken Afrikaner needed help, but it must come to him in such a manner that it neither blurred his consciousness of colour nor anglicized him in language or outlook. In every field, from recreation to welfare, the Broederbond sought to create specifically Afrikaner organizations; it was well aware that the future of Afrikanerdom lay in its suppressed multitudes. That was clear enough from an analysis of the census returns of 1936, which showed that the proportion of those whose home language was Afrikaans increased dramatically as one went down the scale of age. Of Whites over twenty-one, there were 115 Afrikaners for every one hundred English; between seven and twenty-one there were 185; and under seven there were 212. The seeds of Afrikaner supremacy had been sown in the marriage bed; but if those seeds were to be harvested it was necessary to shield the Afrikaner child from contamination, instruct him from an early age in the history and aspirations of his people and warn him of the Afrikaners' natural enemies. With single-medium education, and teachers who satisfied the Broederbond's canons of purity, the task could be done.

It was the popularity of Fusion that gave the Broederbond its chance to expand its political activities into the Transvaal. There was one only Gesuiwerde MP left in that province, J. G. Strijdom, and the Broeders had therefore an uncluttered field in which to manoeuvre.

Hertzog might well feel that his own control was slipping. On 7 November 1935 he attacked the Broederbond in a speech at Smithfield to the head committee of the United Party in the Orange Free State; his theme was South African unity and denunciation of those who would destroy it.

> What do we see surrounding us today? Indefatigable, zealous attempts in all directions to provoke national disunity; to awaken irreconcilable aversion and hatred between the races; to prostitute our cultural assets, our language and religion, our history and origins, as hostile instruments of attack, with which to fight, slander and crush one another . . . What is concealed behind all these excesses?[15]

What was behind it all was the Broederbond; and Hertzog described its organization in detail and derided its claim that it was merely a cultural association. Not only was it political, but also it was the underground branch of the Purified Nationalist Party, and he named Dr Malan as one of its members. Malan admitted it with pride.

Hertzog's Smithfield speech was more important for his own future than for any immediate effect on politics. The high command of the Broederbond never forgave that speech. They had already rejected Hertzog's acceptance of equality between the two white races; now he was personally marked down for political destruction.

The importance which the purified forces of Afrikanerdom now gave to the Transvaal could be seen in the decision to establish a new daily newspaper in Johannesburg, to preach the doctrines of militant racial exclusiveness and, in the process, to counteract the influence of *Die Vaderland*, which preached orthodox Hertzogism. The new paper was named *Die Transvaler*, and its editor was Dr Hendrik Frensch Verwoerd, high in the councils of the Broederbond and lately Professor of Applied Psychology in the University of Stellenbosch. His appointment followed logically from a conference which he had organized in 1934 on the problem of the poor Whites. He was to show himself to be the most charismatic of all Nationalist ideologists. He was an intellectual of formidable abilities who had studied at the universities of Hamburg, Leipsig and Berlin and knew something of Holland, France, England and the United States of America. It seemed that these travels had done nothing to impair his belief in the uniqueness of the Afrikaner *Volk* and his own ability to assist in the God-given work of shaping its destiny. At this stage of his career, at least, the boundaries of his tolerance were straitly drawn. In some ways he was the mirror-image of Lord Milner, not least in not being willing to see the other side of a case on which he had made up his mind. He once told a colleague in his department at Stellenbosch that, if he wished his academic career to prosper, there were two things which he ought to alter – 'your home language and your general outlook'.[16]

In the middle 1930s, however, the Hertzog–Smuts diarchy seemed to be politically impregnable. The country was prosperous, and there seemed to be no acute problems of controversy. Even the most dedicated Nationalist could join with the English in commemorating the exploits of the Springboks, as South African sportsmen were called, after the national emblem. Rugby football was a game which, especially among Afrikaners, evoked a semi-religious devotion, and the victories over the All Blacks in New Zealand had established the Springboks as the most successful rugby players in the world. Enthusiasm here stretched across the boundaries of race and was broad enough to include the Cape Coloured peoples. (Neither the Natives nor the Indians showed either interest or aptitude.) There were tensions within the Government but they did not seem likely to disrupt its unity since very often they took the form of J. H. Hofmeyr versus the rest of the United Party. All of these disagreements concerned the treatment of non-Whites. Hofmeyr might well feel that Smuts gave him less support than he deserved; but Smuts at this period was not prepared to risk the unity of the party for what he regarded as matters of secondary importance: to him the 'racial question' meant co-operation with Hertzog and his followers and steering South Africa away from secession from the Empire. (Even Dr Malan did not dissent from a resolution of condolence on the death of King George V, although he led his followers out of the House when it came to a loyal resolution on the accession of King Edward VIII.) Hertzog behaved with impeccable correctness over the abdication in 1936, and South Africa assented to the Act in accordance with the Statute of Westminster. When the Earl of Clarendon demitted as Governor-General in 1937 he was replaced by what was claimed to be the first indigenous appointment. It was true that Sir Patrick Duncan (the self-denying ordinance against titles was waived on this occasion) was not everyone's idea of a typical South African. He had been born in Scotland, educated at Edinburgh University and Balliol College, Oxford, had come to South Africa as a member of the Milner 'kindergarten', had been a member of Smuts's cabinet from 1921 to 1924, and had then become Minister of Mines under Hertzog in the coalition ministry of 1933.

The results of the general election of May 1938 seemed to have justified Smuts's forbearance; the huge United Party majority was hardly dented. The Purified Nationalists had increased to 29, mostly at the expense of Hertzog's followers. It may have been the knowledge that the threat, if any, came from his Right that induced Hertzog to behave as if he had forgotten that the party which he led was still a diarchy. One of the casualties of the election had been the Minister of Labour, A. P. J. Fourie. Hertzog retained him in the cabinet by appointing him to one of the seats in the Senate reserved for those possessing a 'thorough acquaintance with the reasonable wants and wishes of the coloured races', a category in which no one had previously included Fourie. This was too much for Hofmeyr, who resigned from the Cabinet in protest at what he called a prostitution of the constitution. Smuts said nothing in public.

The next incident awakened the suspicion of the 'English section' that Hertzog was all too eager to appease the Nationalists. In 1918 C. J. Langenhoven, regarded as one of the giants of the second language movement for the promotion of Afrikaans, had written a patriotic poem entitled 'Die Stem van Suid Afrika', which had been set to music in 1921. Those who regarded God Save the King as an affront to their republican sentiments would willingly have seen 'Die Stem' as the official national anthem. On Hertzog's initiative, the Cabinet agreed that 'Die Stem' should be played, as a ceremonial innovation only, at the forthcoming opening of Parliament; this was one of those 'gestures of goodwill' towards Afrikaner sentiment which Hertzog seemed, in the eyes of his critics, to be too anxious to make. It was inevitable that Hertzog should be asked in the House if 'Die Stem' had now become an official anthem. The answer was no, but Hertzog chose to embark on a disquisition that seemed a dangerous retrogression to the emotionally charged debate on the flag issue. There were many who remembered that he had then referred to the Union Jack as 'merely a piece of cloth': he now gave his opinion that God Save the King was merely an invocation to the Almighty, that 'Die Stem' had much more of the character of a national anthem, and one day might become one. Then, on Union Day – 31 May – the military bands at the ceremonial parade at Defence Headquarters played 'Die Stem' and did not play 'God Save the King'. Smuts chose to treat the matter as an oversight (which it was not); in private he was distressed at the way in which Hertzog's mind seemed to be working. 'These mistakes are heartbreaking, and I sit with the broken crockery, even if not with a broken heart! We must endeavour to carry on, but frankly I find it often most trying to work with my old Nat[ionalist] friends. They are more influenced by fear of Dr Malan than of God.'[17]

They had every reason to fear Malan; he was about to enjoy an enormous popular triumph. The year 1938 was the centenary of the Battle of Blood River. The idea of turning this into a festival of Afrikaner solidarity seems to have originated with Henning Klopper, one of the founders of the Broederbond. There would be a symbolic representation of the Great Trek, culminating in meetings of the *Volk* on 16 December, the holiest day in the patriotic calendar. No activity with which the Broederbond was concerned was devoid of political content: Afrikaners were to be reminded of the sacrifices and glories of a past in which the English had no share. Klopper set the tone: 'Disasters, adversity, privation, reversals, and suffering are some of the best means in God's hand to form a people'.[18] The future was theirs – if only brother would unite with brother and reject those who sought to mislead the people. Then would the Afrikaner, at last, come into his own.

On 8 August two ox-wagons, allegedly replicas of those used by Voortrekkers, departed from van Riebeeck's statue in Cape Town on the journey that was to take them to Pretoria. At Goodwood, their first stop, they were met by a crowd of 20,000 Afrikaners, the first sign of the welcome that they were to receive all along their route. There were nine of these wagons, starting from different places, some to go to Blood River and others to what was now named Monument Kop, outside Pretoria, the designated site where the foundation stones of a permanent memorial were to be laid. The wagons visited in all 500 towns and villages in a crescendo of excitement. Welcoming committees dressed in what they believed to be Voortrekker costume; municipalities renamed streets in commemoration; marriage ceremonies were performed in the proximity of the wagons and children were brought there to be baptized. There were the customary excesses that usually accompanied periods of mass hysteria, and some unfortunate babies were afflicted with names such as 'Ossewania' (ox-wagon-girl) and 'Eeufesia' (centenary-festival-girl). Levity and frivolity were sternly discouraged; no liquor was to be drunk in public, and earnest ministers of the Dutch Reformed Church rebuked women who were so far gone in disrespect as to smoke while wearing Voortrekker costume. The wagon routes were designed to pass through the poorer areas of the cities; the object, which was successfully achieved, was to stimulate Afrikaner unity across any emerging class divisions; it was part of the process by which the poor Whites should be reclaimed for the *Volk*.

Although the Government had sponsored the event and contributed large sums towards the cost of the monument, it allowed itself to be elbowed aside, so that this became a festival of the Opposition, looking towards the State that was to come. The national anthem was not to be played; therefore the Governor-General did not attend the laying of the foundation stones at Monument Kop, where over 200,000 Afrikaners had gathered. The Prime Minister was not invited to speak, and he spent the day on his farm. Smuts attended, but in a purely private capacity, as an Afrikaner. Meanwhile Dr Malan spoke at Blood River itself, choosing as his theme the trek of the Afrikaner to the city, where he faced the black man in a new battle for economic survival. The Revd Dr J. D. Kestell, a much-respected chaplain to the Boer forces in the war, had appealed for the rescue of the Voortrekkers' descendants now in need. The result of this appeal was the *Reddingdaadsbond* (Rescue Action Society), which was quietly absorbed into the

Broederbond network. The English were displeased when Oswald Pirow, the Minister of Defence, sanctioned without consultation the renaming of Roberts Heights, the army headquarters, as Voortrekkehoogte. Another consequence, of more substance, was the foundation of the 'Ossewa Brandwag' (Ox-wagon Sentinels).

This originated in Bloemfontein and, like many another South African organization which later underwent a metamorphosis, announced itself as a purely cultural association. The first chairman was the Revd C. R. Kotzé, but since it grew out of the memory of the Great Trek it was natural that it should be organized on the familiar basis of the commando; and it appointed as its first commandant-general a serving soldier, Colonel J. C. C. Laas. It professed an indifference to party politics; its aims, as Colonel Laas expounded them, could reasonably be described as comprehensive:

> the perpetuation of the spirit of the ox-wagon in South Africa; maintaining, amplifying and giving expression to the traditions and principles of the Dutch Afrikaner; protecting and promoting the religious–cultural and material interests of the Afrikaner; fostering patriotism and national pride, and harnessing and uniting all Afrikaners, men as well as women, who endorse these principles and are prepared to make energetic endeavours to promote them . . . The *modus operandi* is as follows: celebrating Afrikaans national festivals and our heroes' birthdays, erecting memorials, laying wreaths at monuments, locating and keeping in repair places of historical interest as well as the graves of Afrikaners who perished on the 'Road of South Africa'; organizing gatherings such as target-practice, popinjay and 'vulture' shooting, playing jukskei [a throwing game, thought to have been popular with Voortrekkers], doing folk-dances and singing folk-songs, holding regular gatherings of an educational and social nature, dramatic performances, lectures on our history, literature . . . debates, camps for men and women, etc.[19]

The Ossewa Brandwag quickly took on the aspect of a paramilitary organization; and in February 1939 the Minister of Defence dismissed Laas from the army and prohibited other army officers from joining an organization which offered so many aspirations that could produce conflicts of interest between it and any established government.

What was clear enough was that events since the general election in May 1938 had profoundly altered the climate of politics; and the

United Party no longer appeared to be as solidly grounded as its parliamentary majority indicated. To the tensions within South Africa there were added the still greater political conflicts that would certainly break out if Great Britain were involved in a European war. It was accepted, by all except the most devoted imperialists of the Dominion Party, that South Africa had no automatic obligation to follow Britain's example; it had been emphasized by ministers, over and over again when questions were asked during the last election, that what South Africa would do would depend on what Parliament decided if ever a choice had to be made. Whatever that decision was, it would almost certainly be disintegrating for the United Party. It was as well that the Cabinet's decision on what it would have recommended to Parliament if war had not been averted by the Munich Agreement of September 1938 did not become public knowledge. Hertzog and Smuts were agreed on a policy of semi-neutrality, a condition unknown to international law or practice. South Africa would not go to war, but it would permit Britain to use the naval base at Simonstown that had long been the headquarters of the South Atlantic command of the Royal Navy.

A year later Hertzog was of the same opinion; Smuts was not. It was by accident that Parliament happened to be meeting in special session at the beginning of September 1939 to prolong the life of the Senate, which was due to expire under the terms of the constitution. It is curious that this constitutional necessity should have been overlooked; but in any event Hitler's annexation of Danzig and invasion of Poland would have made it necessary for Parliament to have been summoned.

The Cabinet was divided, six for Hertzog and 'semi-neutrality', seven for Smuts and war with Germany. Thus on Monday, 4 September, the House of Assembly was faced with a motion from Hertzog with an amendment by Smuts. Both men argued their case on the basis of South African interests; but Hertzog damaged his case, and perhaps swung votes the other way, by a defence of Hitler; there was, he said, not the slightest evidence that he was doing more than seeking to escape from the 'monster of Versailles'. He suggested that he knew and sympathized with Hitler's feelings: 'I know from my own experience what it is to be humiliated and trodden in the dust.'[20]

The voting was 80 for and 67 against Smuts's amendment. The majority was made up of sixty-six members of the United Party, seven of the Dominion Party, four of Labour, and the three Native representatives. Thirty-eight members of the United Party voted in the minority. Hertzog asked the Governor-General for a dissolution of Parliament, which was refused on the grounds that the voting had shown that it was possible for the King of South Africa's Government to be carried on, and that a general election might be productive of public disorder. Hertzog resigned at once, and Smuts became Prime Minister for the second time. A deeply divided country went to war.

The repercussions in the country were profound and immediate. The result of the 'neutrality debate' was greeted with relief by almost all the South African English, partly on simple grounds of attachment to Britain – still the mother country to many of them – and partly because a decision the other way would have pointed towards secession from the British Empire and the coming of the republic, with its consequence of Nationalist domination. For precisely opposite reasons, the decision was deplored by Afrikaner Nationalists. The events of September 1939 reinforced each of these antagonists' views of each other. To the Nationalists, the English were what they had always been – 'imperialists'. This was a word that was never closely defined, but it signified all that republicans found hateful, including the memory of the Boer War and the pretensions of the conqueror and his ally Hoggenheimer, lord of the money-bags. To the English, the Republicans were rebels at heart, and probably Nazis as well. There was just enough truth in both stereotypes for each side to be certain that it was in the right. Neither the English nor the Republicans were likely to face social ostracism for their beliefs. It might be otherwise for Afrikaners who followed Smuts. B. K. Long, a United Party MP who had been editor of the *Cape Times*, wrote in 1945 of what he called the 'ferocity' of Afrikaner politics.

> To this day, Smuts's people in a *dorp* [village] where the majority is Nationalist are liable to be treated, for year after year, without remorse or any remission, as outcasts. They live in an atmosphere of ostracism. Boycott, in church and business affairs, never ceases to harass and pursue them. The Boer nature is tough. The followers of Smuts in these Afrikaans-speaking districts have borne this burden of enmity from their own people for years without bating an iota of their political faith. They still bear it. They do far more than bear it; they glory in it. A strange people, almost incomprehensible to their English-speaking compatriots. In personal contact the Boer will be friendly and extremely hospitable to us English-speak-

ing people; but if we get in the way of his political objects, he will hate us with a deadly hatred, unforgiving and unforgetting.[21]

The outbreak of war offered yet another chance in the perennial effort to bring together in what the Broederbond described as 'a healthy and progressive unanimity' the Afrikaner people, or at least that considerable portion of it that agreed with Hertzog's stance on neutrality. There was, welling up from below, a surge of desire for *hereniging*, reunion, perhaps an attempt to recapture the sentiments that had accompanied the celebration of the Great Trek. Hertzog, then ignored by the faithful, had now apparently seen the error of his ways; the lost leader, who had been seduced from his republicanism by the siren songs of Lord Balfour, doyen of imperialists, had chosen the path of neutrality that would lead, in the end, to secession and the republic; now, it was only a matter of time. Thus on 8 September, four days after the critical vote in the House of Assembly, there was another vast gathering at Monument Kop. There, to the accompaniment of prayers of thanksgiving, amid the panoply of the flags of the old republics, Hertzog and Malan clasped hands in comradeship. On that day, it seemed, the reunion of Afrikanerdom was achieved; and if there were a number of Afrikaners who still followed General Smuts – and their numbers were depressingly large – they could be disregarded in the euphoria of the moment; they, like their leader, stood athwart the path of the Nationalist Afrikaners' destiny, and the forces of history would in due season sweep them aside.

However, those with trained ears might have noted some discordances in the harmony. If there was one characteristic that distinguished the Nationalist, at least when he was not constrained by the limitations of office, it was a tenderness for principle. It was this that made him deficient in the skills of compromise. The speeches of Hertzog and Malan started from different premises. Hertzog talked of moderation, of a broad appeal to all men of good will. This meant that he was not prepared to abandon the English; they, too, if they were prepared to put South Africa first, should have their place in the sun; that, after all, was what he had been preaching for the past twenty-five years. There was now no need for him to muffle his own preference for a republic, but it should not be reserved for Afrikaners only. Malan indicated that the coming of the republic would mean the immediate severance of all ties with Great Britain; to those who understood the code, this meant Kruger's republic with the Uitlanders in their place. Malan was prudently unwilling to describe exactly what that place should be. Dr Verwoerd's idea of the future republic might be discerned through the spume of a cataract of negations.

> It will be a republic in which there will be no place for British public institutions. These things, which are foreign to the spirit of the Afrikaner people, will be annihilated to the very foundations. It will be a republic with a government that is not subject to all sorts of foreign influences. General Smuts's holistic views, according to which the small Afrikaans culture must be dissolved in the great English culture, and South Africa be but a part of the great British Empire, will find no place in this Afrikaans republic. Mr Hofmeyr's negrophilism and liberalism, which would wipe out all colour bars and would make the Afrikaner a backboneless being, will have no place in this Afrikaans republic. Colonel Stallard's imperialism, which would make South Africa subordinate in all respects to British interests, will have no place in this Afrikaans republic . . . The spirit of people who are too afraid to speak about a republic, will also find no entry in this republic. In economic policy, this republic will be no milch-cow of Britain. It will be a republic in which the Chamber of Mines will not have authority. It will be a republic built up on ideals and views of such men as Piet Retief, Paul Kruger, and Marthinus Steyn.[22]

But the complexity of issues could not be resolved, or oversimplified, into a straight argument between the ideas of Hertzog and those of Malan. Whatever might be said of them by their enemies – and the English press was in no humour to see the best of either of them – it could not be denied that they were both constitutional politicians who agreed that the road to the republic ran through Parliament. Where they disagreed was precisely how the republic was to be achieved: would a bare majority be enough, as Malan argued, or should it be based on something more substantial – the broad basis of the people's will, in Hertzog's terminology? But there were other parties to the argument. There was the Ossewa Brandwag, which was looking more and more like a para-military force and, to anxious eyes, one that ominously resembled the *Sturmabteilung* of the Nazi Party, especially when it equipped itself with a militant youth organization called the Stormjaers. They, clearly, had no enthusiasm for parliamentary methods. At the final cabinet meeting of Hertzog's Government, General Kemp, the

Minister of Agriculture, had said that there would be a blood-bath in South Africa unless neutrality were maintained; he spoke with some experience, since he had gone into rebellion himself in 1914.

There was to be no repetition of the rebellion of 1914. Smuts acted with firmness from the first days of his premiership. Parliament was prorogued in September and did not meet again until the following January; in the meantime, Smuts took emergency powers by proclamation, for which he was subsequently indemnified under the War Measures Act of 1940. Any doubts about the loyalty of the security forces were quickly put to rest; Smuts did not hesitate to purge both the professional army and the police forces. He took the portfolios of defence and foreign affairs and began the recruitment of a voluntary army; a new form of attestation, for service 'anywhere in Africa', was signalized by the wearing of orange-red shoulder flashes. Those officers of the professional army who refused to make this commitment were required to resign their commissions. Rifles in private hands were called in; and Smuts used his powers of internment without trial for those whom his intelligence or security forces thought to be dangerous. One of those interned for his activities as an officer of the Ossewa Brandwag was Balthazar Johannes Vorster, a future prime minister, who had declared in 1942:

> We stand for Christian Nationalism which is an ally of National Socialism. You can call the anti-democratic system a dictatorship if you like. In Italy it is called Fascism, in Germany National Socialism, and in South Africa Christian Nationalism.[23]

The Ossewa Brandwag's leadership was strengthened when Colonel Laas was succeeded as commandant-general by Colonel J. F. van Rensburg, formerly Administrator of the Orange Free State. Whatever the aspirations of these organizations, and others like Oswald Pirow's New Order, their common limitation was that they depended for their success on a German military victory. As it was, the Ossewa Brandwag proved to be a greater embarrassment to Dr Malan than to General Smuts's Government, which was never in peril of overthrow from within.

For the sake of intelligibility it is necessary to simplify the intricate and multitudinous negotiations that took place among the various Afrikaner organizations – parties, splinter-parties, groups, groups-within-groups – after the deceptive meeting of unity on Monument Kop in September 1939. Afrikanerdom seemed to be divided more deeply, and more confusingly, than ever before. Unity was, as ever, the aim; but there were those who thought that one of its preconditions was the destruction of rivals who stood in its way – hence the viciousness of some of the in-fighting. What was known to the public came through the press; and much of what was published was mistaken, or incomplete, or written in Aesopian language. The documents amassed by Defence Intelligence during the war were impounded by order of the new Minister of Defence within days of Malan's electoral victory in 1948.

The negotiations between Malan and Hertzog and their respective lieutenants turned in the last resort on the old question of the place of the English in the future of South Africa. Hertzog maintained the position that he had occupied for most of his political life: the English were not to be demoted to second-class citizenship. This meant legal equality of language and civil rights. But not all members of his own former Cabinet agreed with him. The most notable of the dissenters was Oswald Pirow, formerly Minister of Defence. He had, before the war, sent his daughter abroad to a camp for German maidens, and he was now making no secret of his National Socialist sympathies. Eventually he was to enlist fifteen of Hertzog's erstwhile parliamentary followers into his New Order.

The 'English question' underlay even the arguments about what would constitute a sufficient republican majority. N. C. Havenga, Hertzog's most faithful follower, held to the view that a bare parliamentary majority was not enough; the republic must wait until it had broader support, which meant when a sufficient number of the English had become converted to its merits; and that would not come until they were convinced that their own constitutional rights were safe. 'The only majority necessary to proclaim a republic is the majority that can maintain it'; it could not be forced upon an unwilling minority. The Malanites took a different view; some thought that a bare majority was enough and that the republic should come first and the education of the English second, after they had recognized that they must accommodate themselves to an Afrikaner State in which they would have to learn the Afrikaner's language and assimilate themselves to his way of life. This was leaning towards 'Krugerism' and an advance to a mythical past. The republic would be made by Afrikaners, for Afrikaners. To Hertzog, the republic must come through common effort and mutual tolerance. To Malan, it would represent the triumph of Afrikanerdom; to Hertzog it would mean the disappearance of sectional loyalties; the English would have to make sacrifices, but so would the Afrikaner. Hertzog's republic would look very like the existing State, with a president in place of a governor-general. The enemy was 'imperialism'; Malan would have agreed, with the proviso that the imperialists began in the northern suburbs of Johannesburg and Durban.

However, by January 1940 the parliamentary caucuses of the Hertzogites and Malanites had agreed on a formula which could be put to provincial congresses for ratification. There would be a single party under Hertzog's leadership, named 'Die Herenigde Nasionale of Volksparty' (the Reunited National or People's Party); its aim would be 'a free and independent republic, separated from the British Crown and Empire' – a victory for Malan – and the method of achieving that aim would be upon the 'broad foundation of the people's will' – a victory for Hertzog.

It soon became evident that Hertzog's leadership was to be nominal only. He had made many enemies in his long political life, and the most implacable of them all were in the Broederbond, the organization which had never forgiven him for his denunication of it in his Smithfield speech of 1935. He was to discover how dangerous it was for an Afrikaner politician to have enemies on the right. The tempo of politics quickened after the German victories of May and June 1940. Persuasive voices were to be heard arguing that if a German victory over Great Britain was imminent (which seemed likely enough) it would be prudent for South Africa to declare her neutrality while there was still time to dissociate herself from Germany's enemies. Some of Dr Malan's speeches indicated that he had changed his mind on the coming of the republic, and was not averse to considering a quicker way than waiting for the broad basis of the people's will to manifest itself – even, perhaps, a *coup d'état*. Among the obstacles was General Hertzog.

The first challenge to Hertzog came from the Orange Free State, once his impregnable base, where a republican rally was held in spite of his specific instructions. It was a sign of changed times and extravagant emotions that not only did the rally go ahead but also its organizers used the occasion to advocate policies that Hertzog was known to regard as abhorrent; they would have not only the republic, but Christian–National single-medium schools within it, which meant that no Afrikaner child would need to learn English. Bitter tongues were at work, and Hertzog was accused of furthering 'British-Jewish-capitalist influence' in promoting fusion in 1934. What was said about Hertzog is less surprising than the fact that some of the slanders against his reputation should have been believed. The most outrageous of these was contained in what came

PLATE 13. *C. R. Swart* (Courtesy of Popperfoto).

to be known as the affair of the Freemason's letters. These were supposed to have been discovered in a chest belonging to an unnamed
Freemason and to prove that Hertzog and Havenga were in league with
Smuts to turn South Arica into a republic within the British Empire,
incorporating the two Rhodesias and other adjacent British territories.
(The story bore a remarkable resemblance to the 'Black Manifesto' put
out under the signatures of Hertzog, Malan, and Tielman Roos before
the general election of 1929, accusing Smuts as 'the apostle of a black
Kaffir state . . . extending from the Cape to Egypt'.)

   What lay behind the rumours and intrigues was a direct challenge to
Hertzog's leadership. Matters came to a head at the meeting of the
provincial congress of the Party in Bloemfontein in November 1940.
Beneath the details of procedure the principle at issue was whether

Hertzog's or Malan's view of the future republic should prevail, and the vote went in Malan's favour. Hertzog at once resigned both his leadership and his membership of the party in the Orange Free State, and for the second time in his life walked out of a party conference, uttering this time the bitter words: 'Havenga will follow me; Pirow, too, must go; and Malan will follow later'. He was succeeded as leader in the Free State by C. R. Swart, his local antagonist, who had greeted Hertzog's departure with the words 'we dare not separate over personalities or the rights of the English'.[24]

In December 1940 Hertzog resigned from the Smithfield seat in Parliament which he had held for the past thirty years. For him, the struggle was over. He died, sad and discouraged, on 21 November 1942. By then he had ceased to count; his death, as Talleyrand said of Napoleon's, was not an event but merely an item of news. His followers formed the Afrikaner Party; it was small and ineffective. By the beginning of 1942 two-thirds of Hertzog's last prophecy had been fulfilled: Havenga had followed him at once, and now Pirow took himself and his New Order group out of the caucus of the party. *Hereniging*, reunion, was dead; but then Malan and those behind him in the shadows had always been determined that re-union should be achieved only on their own terms. Malan turned next against the Ossewa Brandwag, whose increasing rejection of parliamentary means ran counter to Malan's own beliefs and to his strategy for an eventual Nationalist electoral victory. The battle was long, bitter and, to those unskilled in interpreting the nuances of statement and counter-statement, only partly intelligible. The rights of the English were no longer an issue; what now mattered was who was to represent the aspirations of Afrikanerdom.

That question was answered at the general election of July 1943. General Smuts fought it on the issue of South Africa's continuation in the war. After the Allied victories at El Alamein and Stalingrad that issue was not in doubt, and Smuts's coalition increased its membership in the House of Assembly to 110 out of 153. The other 43 seats all went to Malan's Nationalists. The comprehensiveness of Smuts's victory could not be denied; but under the surface there were encouraging signs for Nationalists with patience and foresight. One estimate was that the percentage of the Afrikaans-speaking population voting for Smuts's Government had fallen from about 40 per cent to about 32 per cent.

No doubt Malan's first reaction was a feeling of disappointment as he looked at the overwhelming numbers against him, but a cooler analysis must have given him very solid grounds for hope . . . The question posed so often during the last two years had been answered without a shadow of ambiguity. The rebels against Malan's leadership had been simply annihilated: not a single seat survived from the wreck . . . The Hertzogites, the Pirowites, the Ossewa Brandwag had all challenged the claim of himself and the Herenigde Nasionale Party to be the sole representatives of Nationalist Afrikanerdom. The challenge had been met and from the electoral battle the H.N.P. had emerged victor. It had made good its boasted monopoly. It stood now, the sole effective organ of Afrikanerdom, compact, purified, and beyond the reach of revenge. The process begun when Hertzog was extruded in 1940 had reached its end. The Opposition was *gleichgeschaltet* at last.[25]

9 THE TRIUMPH OF REPUBLICANISM

South Africa fought on the side of Great Britain in two world wars; this could be accounted as part of the reward reaped through the 'policy of magnanimity' adopted by Campbell-Bannerman's Government in granting self-government to the former Boer republics in 1907.

With South Africa divided on the issue of the war, conscription was out of the question. In all, 186, 218 White men and 24, 975 White women enlisted, and in addition there were 123, 131 non-Whites who, in principle, were employed as non-combatants.[1] South Africa was one of the locations of the Empire training scheme for air crews of the Royal Air Force. South African forces served with distinction in the East African campaign against the Italians in Eritrea and Abyssinia, and then took part first in the campaigns in the Western Desert, and then in Italy. This time, the analogue of Delville Wood was the battle of Sidi Resegh in the Western Desert. The greatest disaster came in June 1942 when Major-General Klopper, commanding the South African 2nd Division, surrendered the fortress of Tobruk; there were those who thought that resistance had not been prolonged to the utmost of the garrison's capacity.

South African industry was adapted to the construction of weaponry. Once the entry of Italy into the war in 1940 had closed the Mediterranean the South African ports found themselves working to capacity and beyond as British convoys made the long journey around Africa to the Middle East.

Smuts himself travelled constantly and established himself as second only to Churchill as an imperial statesman. This redounded not at all to his credit with the Nationalist Opposition; the bitterness of party strife continued unabated.

Smuts played some part in the drafting of the charter of the United Nations; ironically enough, it was at his initiative that the words 'fundamental human rights' were introduced. At the first meeting of the General Assembly, South Africa came under attack for the denial of those rights to her Indian inhabitants. It was the first of many attacks. It had been the custom, at imperial conferences, not to criticize the domestic policies of the Dominions; no such protection was forthcoming at meetings of the United Nations. It took white South Africans some time to realize how rapidly, and in what directions, international opinion had moved during the war. Anti-colonialism was one of the moods of the moment; and at the end of the war South Africans found themselves demoted from the status of 'gallant allies' to that of oppressors of the non-white peoples, with a hostile international opinion being mobilized against them. Many found this to be bewildering; it was not they, but the world, which had changed.

To new attitudes abroad were added new troubles at home. The development of the South African war economy had brought problems that were world-wide – manpower difficulties (that were compounded by the industrial colour bar), shortages of consumer goods, inflation and the consequent stirrings of industrial unrest. There was a serious strike of Native mineworkers on the Rand in 1946; and although this was concerned with low wages, the line between economics and politics in South Africa was sometimes non-existent. There was, growing up among the elite of the non-white peoples, a disposition towards political organization and attempts to form a united front. What all this meant was that the 'racial question' in South Africa had acquired a new dimension. The non-Whites were ceasing to be passive. The 'Native question' had become more urgent, and it was clear that the Native himself was demanding to be heard; so, too, was the Indian and the Cape Coloured. The African National Congress was divided between those who were content to petition and those who preferred direct action – strikes, boycotts, passive resistance.

One consequence of the war was a general hardening of attitudes, throughout South Africa, on the place of non-Whites within a framework of society that suddenly seemed to have lost the solidity of its base. One perennial theme in South African politics had been the attempts to unify the Afrikaner; another had been attempts at reconciliation between English and Afrikaner, usually at the expense of the non-Whites. The Peace of Vereeniging had excluded non-Whites from the franchise in the former republics. The compact of union in 1909 had been achieved at the price of a colour bar in Parliament; the pact between Hertzog's Nationalists and the Labour Party had extended the colour bar into industry. The price of fusion had been the removal of the Natives in the Cape from the common voters' roll.

Now the price of Smuts's coalition was the restriction of Indians' rights to buy land, to appease the English voters of Natal. It was this measure which had touched off the attacks at the United Nations.

The census of 1946 showed that the urban Native population had risen by half a million since 1936 to nearly 1,700,000 and now was approaching parity with the Whites in the cities. The Afrikaner sociologists who had laid their emphasis on the importance of the cities as the focal point of the politics of survival found themselves suddenly required to transfer their attentions from the misfortunes of the poor Whites (which no longer seemed to be acute) to the ways by which the urban Native could be constrained within a structure of society that he was no longer prepared to accept without argument. In South Africa, as elsewhere, the war had been a mighty accelerator of social change. A single generation was confronted with a problem that had been accumulating, in complexity and scale, for generations.

It was logical that the Nationalists should have concentrated their attack upon the 'Native policy' of the Smuts coalition, which was indeed its point of greatest weakness. In particular, they fixed upon J. H. Hofmeyr as the proponent of 'liberalism' and attributed to him every variety of malevolent purpose in undermining the status of the white man. Hofmeyr's own position was a more sophisticated version of the old 'Cape liberalism', but the efficacy of the Nationalists' attacks on him was a sign of how far that spirit was in retreat. Smuts himself had little to offer except high generalizations: the caravan of humanity was once more on the move, but time would take care of all things. He had never opposed racial segregation. Moreover, in domestic politics, he was never one to move faster than his followers, and he had learnt from experience that accusations of negrophilism, however preposterous, could always sway a white electorate. He did introduce an assisted immigration policy, which brought 60,000 new settlers to South Africa, mostly from Great Britain, as an attempt to do something about the shortage of skilled labour without breaching the colour bar. In 1947 King George VI and Queen Elizabeth, accompanied by their daughters, visited South Africa at Smuts's invitation. They were received with enthusiasm; but their visit did nothing to change either social or political attitudes. *Die Transvaler* referred to them, if at all, as 'distinguished foreign visitors'; Dr Malan and his parliamentary followers declined invitations to all official occasions (although a private and 'accidental' meeting between him and the King was contrived).

Smuts had little to offer the non-Whites except the vague hope that somehow things would get better. He did realize, almost with surprise, that Native aspirations went further than improvements in their material condition. On 6 February 1947, he wrote:

> The fact is that both Native and Indian leaders want *status* . . . in social and economic advances we have a strong case, but the Natives want *rights* and not improvements. There we bump up against the claim for equality which is most difficult to satisfy except in very small doses[2]

Even the docile and conservative Native Representative Council was now talking of rights. In 1946 it had passed a resolution deprecating the Government's 'post-war continuation of a policy of Fascism which is the antithesis and negation of the letter and the spirit of the Atlantic Charter and the United Nations Charter', and had called upon Smuts 'forthwith to abolish all discriminatory legislation affecting non-Europeans in this country'. That was to make demands that no South African government, with the existing electorate, could meet and still hope to remain in power. In short, the 'Native problem' was insoluble within the existing structure of politics. Smuts had no answer. Dr Malan believed that he had. The Nationalists began to talk about something which they called *apartheid* – 'apartness'.

It was this word that was new in the general election campaign of 1948. Otherwise, there was much that was familiar in the usual clamour of denunciations and counter-denunciations. The Nationalists were able to exploit all the accumulated grievances and disenchantments of the war years and their aftermath. They spoke of rising prices and appealed to ex-servicemen discontented with their peace-time status. The old cries were repeated about South Africa's being dragged into Britain's wars, and to this was added a new complaint – association with 'godless Communism' at the United Nations. 'A vote for Smuts', in the words of one mysterious assertion, 'is a vote for Stalin.' A new enemy had emerged – the 'liberalist', the ally or dupe of the communist, and identified with J. H. Hofmeyr, Smuts's deputy prime minister. There were the customary

PLATE 14. *H. F. Verwoerd* (Courtesy of the South African High Commission).

reminders of the persecution of the Afrikaner in the past and appeals to the call of the blood. But what distinguished this election was that the electorate was being offered a distinctive choice on the 'Native question' instead of blurred variations of the 'traditional policy' of segregation. The United Party based its colour policy on a recognition of the economic interdependence of the races, coupled with social and political segregation, and offered a hope that economic development might provide an answer without tears. The Nationalists offered resolute action. *Apartheid* was a new addition to the political vocabulary, but the ideas behind it had been germinating in the minds of Afrikaner intellectuals, in the universities, in the churches, and in the confabulations of the Broederbond, for many years.

Those ideas had many sources. Central to the concept was the assertion that the unit of creation was not the individual but the group, of which the nation was the highest expression. Something of this could be extrapolated from the writings of Abraham Kuyper in the Netherlands, which were familiar to some theologians of the Dutch Reformed Churches in South Africa. More pertinently, there were echoes of the doctrines of Herder and Fichte, brought back by Afrikaners who had studied in Germany in the 1920s and 1930s – men such as Nico Diederichs, Hendrik Verwoerd and Piet Meyer, all of whom were men of weight in the Broederbond. These ideas were assimilated into older traditions and the more familiar ambitions of Afrikanerdom.

What was especially seductive about the theory of *apartheid* was its appeal to tender consciences. It could be put forward as a moral solution to the racial problem. It could not be denied that segregation was difficult to justify to world opinion by references to the Book of Genesis and the curse of Noah. Times had changed since Kruger had resorted to the Old Testament to dismiss a petition from the Transvaal Indians: 'You are the descendants of Ishmael and therefore from your very birth bound to slave for the descendants of Esau. As the descendants of Esau we cannot admit you to rights placing you on an equality with ourselves. You must rest content with what rights we give you.'[3] This would no longer suffice as a justification for perpetual inequality. *Apartheid* offered equality, but of a particular kind. Whereas segregation meant a horizontal division between superior and inferior races, *apartheid* would mean a vertical division between equal ethnic groups.

This might sound meaningless unless it were considered in relation to the whole landscape of Afrikaner nationalist aspirations. Thus J. C. van Rooy, Chairman of the Broederbond in 1944, could postulate that the Afrikaner was the bearer of that divine purpose which God had set out for each national group: 'So God created the Afrikaner *Volk* with a unique language, a unique philosophy of life, and their own history and tradition in order that they might fulfil a particular destiny and calling here in the southern corner of Africa.'[4] But God would not deny to others what he had granted to the Afrikaners, not as individuals but as members of divinely ordained groups. This was a switch from the idea of the equal value of all individuals to the equal value of all races. In 1947 the Dutch Reformed Church issued a statement of belief and intention:

Dutch Reformed Church policy amounts to the recognition of the existence of all races and nations as separate units foreordained by God. This is not the work of human beings. Accordingly the Dutch Reformed Church considers it imperative that these creations be recognized for the sake of the natural development through which they could fulfil themselves in their own language, culture, and community. Although God created all nations out of one blood, He gave each nation a feeling of nationhood and a national soul.[5]

It was not difficult to criticize these and other statements as hypocrisy, an expression of the divine right of the Afrikaner to domination. It appeared to the cynical that there was a suspicious correlation between the ideas attributed to God and the ideas of the Broederbond. Thus Dr E. G. Greyling could say (this was in 1944) that 'God has willed it that there shall be separate nations each with its own language, and that mother-tongue education is accordingly the will of God. The parent should . . . have no choice in this case';[6] for this dictum was one of the prime objectives of the revived movement for Christian national education, which seemed to have as its main purpose the isolation of the Afrikaner child from English influences and to counteract the debilitating effects of foreign culture. Thus Broeder van Zyl warned against study abroad, especially in Britain, and regarded the Rhodes scholarships as a means of denationalizing the Afrikaner and possibly marrying him off to an English woman. Piet Meyer, later to become the directing mind of the South African Broadcasting Corporation, claimed to have discovered that 'godlessness is more prevalent among bilingual people than those who are unilingual'.[7]

What seemed undeniable was that *apartheid*, if it were to be put into practice, would require the use of State power on a scale never before attempted in South Africa. It would involve not only huge movements of population, but it would also entail a radical transformation of men's minds and aspirations, affecting both Whites and non-Whites. Afrikaner ideologues seemed to assume that other racial groups had ethnic and nationalist aspirations similar to their own; and those who dissented should be told that they were mistaken about the 'general will' of their own national group and that they themselves, in Jean-Jacques Rousseau's phrase, might be 'forced to be free'. Furthermore, *apartheid* would eliminate certain evils regarded by Afrikaner Nationalists as especially abhorrent. G. Cronjé, a Pretoria sociologist, held that a 'just separation' of the races would eliminate miscegenation, liberal ideas of individual equality and Marxist ideas of class conflict.[8]

The choice was presented to the electorate in 1948 as a simple alternative – integration of the races, or *apartheid*, the 'just separation'. There was, it was asserted, no middle way: this was the argument of the irreconcilable alternative, the logic of the ultimate consequence. In the words of one election manifesto:

> We can act in only one of two directions. Either we must follow the course of equality, which must eventually mean national suicide for the white race, or we must take the course of apartheid through which the character and the future of every race will be protected . . . the [National Party] therefore undertakes to protect the white race properly and effectively against any policy, doctrine or attack which might undermine or threaten its continued existence. At the same time, the Party rejects any policy of oppression and exploitation of the non-Europeans by the Europeans as being in conflict with the Christian basis of our national life, and irreconcilable with our policy.[9]

Elaborated in more detail, *apartheid* promised barriers not only between Whites and non-Whites, but between the different non-White peoples. The Cape Coloureds would be isolated from Whites, on the one hand, and from Natives on the other. The Indians, the familiar scapegoats, were described as a 'foreign element' which could not be assimilated. It would be best if they went back to India; if they remained, they could not expect to be treated other than as an unwanted immigrant group. As for the Natives, they would be encouraged to develop 'along their own lines' in their own areas; but while they were in the 'White man's territory' (the whole of South Africa, except for 13 per cent allocated as Native reserves) they would be treated as migrants. 'The process of detribalization should be arrested.'

Amid the clang and clamour of the election, it might seem that the manifesto offered no more than a deodorized version of the old Nationalist election slogan, dear to audiences in the *backveld*, of '*die kaffir op sy plek en die koelie uit die land*' (keep the black man in his place, and send the Indian back to where he came from'). As an electoral cry, *apartheid* offered firm but indefinite action to answer 'the Native question', as contrasted with the *laisser allez* attitude (since it could hardly be called a policy) of the United Party. *Apartheid* was vague enough to be hard to attack in detail and those who questioned its premiss could be denounced as 'liberalists', '*kaffir-boeties*' (nigger-lovers) or advocates of race suicide (J. H. Hofmeyr could conveniently be portrayed as all three). It is impossible to say just how much it had to do with the Nationalists' victory, or how many of those who voted for Malan understood just what kind of mandate he was claiming; *apartheid* was one of many election appeals. On the other side, the United Party and its allies offered the towering figure of Smuts, their war record and the concepts of the 1930s in which they denied that they advocated racial equality, and talked of trusteeship and the development of the non-Whites under white guidance. In short, the United Party scarcely recognized the changing tides of world opinion. The National Party did – and promised to swim against them.

Malan fought the election in alliance with the ghost of Hertzog, as represented by the Afrikaner Party, under the leadership of N. C. Havenga. The existence of this alliance was a guarantee that the constitutional rights of the English were safe enough: the exclusiveness of Afrikanerdom was kept well in the background during the election.

Smuts had been urged by his own supporters to correct the anomalies of the electoral system by which rural consntituencies enjoyed a favourable weighting which might be as high as 30 per cent against the urban areas. He refused to listen. The result was that although the United Party and its allies had the votes of over 53 per cent of those who voted, compared with 40 per cent for the Nationalists and their auxiliary, they found themselves in a minority of five in the House of Assembly – 74 seats against 79. General Smuts himself was defeated in his old seat at Standerton; he returned at a bye-election after one of his supporters had made way for him. It was a humiliation as staggering as it was unexpected. 'To think', he exclaimed, 'that I have been beaten by the Broederbond!' He complained to a friend, 'My old comrades have turned against me', and received the reply, 'how could they turn against you? They are all dead'. Sir Keith Hancock, Smuts's biographer, commented: 'If that reply was comfort of a kind, it was also a devastating truth. It meant that Smuts and his ideas and his loyalties had lost their appeal to Afrikaner youth. It meant the end of an epoch; of his epoch.'[10] In May 1948 Dr Malan formed the only purely Afrikaner government since Union.

In retrospect, it is clear that the general election of 1948 initiated a constitutional revolution in South Africa – a change in the political leadership, a change in the administrative elite, and a change in the philosophy and purpose of government. The immediate effects were not felt by the non-Whites – that would come later – but for the moment they might feel that they had enjoyed little and been promised less. For the South African English, the shock was stunning and immediate, the more so for being wholly unexpected. It might be said that they had suffered a just retribution for their neglect of politics. Since Union, the English had not produced a political figure of the first rank. Theirs had been the world of commerce and industry, and especially of gold mining and the professions. For years the Nationalists had taunted them with the reproach that they could not be wholly South African until they had shed their sentimental ties to the monarchy, had taken more pains to learn Afrikaans, to cease from mocking the Afrikaner as a being both crude and uncouth, and to desist from referring to England as 'home'. There was some truth in these charges; but many of the English knew little more of the country of their ancestors than the urbanized Africans of the Witwatersrand did of the history and traditions of the tribes from which they came. What could not be denied was the political complacency of the English; they had got into the habit of depending on General Smuts. Now, for the first time, they experienced a total exclusion from power at the national level.

The Nationalists were understandably exultant in victory. As they saw it, their country was now their own at last. The mills of God were grinding small at last: the republic was in sight, and the verdict of the Boer War could be set aside. The commanding heights of politics had been captured; now was the time to make them secure, to reward friends and allies and to settle some old scores with renegades and backsliders. There was something like a purge in the senior ranks of the civil service, the army and the police. Some 'nationally minded' professional soldiers who had resigned their commissions in 1939 were reinstated, sometimes with back-dated promotion. Bilingualism was taken seriously in public employment, to the detriment of those whose command of Afrikaans was considered to be inferior. Some municipalities changed their street names – there was a tendency for 'Alamein Avenues' to disappear – and switched their banking accounts to Volkskas. Government contracts went to good Nationalist firms, where possible. The Broederbond could pride itself that its labours had at last been justly rewarded.

Wherever possible without material damage, purely sentimental links with the British Empire were weakened. Smuts's immigration scheme was suspended, and when it was started again the emphasis was switched from the Commonwealth to the European continent. The South African Citizenship Act of 1949 made it harder to become naturalized. There was a division of opinion within the

Cabinet on the future status of South Africa. In 1949 a precedent had been set when the Republic of India chose to remain within the Commonwealth. Malan, who had been present, was content with the conference's decision that former colonies which became republics might remain within the Commonwealth, provided that existing members agreed. The implication that a South African republic might keep its Commonwealth membership was not to the liking of the hard-liners, especially from the Transvaal, who now looked to Johannes Strijdom to uphold the secessionist tradition that Malan seemed to have abandoned. As it was, the Government was in no hurry. In spite of its majority in Parliament it was well aware that it was still in a minority among white voters. Moreover, it was dependent for its majority on Havenga and his eight followers, all of them Hertzogites and faithful to their dead leader's insistence that the republic could come only when it had a broad base of public support.

In 1951 the Government began a long-running battle with the Supreme Court over the interpretation of the South African constitution, now embodied in the Status of the Union Act of 1934 and thus, in Hertzog's phrase, 'autochthonous'. This turned on the validity of one of the entrenched clauses, safeguarding the voting rights of the Cape Coloured people. The point at issue was whether the Statute of Westminister, 1931, had freed the South African Parliament from the necessity of a two-thirds' majority in a joint session of the House of Assembly and the Senate. It is possible that the Government might have avoided this conflict if their law officers had not given them advice which turned out to be an incorrect prediction of what the courts would decide. They had relied on remarks from the bench in the case of *Ndlwana* v. *Hofmeyr* (1937) in which the Act removing the Natives from the common voters' roll had been challenged in the courts. That Act had been passed in a joint session with the requisite majority, and the challenge was unsuccessful. However, the Chief Justice took the view that, since the passage of the Statute of Westminster, the South African Parliament could 'adopt any procedure it thinks fit; the procedure expressed or implied in the South Africa Act is so far as Courts of Law are concerned at the mercy of Parliament like everything else.'[11]

The Government had nothing like a two-thirds' majority in either House, and no likely chance of obtaining one; but on the strength of the law officers' advice it passed the Separate Representation of Voters Act, 1951, by simple majorities in each House, sitting separately. In

March 1952, in a unanimous decision, the five judges of the Appellate Division of the Supreme Court declared the Act to be unconstitutional on the grounds that the provisions of the entrenched clauses had not been affected by the Statute of Westminster. Counsel for the Government contended unsuccessfully that no country which had emerged from Colony to Dominion within the framework of the British constitution could be a sovereign state unless it possessed a sovereign parliament functioning in the same manner as the Parliament of the United Kingdom. The Court did not agree.

The struggle over the Coloured vote dragged on for five years. It could be considered as much a matter of political theory as of constitutional law. The Nationalists were contending both that Parliament was sovereign, and that it had a mandate from the electorate which it must regard as binding: it was unimpressed by opponents who contended that this argument was a logical contradiction. The long debate involved the nature of parliaments, the place of the courts in the process of government and, in the background, the status of English as an official language: that, too, was entrenched, but if one entrenched clause could be abolished in a manner which went outside the compact of Union, why not another? The Government's immediate reaction to the Supreme Court's judgment was to pass an ill-digested Act setting up a 'high court of Parliament' to be the final appellate body in all constitutional cases. The Supreme Court declared this Act invalid on the grounds that the 'high court of Parliament' could not be considered a court of law in any meaningful sense. There, for the moment, the matter rested.

The constitutional crisis was the occasion for the emergence of a number of extra-parliamentary pressure groups; of these, the Torch Commando was the most flamboyant, the Women's Defence of the Constitution League (later called 'the Black Sash') the most original. The Torch Commando took its name from its first dramatic march by torchlight to Parliament. Its aim was the 'preservation of the constitution'; its titular leader was Group-Captain 'Sailor' Malan, an Afrikaner hero of the Battle of Britain. The Torch Commando recaptured something of the camaraderie of the war and canalized resentment against the tone and content of Nationalist government. It was only indirectly concerned with the fate of the Coloured voters; it took its stand on the compact behind the Act of Union, and there were embarrassed internal debates about whether Coloured ex-servicement should be admitted to membership. The Torch held some impressive parades. From time to time there were brawls with Nationalist supporters, which gave the Afrikaans press the chance to argue that the atmosphere of the early 1940s was being recreated, with the Torch commando playing the role of the now-defunct Ossewa Brandwag. The Torch Commando generated a transitory enthusiasm but made few converts. As the general election of 1953 approached, it turned its energies to canvassing and became something like an extra-mural branch of the United Party.

The Black Sash appeared in the second phase of the conflict over the Coloured voters, which began in 1955. Its method was that of passive protest, an appeal to the conscience of the governors. Members of the Black Sash, mostly white women of the middle classes, some with impeccable Afrikaner credentials, took to the 'haunting' of cabinet ministers. Wearing black sashes and displaying the slogan *Eerbiedig Ons Grondwet* (honour and respect our constitution) they positioned themselves on public occasions in such a way that cabinet ministers had to pass through a double line of 'mourners'. Many ministers found these attentions to be extremely embarrassing; some showed energy and ingenuity in avoiding them. They had no effect on government policy.

There were other, and shorter-lived, organizations, such as the Covenant Movement and the Anti-Republican League. They, and others, were careful to deny that they had any connection with the United Party; this was a tactical decision, in the hope that it would not repel the 'moderate Nationalist'; it took a long time to learn that 'moderation' among Nationalists began a long way to the right of any of the protest movements.

Thus far, the progress of *apartheid* looked very little different from merely an extension and intensification of the 'traditional policy' of segregation. There was legislation to prevent mixed marriages and to criminalize sexual intercourse across colour lines. The latter produced some bizarre court cases. Because accused persons of different races were tried separately, it happened from time to time that one partner was acquitted and the other found guilty. Irreverent critics mocked at 'unilateral fornication'; there was, however, no joking about the reality of the gaol sentences or the ruin of the social reputations of those Whites who were convicted. Dr Edgar Brookes, once a senator representing Native interests, pointed to the contradiction in the ideas of legislators who simultaneously asserted: '(a) Right-thinking South Africans have an instinctive horror of miscegenation. (b) Very strict laws are necessary to prevent them from committing it.' A population register was compiled in which men and women were classified by race; there would be no more 'passing for White'. The Group Areas Act of 1950 empowered the Government, by administrative action, to enforce residential segregation in towns not merely between Whites and non-Whites, but between different categories of non-Whites. There was an insistence on what came to be called 'petty *apartheid* – enforced separation on bathing beaches and in the use of public transport, lavatories, lifts and the entrances to public places: there were, for instance, separate entrances to the Johannesburg Zoo, though once inside visitors of every racial group could mingle as much as they chose, provided that persons of different colours did not sit down together on benches labelled 'For Whites Only'.

The promised positive side of *apartheid* was slow to appear; the Government claimed that it was waiting for the reports of committees, on primary and secondary education, on the universities and on the development of the Native reserves, It was doubtful whether Dr Malan shared the millennial doctrines of some of his more radical social engineers, such as ex-Professor H. F. Verwoerd, who became Minister of Native Affairs in 1951, and Professor W. W. M. Eiselen, who became permanent secretary of that department and had already described *apartheid* as meaning the separation of 'heterogeneous groups . . . into separate socio-economic units, inhabiting different parts of the country, each enjoying in its own area full citizenship rights' – a statement that was as high-minded as it was unquantified. Dr Malan's head was never in the clouds. Territorial separation would, he said, be ideal, but it was not practicable in a country where the economy was so heavily dependent on Native labour. But *apartheid*, he insisted, was not a policy of oppression. 'On the contrary, like a wire fence between two neighbouring farms, it indicates a separation without eliminating necessarily legitimate contacts in both directions, and although it places reciprocal restrictions on both sides it . . . serves as an effective protection against violations of one another's rights.' It might be asked whether *apartheid* was anything more than a euphemism for the enforcement of white privilege. Malan came close to admitting this in a letter of remarkable candour to the Revd J. E. Piersman, an American divine:

> The deep-rooted colour consciousness of the white South African – a phenomenon quite beyond the comprehension of the uninformed – arises from the fundamental differences between the two groups, white and black. The difference in

colour is merely the physical manifestation of the contrast between two irreconcilable ways of life, between barbarism and civilization, between heathenism and Christianity, and finally between overwhelming numerical odds on the one hand and insignificant numbers on the other . . . Small wonder that the instinct of self-preservation is so inherent in the white South African. He has retained his identity all these years. He is not willing to surrender it now.[12]

J. H. Hofmeyr died in 1948, General Smuts in 1950. In Smuts's place, the United Party chose as its leader another Afrikaner, J. G. N. Strauss, under whom the party drifted to the right in its search for the 'moderate Nationalist'. The leadership was in haste to purge itself from the imputation of liberalism which, it began to believe, was the cause of its defeat in 1948. It approached the election of 1953 in an optimistic mood. It had convinced itself that the result of 1948 had been no more than an untoward event, something accidental that could be explained by a protest vote or abstention by many habitual supporters who, now that they had tasted Nationalist rule, would return to their habitual allegiance. Nothing, therefore, must be done to ruffle the feathers of these birds of passage.

Its attitude therefore was equivocal when the Government equipped itself with formidable new powers of executive discretion which evaded the rule of law. In 1950 the Suppression of Communism Act outlawed the Communist Party and enabled the Minister of Justice to declare kindred organizations unlawful, to 'name' office holders and supporters of such organizations and to restrict 'named' persons from taking part in any gatherings which in the Minister's opinion furthered the aims of Communism. 'Statutory Communism', as it came to be called, was defined in very wide terms – not only Marxist–Leninism but also 'any related form of that doctrine' which sought to bring about the dictatorship of the proletariate or 'any political, industrial, social or economic change within the Union by the promotion of disturbances or disorder'. Under this Act the Government moved against multi-racial trade unions, some of which had Communists as members. There was further legislation in 1951 and 1952 to deal with concerted non-White political activity. Demonstrations were planned to coincide with the celebrations on 6 April 1952 of the tercentenary of van Riebeeck's arrival at the Cape. This was the so-called defiance campaign, and it attempted to use the tactics of peaceful disobedience which Gandhi had devised forty years earlier. The tactics of peaceful disobedience depend for their success on two necessary conditions – a split mind in the governing body which is the object of protest, and that which the protesters are asking for is not regarded by the governing body as essential to its existence. Neither of these conditions was present. What the protesters were asking the Government to do was to reverse its colour policies. The organizers of the campaign had emphasized that it would be peaceful; but they could not control some of their followers. The worst of the violence was in East London where twenty-six non-Whites and six Whites were killed, including a nun who was murdered in brutal circumstances. This lost much of such white sympathy as the demonstrators had on their side.

Some of the demonstrators arrested for occupying premises reserved for Whites won a court action on the ground that separate premises and facilities must be equal in quality to those for Whites. This gap in the façade of petty *apartheid* was closed by the Reservation of Separate Amenities Act, which made equality unnecessary. The Government was demonstrating that it would circumvent the courts of law by legislating to prevent the repetition of legal decisions which invalidated government policy. The Public Safety Act enabled the Government to declare a state of emergency during which it might make regulations with the effect of law; and a Criminal Law Amendment Bill prescribed heavy sentences of imprisonment, fines and flogging for breaches of the peace. The United Party decided that it would be electorally damaging for it to oppose this legislation.

The United Party's optimism over the coming election was not blunted when the Government created six new seats in the House of Assembly for the mandated territory of South-West Africa, and then won all six of them: opinion in this former German colony was not thought to be representative of the country at large. There was no question this time of want of energy or shortage of money. The Opposition mobilized its total strength, and the result of the election was a bewildering blow. Disregarding the Speaker, the Nationalists increased their seats from 87 to 94; the United Party dropped from 64 to 57 and Labour from 6 to 4. The Afrikaner Party had been absorbed in 1951; thus for the first time since Union political power lay in a monolithic Afrikaner party, not in a coalition. The Opposition now had to face the bleak fact that it had become a permanent minority. It was clear that 1948 had marked a lasting shift of power. Given the demographic trend, there would be more Afrikaners than English of voting age with each succeeding year;

and given the political trend, most of them would vote Nationalist. The United Party's search for the 'moderate Afrikaner floating voter' had plainly come to nothing. Thus, if a change were to come, it would have to be because of a split in the National Party. This, it was quickly seen, was a forlorn hope. What splits there were came on the other side. The right wing of the United Party began to crumble and to drift towards the Nationalists.

Malan retired at the end of 1954; he was eighty. It was no secret that he tried to influence the succession against the hard men of the Transvaal. His own preferred candidate was N. C. Havenga. The party's choice was Johannes Strijdom, yet another 'Lion of the North', who had been known as both a republican and a secessionist. He embodied the spirit of *kragdadigheid* (tough and vigorous action) which appealed to those backwoodsmen of the party who preferred the traditional subjection of the black man to millennial

PLATE 15. *J. G. Strijdom arriving at No.10 Downing Street, 27 June 1956* (Courtesy of Hulton Deutsch Collection Limited).

theories about his 'development along his own lines in his own areas'. As it turned out, the party got both, for Strijdom's premiership meant an enhanced status for Verwoerd, who had been demonstrating a form of 'vertical segregation' on his own account by building up the Department of Native Affairs into a private empire which came to control nearly all matters concerned with the non-White peoples.

Strijdom's immediate preoccupation was to end the long-drawn controversy over the Coloured vote. He possessed none of Malan's scruples about the spirit of the constitution. Chief Justice Centlivres, giving judgment in *Harris's Case*, had dismissed the contention that a sovereign parliament, such as that of the United Kingdom, could adopt any procedure that took its fancy. 'It would indeed be surprising', he said, 'if a Government which is in a minority in the House of Commons could, by advising the Sovereign to convene a joint sitting of the House of Lords and the House of Commons, swamp the majority in the Commons by the vote of the Lords.'[13] Strijdom's mind was working in that 'surprising' direction. There was nothing in the constitution which entrenched the procedure by which the size of the Senate could be enlarged or diminished; that could be done by simple majorities in either House. Thus the Senate was increased in such a way that the Nationalists had all seats in every Province except Natal; thus, with a manufactured two-thirds majority, the Bill removing the Coloured voters in the Cape from the common roll was passed into law in a joint session of both Houses, amid considerable political bitterness. The Government had also taken the precaution of enlarging the Appellate Division of the Supreme Court from five to eleven and appointing six new judges who were believed to be safely 'nationally minded'. The legislation was validated by a majority of ten to one in the Appellate Division, the lone dissenter being Mr Justice O. D. Schreiner. Having been enlarged for a specific purpose, the Senate was quietly allowed to shrink again.

The twelve years between the election of Strijdom in 1954 and the murder of Verwoerd in 1966 were a period of extraordinarily rapid social and political change in which the social engineers came into their own and the ideologists of the National Party were given their head. It was also the period in which South Africa became, in the elegant phrase of the Minister of External Affairs, E. H. Louw, 'the pole-cat of the world'.

One matter, at least, had been settled: the 'racial question' now required a different answer. The place of the English in the body politic had been decided; there was no possibility within the existing structure of their achieving power in any conceivable political combination. In 1958 the Nationalists won their fourth successive general election, this time increasing their seats to 103 out of 159. It would require a cataclysm to dislodge them from office. The South African English did not theorize about racial discrimination; they merely practised it. Thus any fears, sometimes expressed among Nationalists, of an electoral alliance with non-Whites (in the days when non-Whites still had votes that mattered) were groundless. The 'racial question' now asked how Afrikaners were to maintain their social and political privileges in a country in which the black population was multiplying more quickly than the white. The English were not invited to contribute to this debate, but they were not be be excluded from social and economic privilege. They could be enlisted in the battle for Afrikaner survival, if not as full partners at least as auxiliary troops. One consequence of the Government's policies was that the various tribes and peoples of southern Africa were being compressed into a united movement, however transient, against white supremacy. If there ever were to be a racial revolt, the English would have to take refuge in the Afrikaners' *laager*; there would be nowhere else to go. There was hardly a protest when, in 1957, both God Save the Queen and the Union Jack lost their official status; South Africa now had one national anthem and one flag. Surprisingly, perhaps, Strijdom did not force the republican issue.

Meanwhile, Verwoerd's administrative empire was growing. The name 'Bantu' now came into general official use instead of 'Natives'; liberal Whites preferred to speak of 'Africans'. The legislative landmarks which marked Verwoerd's progress included the Bantu Authorities Act of 1951, which followed the old British colonial practice of indirect rule through tribal chiefs in the lands reserved for Africans; the Native Laws Amendment Act of 1952, which restricted the rights of Africans to live permanently in urban areas to those who had been born there, those who had lived there continuously for fifteen years and those who had worked for the same employer for ten years; the Natives (Abolition of Passes and Co-ordination of Documents) Act, which required all Africans, including for the first time African women, to carry comprehensive 'reference books' (passes by another name); and the Bantu Education Act of 1953, which transferred responsibility for schools from the Department of Education to the Department of Bantu Administration, which then devised curricula which would encourage Africans to 'develop along their own lines'. The Extension of University

Education Act set up ethnic university colleges, each for a specific category of non-Whites, who were then excluded from the so-called 'open universities' of Cape Town and the Witwatersrand. By the end of the 1950s the non-White peoples were compressed within an increasingly elaborate mesh of controls, depicted as the intermediate stage of a new society. The word *apartheid* had travelled round the world, gathering odium as it went. Its supporters now preferred to speak of '*aparte ontwikkeling*', separate development.[14]

But development to what? The purpose seemed often to be occluded behind a cloud of rhetoric. Thus in 1954 Verwoerd spoke as if his policy encompassed the whole of human existence:

> Apartheid comprises a whole multiplicity of phenomena. It comprises the political sphere; it is necessary in the social sphere; it is aimed at in Church matters; it is relevant to every sphere of life. Even within the economic sphere it is not just a question of numbers. What is of more importance there is whether one maintains the colour bar or not.[15]

It was becoming clearer every year that Malan had been right when he said that territorial separation was not possible. The difficulties were interlinked. The African reserves could not support anything like the total African population of the Union. There remained the problem of the urban Africans, economically essential to industry, desirable as domestic servants, and yet by their presence and the demand for their services demonstrating the impossibility of separate development. Verwoerd's demographers estimated in the 1950s that it would take another twenty years before the flow of Africans to the urban areas would be reversed; and that would depend on the siting of industries in or around what were now coming to be known as African 'homelands'. There was a fictitious exactitude about all predictions relating to the growth or movement of the African population.

Apartheid had originally been justified on moral grounds – equality within separate spheres. Yet what had so far been done was purely negative and restrictive. Residential areas that had been occupied by Africans or Coloureds for generations were now proclaimed for Whites only, and those who lived there were moved to new localities, by force or the threat of force. Two spectacular examples were Sophiatown, an African enclave in the western suburbs of Johannesburg, and District Six on the slopes of Table Mountain, where Coloureds had lived for over a century. Indians were moved from the suburbs of the cities or the centres of provincial towns, sometimes to bare *veld* where they existed in tents or makeshift dwellings until they could build something more permanent. African men and women were 'endorsed out' of urban areas where they might have lived for most of their lives and deported to 'homelands' where there was little room for them and small chance of making a living. An ever-growing bureaucracy was employed in manipulating Africans; many decisions resulted in human tragedies. The price of *apartheid* was paid in African suffering.

Unsurprisingly, the process of racial separation evoked protest and occasionally physical resistance. The reaction of the Government was to fortify the apparatus of coercion, either by using powers that had lain dormant or by creating new powers under statutes passed by a docile Parliament. Increasingly the Government was facing difficulties of its own making. A golden age had been promised when *apartheid* was complete and racial tensions had vanished. But what would happen if the measures taken to achieve that golden age stimulated those very resentments and occasions of conflict which it was the purpose of *apartheid* to banish for ever?[16] The Government seemed to have no answer beyond the use of force.

Two assumptions underlay the official policy: the African would want what the Government told him that he wanted, and he would accept it peacefully. Verwoerd seemed to be coming closer and closer to the claim that he understood the 'real will' of the African better than the African understood it himself. (The Boer of the Transvaal in the 1870s had watched British administrators making the same claim about him, and that had made him justly angry.)

The official leadership of the African National Congress had been traditionally mild to the point of blandness; now, under the stimulus of Verwoerd's activities it was pressed towards a more militant attitude. A new generation was coming to the fore. Albert Luthuli, a minor Zulu chief, had been elected as president in 1953; his past approach had been, as he put it, 'knocking in vain, patiently, moderately and modestly at a closed and barred door'. Behind him were the young lions, such as Nelson Mandela, Walter Sisulu, Oliver Tambo, Potlako Leballo and Robert Sobukwe, educated men who were unwilling to wait, as their elders had done, for some indefinite future when white men should have experienced a change of heart. To these men, economic improvement as a by-product of European development was not enough. (These were the people whom Smuts had despairingly recognized as wanting rights.) Luthuli himself had been deposed from his chieftainship by the

Government when he became president of the A.N.C. He was a man of massive simplicity and integrity, but behind him, in what came to be known as the Congress Alliance, were men of nimbler minds and more devious purposes. One of the unexpected consequences of the Government's banning of the Communist Party had been to promote links between Communists and African Nationalists. There were not many Marxist–Leninists among the African intelligentsia, but there were many who were willing to accept help from any quarter from which it was offered, and the fact that the Communists were officially stigmatized as enemies of the Government was enough to commend them in some African eyes. Some of these new allies had studied in China and the Soviet Union, and there had been unofficial delegates from South Africa at the Bandung conference on Afro–Asian unity in April 1955. (It was to prevent such contacts in the future that the Government made it a criminal offence to leave South Africa without a valid passport.)

In June 1955 a 'Congress of the People' met at Kliptown, near Johannesburg. There were nearly 3,000 delegates, from the African National Congress, the South African Indian Congress, the National Union of the Organization of Coloured People and the Congress of Democrats, a white group with Communist connections. The meeting endorsed a document known as the Freedom Charter. In some ways, this resembled the *cahiers des doléances* of the French Revolution, a series of grievances for redress; it amounted to a rejection of the existing political, economic and social structure of South Africa. The charter combined millennial hopes – 'The people shall share the country's wealth'; 'The doors of learning and culture shall be open'; 'There shall be peace and friendship' – with specific demands for the nationalization of banks, mines and industry; redistribution of the land; universal suffage; and the abolition of *apartheid* in all its forms. The slogan 'The people shall govern' now began to appear as graffiti.

The Government's response was to carry out a series of police raids, during which large quantities of documents were impounded. A year later, at the end of 1956, 156 people, drawn from all races, were arrested and accused of high treason. The trial, in all its stages, lasted five years. The accused persons were defended by what was probably the most eminent team of legal counsel ever to act in a South African trial. In 1961 a bench of three judges delivered a unanimous verdict of 'not guilty'. By then, however, the South African scene had dramatically altered.

Strijdom died in office on 24 August 1958. This time the succession was openly disputed, but Verwoerd was preferred to C. R. Swart, of the Orange Free State, and Dr T. E. Dönges, of the Cape. Hertzog, Malan and Strijdom had all in their time 'emerged'; Verwoerd was elected. Those who saw in this contest seeds of open division within the National Party were mistaken. The choice made, the party clicked into line once more. It is doubtful whether Verwoerd was ever a figure of affection to his followers as his predecessors had been; but he dominated by reason of his intellect, his personality and his passionate conviction that his policies could be made to work. To those who did not possess his vision of the future there seemed little sign of development towards the territorial separation which Verwoerd still insisted was the only answer to South Africa's racial problems. To the outside observer it might seem that after ten years the pursuit of *apartheid* had brought little but misery and humiliation to the non-White peoples. In spite of population removals, influx control and attempts to encourage migration to the Reserves, the problem of the cities seemed to be as intractable as ever. Twelve of the thirteen largest towns in the Union, with Pretoria as the only exception, had non-White majorities. The crux of the problem was where it always had been, in the cities. Without non-White labour South African industry could not survive, let alone prosper. To the world at large apartheid seemed to be no more than a euphemism for a policy of social segregation, economic exploitation and political oppression. Those who professed to be South Africa's friends pressed the Government to make some concessions that might mitigate mounting hostility at the United Nations; Great Britain was additionally concerned that *apartheid* might disrupt the Commonwealth, which was on its way to becoming a multiracial association no longer dominated by the metropolitan country and the old white dominions.

Verwoerd believed with passionate intensity in republicanism and that 'separate development' could be made to work. In 1959 he pushed through Parliament the Promotion of Bantu Self-Government Bill which envisaged eight 'national units' for the African people. He now bedazzled the faithful with a vision of white South Africa as the suzerain power at the core of a cluster of African States.

My belief is that the development of South Africa on the basis of this Bill will create so much friendship, so much gratitude, so many mutual interests in the propulsive development that there will be no danger of hostile Bantu states, but that there will arise what I call a commonwealth, founded on common interests and linked together by common interests in this southern part of Africa.[17]

It was Verwoerd's hope that South Africa would be permitted to include within this 'commonwealth' the British protectorates of Swaziland, Basutoland and Bechuanaland. These hopes were dashed by the address delivered by Harold Macmillan, the British Prime Minister, when he addressed the South African Parliament in Cape Town in February 1960. It is possible that Macmillan himself would have been satisfied with some gestures of conciliation towards Africans. He told one of his entourage that South Africa's foolishness was that of 'elevating segregation into a doctrine. If they didn't make an ideology of it they would almost certainly succeed in getting the results they seek with a minimum of concession. Economic differences between black and white would alone be sufficient to achieve practical separation'.[18] If this was Macmillan's considered opinion, it did not survive his meeting with Verwoerd, who was his host in Cape Town. Macmillan, who loved to toss ideas into discussion, and often used his erudition to conceal his thoughts, turned a private conversation towards theology; this, to Verwoerd, included *apartheid* which, Macmillan noted, was 'more than a political philosophy, it was a religion based on the Old Testament rather than on the New . . . he had all the force of argument of some of the great Calvinist leaders of our Scottish kirk. He was certainly as convinced as John Knox himself that he alone could be right, and that there was no question or argument but merely a statement of his will . . . nothing one could say or put forward would have the smallest effect upon the views of this determined man.'[19] It was after this conversation that Macmillan made the speech in which he remarked that the 'wind of change' was blowing through Africa, by which he meant a growth of national consciousness. He then dissociated his Government from a basic tenet of *apartheid* by insisting on the criterion that individual merit alone was the 'criterion for a man's advancement, whether political or economic'. He ended with a warning:

As a fellow member of the Commonwealth it is our earnest desire to give South Africa our support and encouragement but . . . there are some aspects of your policies which make it impossible for us to do so without being false to our own deep convictions about the political destinies of free men to which in our own territories we are trying to give effect. I think we ought, as friends, to face together ... the fact that in the world today this difference of outlook lies between us.[20]

Verwoerd had never been one to bow to pressure from without. He was indeed moving faster on the racial issue than any of his predecessors. He was now linking together two issues – 'Bantu self-government' and, at last, South Africa as a republic. He was proposing to bring *apartheid* down from the clouds of theory into the realities of administration and to graft on to the practice of segregation the granting of political powers, however limited for the time being, to Africans. He spoke the language of sacrifice: the white South African would have to pay a price for his privileges. He could not have it both ways, enjoy both affluence and security, retain the African as labourer and servant, and be protected against the claims of a black proletariate. Verwoerd himself set what he hoped was an example by having no black servants in the Prime Minister's official residence. He hinted that the physical partition of South Africa might come about some day, when the Whites would have to be content with a lesser share than they possessed at present. For himself, if the choice ever came to that between a smaller white State and one that was multiracial, his own choice would be for the smaller.

Verwoerd's critics pointed out that 'political' *apartheid* – political rights to be confined to Africans in their own homelands – was no answer to the problem of the growing African majorities in the cities, where they were to have no political rights at all. Verwoerd claimed that this involved parity of treatment, because Whites would, reciprocally, have no political rights in African areas. This, his critics replied, was a specious argument: there was no need for any Whites to go to African areas to earn their livings, whereas most Africans could maintain themselves and their families only by selling their labour, regularly or irregularly, in 'white' areas. The Department of Bantu Administration constantly reiterated the prophecy that some time in the future – the year 1978 was cited in the late 1950s – the movement of population would change direction and a term would be set to the growth of the urban African population. In the meantime Africans were to live, segregated, in what were previously called 'locations' and were now known as 'townships' on the fringes of the 'white' urban areas, such as Soweto (an abbreviation of 'South-western Township') outside

PLATE 16 *The Sharpeville Massacre* (Courtesy Argus South African Newspapers).

Johannesburg. These townships, wherever they occurred, were joyless places, a prey to a growing breed of petty criminals and often the arenas of gang warfare.

To those conservative Afrikaners who believed that Verwoerd was moving too fast he held out the attraction of the republic, an issue that was likely to unite Nationalists. In January 1960 he announced that a referendum (for Whites only) would be held later that year on whether South Africa should become, at once, a republic within the Commonwealth.

Before then, however, South Africa found itself the object of world-wide condemnation when, on 21 March 1960, the police opened fire on unarmed Africans demonstrating at Sharpeville, near Vereeniging in the Transvaal, killing 69 and wounding 180. The demonstrations, which had been taking place all over the country, were against the 'pass laws' that restricted the free movement of Africans, and had been organized by the Pan-African Congress, a more radical offshoot from the African National Congress. Most of these demonstrations passed off without violence, but at Sharpeville the police lost their nerve. It was an episode which shocked the world, and Sharpeville took its place at once in the international catalogue of outrages against humanity. Richard

Dimbleby, a commentator of the British Broadcasting Corporation, compared Sharpeville to Guernica and Lidice – the first a town devastated from the air in 1937 during the Spanish Civil War, the second a village in Czechoslovakia wiped from the earth in 1942 on Nazi orders in retaliation for the assassination of Heydrich, the German 'Protector of Moravia'. These comparisons were grotesquely exaggerated, but it was a sign of the emotion generated by the Sharpeville shootings that they could be made at all. There was no premeditation at Sharpeville; it was a disastrous accident, but of a kind that was likely to happen where the police had long been encouraged to shoot if they felt themselves to be endangered.

In South Africa it seemed that the long-threatened revolt of the masses had occurred at last. There were calls for a general strike of Africans, and in most of the larger towns there were protest marches of impressive size. The Government declared a state of emergency, mobilized the Active Citizen Force and arrested as many as 18,000 people of all races, including for the first time a number of white liberals. Police were used to force strikers back to work; legislation was pressed through Parliament declaring both the African National Congress and the Pan-African Congress to be illegal organizations; the state of emergency was enforced in nearly half of the country's magisterial districts. On 9 April a South African Englishman shot and wounded Verwoerd in the head as he was opening the annual trade and agricultural fair in Johannesburg. With Verwoerd in hospital some members of his Government seemed ready to make major concessions, to stave off further domestic violence and do something to restore South Africa's battered reputation abroad. It seemed that change by shock was coming to South Africa at last.

It did not happen. Sharpeville was the turning-point where nobody turned. Verwoerd's wounds were not fatal, and by an astonishing demonstration of will-power he reasserted his authority over his Cabinet. There would be no concessions of any kind. But a new ruthlessness now made its appearance in South African government. The role of the 'special branch' of the police force was enhanced. Superficially at least, the country reverted to normality.

The referendum on the republic was held in October 1960. The result was the triumph of Verwoerd's career. The republican majority was 70,000 out of 1,600,000 votes cast – slender but sufficient. He put his case with persuasive skills: vanished were the anti-English polemics of the former editor of *Die Transvaler*, and in their place appeared the subtler arguments of the professional psychologist. Each voter received a letter, in both English and

Afrikaans and in a facsimile of Verwoerd's handwriting, beginning 'Dear Friend' and representing republican unity as a defence against those who were willing to appease the forces of black Nationalism. 'The struggle between Eastern and Western nations, between Communism and Christendom, is such that both groups of nations will grant and concede anything (including the white man of Africa, his possessions and his rights) to seek the favour and support of the black man. This has led to chaos in the Congo.' Therefore Whites in South Africa must stand together; and for that a republic was necessary, for until then the Afrikaner Nationalist would not be satisfied, and the English could not count on his friendship until they, too, gave an undivided loyalty to South Africa. It was an old argument but there was a new twist, in that it was now directed at the 'moderate Englishman', who was being invited to give up what sentimental attachment to the monarchy he might possess for the sake of the protection that the Afrikaner could give him. He was being asked to sacrifice his allegiance to the Queen but to retain membership of the Commonwealth of which she was the head.

However, Commonwealth membership was not something that South Africa could choose at will; and at the Commonwealth Conference in London in March 1961 it was made clear that, as a republic, South Africa would have to apply for readmission. The opposition to this application was led, surprisingly enough, by Canada, which made it clear that its own support would be conditional on 'significant changes' in South Africa's racial policies. Where Canada led, the Asian and African members could not but follow. Verwoerd was as intransigent to the heads of Commonwealth governments as he had been to Macmillan in Cape Town; and he eventually withdrew his request rather than experience a hostile vote. Thus when South Africa became a republic, on 31 May 1961, the fifty-ninth anniversary of the Peace of Vereeniging, it was separated at last from the British connection. This had not come about in the manner which the most ardent of Nationalists could wholly welcome – a virtual expulsion was not the same thing as secession – but none the less Verwoerd was welcomed back from the conference as a Nationalist hero. The first State President of the Republic of South Africa was C. R. Swart, Hertzog's old antagonist; the Cabinet decreed that his official dress should include a sash and a top-hat, much as President Kruger had worn. It was a gesture to the past by a prime minister whose thoughts roamed over a future that he believed could be moulded by his will. Some might think that if South African history were to be searched for a predecessor to Verwoerd, the would-be transformer of society, Alfred Milner might be a more suitable candidate than Paul Kruger.

10 APARTHEID:
ITS VARIATIONS AND ITS COLLAPSE

Piet Cillié, a former editor of *Die Burger* and hence an Afrikaner sage ex officio, in a celebrated essay published in 1985, denied that *apartheid* had ever been a coherent ideology.

> A system? An ideology? A coherent blueprint? No, rather a pragmatic, tortuous process of consolidating a nationalist movement's leadership, of establishing the Afrikaner's right to self-determination, not primarily against a coloured force, but by preventing the return of the United Party.[1]

Cillié's assertion is a matter of dates: *apartheid* meant different things at different times to different people. In 1948 the Nationalists adopted it as an electoral weapon against the United Party, to distinguish their own clear-cut 'Native policy' from that of their opponents. This was not difficult. The United Party had little to say besides a recognition of the obvious – that the black man was in the cities to stay, where he was to be regarded, now as in the past, as a disagreeable necessity; as for the future, that would have to take care of itself. It is a matter for argument whether *apartheid* signified a new departure, or merely a more rigorous and systematic application of the old expedients of racial segregation. The Nationalists' electoral victory in 1948 had been a close-run thing, and it would not have been won at all if Smuts had listened to those of his supporters who had urged him to alter the electoral arrangements which simultaneously inflated the value of rural votes and diminished that of the cities. There were certainly Nationalist theorists who, as they contemplated the apparent precariousness of their party's position, visualized a potential alliance between their white opponents and the Cape Coloured people. Malan was on record as regarding the voting system of the Cape as an example of the imperialist subjection of the Afrikaner.

> How did the non-European come by his vote? There is only one answer. Overseas imperialist authorities, when it came to granting self-government, were afraid because Afrikanerdom was in the majority and would strive for freedom. So non-Europeans were not only enfranchised, but were set against the Afrikaners.[2]

Nationalists had long feared that their political opponents might make common cause with non-White voters in an electoral alliance. That was one reason for Hertzog's removal of Africans from the common voters' roll in the Cape, as part of the price of fusion with the old South African Party; it helps to explain the preoccupation of Malan's Government with the Cape Coloured vote. Malan himself approved of *apartheid* in theory but doubted whether it could be achieved. He was conscious enough of its value as an electoral slogan; beyond that, his thinking on the 'Native question' was little more penetrating than that of General Smuts: it was a matter for posterity. The views of Malan's successor, J. G. Strijdom, were relatively simple: he was for *baasskap*, white mastery, which he considered to be essential for the maintenance of Afrikaner racial purity. He was especially worried about the black influx into the cities. Back in his own environment – which to Strijdom probably meant his *kraal* – the African was satisfied with his 'natural' condition and did not aspire to become an 'imitation white man'. In 1946 he had warned Malan: 'If we allow the natives in their millions to settle among us and in our towns, and they gradually develop and become civilized . . . the existing colour line will slowly disappear and . . . equality will also slowly be established.' To those of Strijdom's persuasion *apartheid* was a more rigorous form of segregation, aimed especially at the protection of the Afrikaner poor in the cities. It was unapologetically defensive.

This was not Verwoerd's standpoint. To him, *apartheid* went beyond politics; it was part of a vision of South African society which, as it developed, became the core of an ideology which would not only ensure the survival of the Afrikaner (and other white men as well) but would be in the best interests of the African peoples. Where others thought of the next election, Verwoerd thought of the next generation, or perhaps the one after that. For a time, he convinced many Afrikaners – and not a few of the English – that *apartheid* could be morally justified. He might even convince himself that it was not only in the best interests of the African peoples, but was also their 'real will' – what they would desire for themselves if they thought clearly or were not led astray. Thus to separate the African from the white man and confine him to his own geographical areas and to his own spheres of life was justifiable; the African would be forced to be free. True, he would have some rights taken away from him, but in compensation he would 'receive something better'. He would become himself and not a distorted European. Thus Verwoerd devised a system of 'Bantu education' to replace a former system that he considered harmful in that it drew the black man away from his own community and 'misled him by showing him the green pastures of the European but still did not let him graze there'.[3]

All this would take time; and it would entail an enterprise of social engineering vaster than anything envisioned by Milner. In his own areas the black man would be autonomous. There would be no rights for him in the white man's areas; but there was nothing vexatious in this, since the white man would, likewise, have no rights in the black man's areas. In 1952 Verwoerd was claiming that 'the various Acts, Bills, and also public statements which I have made, all fit into a pattern and together form a single constructive plan'.[4] By 1959 he was introducing legislation which aimed at producing, in due season, self-governing tribal enclaves. Unsurprisingly the press called these 'Bantustans', on the mistaken analogy of Pakistan.

All this was in the future. There remained the urgent questions of internal security and of foreign relations. Internal security was the business of the Minister of Justice, and to this office Verwoerd appointed, in 1962, Balthasar Johannes Vorster, a former 'general' of the Ossewa Brandwag and as such interned by Smuts in 1942. Vorster's political creed, as stated by himself, was in those days an extreme form of authoritarianism:

> We stand for Christian Nationalism which is an ally of National Socialism. You can call the anti-democratic system a dictatorship if you like. In Italy it is called Fascism, in Germany National Socialism, and in South Africa Christian Nationalism.[5]

As Minister of Justice, Vorster announced that 'you could not fight Communism with Queensberry rules'. He was as good as his word. His definition of Communism encompassed almost any attempt to change the system of government other than through parliament.

Acts of Parliament gave still wider powers to the police, including the right to detain suspects without charge and in solitary confinement for periods which started at twelve days in 1962, were extended to ninety days in 1963, to 180 days in 1965, for an unlimited period if authorized by a judge in 1966 and without any judicial authorization during a proclaimed state of emergency. Sabotage and terrorism were defined by statute. Vorster also took powers to place persons under partial or total 'house arrest' – a harrowing penalty inflicted at the Minister's discretion, which made it practically impossible to practise a profession or, at its most extreme, to earn a living. These measures were effective in breaking the power of the African National Congress and its armed wing, Umkonto we Sizwe ('Spear of the Nation'). In 1964 Nelson Mandela, Walter Sisulu and other members of the African National Congress were sentenced to life imprisonment on charges of sabotage. A small group of young white men and women who called themselves the African Resistance Movement went, like black activists, either to gaol or to refuge abroad. The scope of rebels in exile was hampered by the necessity of operating from bases beyond a cordon of buffer states – Mozambique, Rhodesia, South-West Africa and Angola – running like a horseshoe around South Africa's frontiers.

South Africa's international standing became increasingly precarious. South African governments continued to argue that their internal affairs were nobody else's business; they found themselves increasingly confronted with accusations that they had infringed universal standards of conduct and deprived many of their own citizens of what the Western world regarded as 'fundamental human rights'. During the Korean war a South African Air Force contingent had been among the armed forces of the United Nations. After Sharpeville in 1960, and the breaking of the Commonwealth connection in 1961, South Africa found itself becoming an international outcast. Its pronounced anti-Communism was found not to be an automatic assurance of Western friendship: Western governments seeking to woo African states away from the embrace of the Soviet Union found it embarrassing to be too closely linked to South Africa. Anti-*apartheid* movements grew up in many Western states, demanding boycotts of all kinds. Sanctions against the export of armaments began in the 1960s; South Africa's response was to set up its own manufactory, ARMSCOR. But although there was widespread propaganda against South Africa, those states that were avowed enemies had not the capacity to inflict crippling damage, and those that did possess the capacity lacked, for the time being at least, either the will or the desire to use it.

Thus, in spite of international unpopularity, the South African Government could remain apparently unmoved by the ritual picketing of its embassies, the refusal of liberal zealots in foreign lands to drink South African sherry, the disruption of sporting events abroad and the spreading reluctance of European celebrities to accept invitations to South Africa. The 1960s were years of economic prosperity. Moreover, the prophecy that relations between the two white groups would improve once the country became a republic seemed to be on the way to fulfilment. Socially, Nationalists and their political opponents were as far apart as ever; but in the privacy of the ballot the Nationalists were clearly gaining English support. Many things contributed to this. One was the dislike of British decolonization: in particular, refugees from Kenya

PLATE 17. *B. J. Vorster* (Courtesy of the South African High Commission).

and Zambia (lately Northern Rhodesia) were attracted by the Nationalists' racial policies and spread depressing stories of the gaucheries of black majority rule in the lands they had abandoned. One of the most remarkable things about the coming of the republic was the absence of popular resentment among the English; there was little of the bitter rejection that had for so long characterized Nationalist attitudes to the British connection. Such sentimental regret as they might feel because the Queen of England was no longer the Queen of South Africa was tempered by their altered status when they visited England, where they had now become aliens with limited rights of abode and required to register with the police. Moreover, England was fast becoming a multiracial society on its own account, a circumstance that had little appeal for colour-prejudiced South Africans.

When Verwoerd began to move resolutely towards the republic he had correctly calculated that there was a swing to the right in the white electorate. In 1959 the United Party shed its liberal wing when nine of its Members of Parliament seceded and formed themselves into the nucleus of a new Progressive Party, advocating a non-racial society under the slogan 'merit, not colour'. In the general election of 1961, following the proclamation of the republic, the Progressives won only a single seat, that retained by Helen Suzman, MP, in the Houghton division of Johannesburg; they did not win another seat until 1974, three elections later. Thus for thirteen years the lonely voice of Mrs Suzman was the only parliamentary opposition on the principles of racial discrimination and civil liberties.

Few things were more remarkable about the career of Dr Verwoerd than his ability, as his premiership continued, to win the support, tacit or avowed, of those of the English who had previously damned him as one of the deadliest of their political enemies. He was able to include two of them in his Cabinet – A. E. Trollip and F. W. Waring (the latter a distinguished Springbok rugby three-quarter). Many of the English were becoming weary of the posture of unavailing protest: by 1961 the Nationalists had won four general elections in succession and increased their majority each time. Constitutional opposition seemed hopeless and unconstitutional opposition unthinkable. Verwoerd's personality was strong enough to discourage opposition within Afrikanerdom. In 1960 representatives of the main branch of the Dutch Reformed Church had voted for a resolution condemning apartheid moved at a conference at Cottesloe, in Johannesburg, sponsored by the

World Council of Churches. The erring representatives were swiftly told to mend their ways, and the findings of the conference were repudiated by provincial synods in the Cape and Transvaal. In 1962 the first national synod of the Dutch Reformed Church was made the occasion of a bland demonstration of unity and support for the Government.[6]

White opinion, then, was hardening against 'liberalism'; this attitude was strengthened by the general white revulsion against sporadic acts of sabotage, especially when a white member of the African Resistance Movement planted a lethal bomb in the concourse of the Johannesburg station; he was subsequently convicted of murder and hanged. In the 1950s protest marches in the cities against the Government's proposals or actions had been greeted by many onlookers with sympathy; a decade later the mood was one of apathy or hostility. Furthermore, it was clear that 'separate development' – now the preferred name for *apartheid* – was having some success: in 1963, the Transkeian Constitution Act set up the first of the African territorial authorities, this one for the Xhosa tribe. Demonstrably there were some Africans who were willing to collaborate with the Government. The rewards of the collaborators were correspondingly large.

On 6 September 1966 Verwoerd was stabbed to death in his seat in the House of Assembly as he waited to open a debate. The killer was an official messenger of the House, of Greek origin, who was found unfit to plead at his trial and was confined as insane. There was, it seemed, no coherent motive for his crime. The assassination produced public shock but no political crisis. The National Party elected Vorster as its leader and hence as Prime Minister. Apparently there was no break in continuity; but this, it now appears, was a superficial view. Verwoerd had once declared that he would entrench *apartheid* so deeply that it could never be uprooted. In that process he had turned what was originally the Ministry of Native Affairs, and had then been rechristened the Department of Bantu Affairs and Administration, into what was almost a state within a state, a huge and growing bureaucracy charged with oversight over all affairs which concerned the African peoples. This had developed a momentum of its own, administering laws which touched the lives of twenty million African people. It was as insensitive as it was vast; it could not change direction easily, and those who did its work could cushion themselves against accusations of inhumanity only by accepting both the rightness and the necessity of the ideology which shaped their actions. There is evidence that, once the first shock had been absorbed, the departure of Verwoerd was greeted with a certain relief among Nationalists. It was not merely that he was an authoritarian personality armoured in the certainty of his beliefs who treated disagreement as heresy and opposition as akin to treason; questions could increasingly be asked about whether the price to be paid for Verwoerd's ideology might be too high for what it could achieve. What had once been an item in an electoral programme which aimed at Afrikaner survival through political means had now become an end in itself, entailing irreversible changes in the structure of South African society which would affect Whites as well as Blacks.

Vorster was no visionary. Early in his premiership he repudiated Verwoerd by implication when he said:

> The cardinal principle of the National Party is the retention, maintenance and immortalization of the Afrikaner identity within a white sovereign state. Apartheid or separate development is merely a method of bringing it about, and making it permanent . . . If there are other better methods of achieving this end, then we must find those methods and get on with it.[7]

This was to degrade what Verwoerd had regarded as an end in itself to a mere means to an end, capable therefore of adaptation. For the moment, the machine of separate development – the new sanitized name for *apartheid* – continued its momentum unchecked. Moreover, disorder at home was suppressed with a rigour that verged on the ferocious. At the same time Vorster began to seek for allies abroad, even to the extent of welcoming black diplomats to Pretoria, although for the moment only the State of Malawi chose to take up the offer. Vorster lacked both the charisma and the certainty of Verwoerd, and he did not possess the same authority over the National Party. The beginning of his premiership was marked by a public manifestation of the *broedertwis*, that 'strife between brothers' which lingered just beneath the surface of Afrikanerdom. This time the contending factions were felicitously entitled *verkramptes* and *verligtes* – cramped ones against the enlightened.

Few Afrikaner controversies are simple for the outsider to understand, and this was no exception. At its core was the *verkramptes'* suspicion that the Afrikaner was being permitted to deviate from the fundamental principles of his ancestors. Some have attempted to interpret the quarrel according to Marxist ideology; Afrikaner unity entailed surrender to the susceptibilities of the most reactionary of the tribe and this had become an obstacle to the accumulation of Afrikaner capital.[8] But the Afrikaner Nationalist does not fit easily into the confinement of Marxist man, and one is on safer ground in assuming that the matters at issue were what those involved said that they were; and these are not easily explainable as the results of 'false consciousness'. Among the predisposing conditions of discord was the long-existing rivalry between the Cape and Transvaal branches of the Party which extended to the National Press, which published *Die Burger* in Cape Town, and the Voortrekker Press which published *Die Transvaler* (once notable for the polemics of Dr Verwoerd) in Johannesburg. It was resented in the Transvaal when the National Press decided to publish a new Sunday newspaper, called *Die Beeld*, in Johannesburg; this was an invasion of territory and, perhaps, of ideology as well. It was *Die Beeld*, notably *verligte* in sentiment, which publicized Dr Albert Hertzog's attempts to undermine Vorster's 'outreach' policy towards black states in Africa. (Hertzog was an unapologetic *verkrampte*; as Minister of Posts and Telegraphs he had blocked the introduction of television into South Africa, believing with Verwoerd that it would be detrimental to Afrikanerdom. Television did not arrive until 1976.) Nor were all Nationalists happy at Vorster's softer attitude towards the English and his attempts to enlist more of them as collaborators. One of the principal *verkramptes* on English influence was Piet Meyer, who held a lofty position in the Broederbond and whom Verwoerd had appointed as head of the South African Broadcasting Corporation.

In 1966 Meyer restated a demand for Afrikaner cultural hegemony. He found it deplorable that the political realm was still dominated by institutions of British origin, such as the parliamentary system and the concept of citizenship as 'a collectivity of all state subjects, irrespective of differences of origin and culture'. What he wanted was an ethnically homogeneous state, which not only meant the continuation of the Verwoerdian policy of total apartheid, but also the Afrikanerization of the English.

> [This would mean] that the English-speaker has to make the Afrikaans world-view his own; that he will integrate his ideals and life style with those of the Afrikaner; that he will adopt Afrikaans history as his own; that he will accept Afrikaans as his national language, alongside English as the international community language ... We shall then be able to speak of Afrikaans-and English-speaking South Africans.[9]

Meyer was contradicted by Professor H. B. Thom of Stellenbosch University, one of the intellectual heavyweights of Afrikanerdom and presently chairman of the powerful Federation of Afrikaans Cultural Societies, who declared that 'the gates of the laager have to be thrown open; our Afrikanerhood must be extended fearlessly'. It was the word 'fearlessly' that, to *verkramptes*, was charged with menace: it was one thing to admit to the laager the well-disposed and 'right-thinking' English (creatures that were much thicker on the ground than they had been a decade earlier); but might not inclusion also be offered to the Cape Coloured people? Other matters to which the *verkramptes* took exception were moves towards multiracial sporting encounters, hospitality to black diplomats, indiscriminate white immigration which might include Roman Catholics (to Nationalist purists the 'Roman peril' had been high on the list of potential calamities), excessive spending on African 'homelands' and the disposition among some local authorities to dispense with 'petty *apartheid*'. To *verkramptes* all this meant a dilution of Afrikaner exclusiveness and eventually, therefore, of Afrikaner supremacy, a squandering of the achievements of the heroic past.

They were also distressed at matters rather more remote from party politics – the corruption of the 'soul of the Afrikaner' by a new breed of Afrikaans writers, calling themselves *die sestigers* (people of the sixties). This was indeed a new departure: Afrikaans literature in the past had been linked with politicial emancipation from 'British imperialism' and the corresponding language movement to replace High Dutch with Afrikaans. The generation which drew its inspiration from the Boer War had long served as accepted models: every Afrikaner schoolchild would have been exposed to poems such as 'Winternag' by Eugene Marais and 'By die Monument' by J. D. du Toit, son of a father famed in the struggle for a language that the Afrikaner could call his own exclusive possession. It was sometimes difficult to draw a line between literature and politics: C. J. Langenhoven (1873–1932) had served on the Cape Provincial Council and had been instrumental in that capacity for introducing Afrikaans into primary schools. He had also glorified the Bezuidenhout who had touched off the Slagtersnek rebellion as a lonely standard bearer of liberty against the imperial oppressor. He wrote the poem 'Die Stem van Suid Afrika' which, set to music by M. de Villiers, was eventually to become the national anthem. However, it might be said that Afrikaans prose did not match the achievements of Afrikaans poetry; the great Afrikaans novel had yet to be written. D. J. Opperman, one of the prestigious figures of the literary establishment, touched a raw nerve when he said that it was time that the Afrikaner realized that he was part of a governing nation, not one perpetually in opposition. Those who did not recall imperialist iniquities were disposed to write about Afrikaners in distress or to romanticize the simple life of the farm compared with the meretricious glitter of the English-dominated cities where, by tradition, the unsophisticated Afrikaner was perpetually led astray.

In the 1960s a group of young men and women, some of whom had spent time in Europe, and especially in Paris, initiated a more cosmopolitan strain in Afrikaans writing. André Brink, one of the most prominent members of the new school, said that they 'introduced the then current vogues of experimentalism, existentialism and postmodernism into a literary scene still largely determined by nineteenth-century techniques and by the severely localized expression of themes like drought, locusts and poor whites'.[10] As well as Brink himself the movement included unorthodox figures such as Breyten Breytenbach (who was subsequently gaoled under the Terrorism Act of 1967), Chris Barnard, Jan Rabie, Welma Odendaal and André le Roux. There was something here which was akin to American writing about involvement in Vietnam. It was all deeply disturbing to traditionalists. It has been suggested that the quarrel between the cramped and the enlightened ones within Afrikanerdom became acute in 1966 when the Akademie vir Wetenskap en Kuns (Academy for Science and Art) awarded the prestigious Hertzog Prize to Etienne le Roux for his novel *Sewe Dae by die Silbersteins*.

Some of the new school suffered the fate of the literary heretic – ostracism, pressure on printers and publishers and the use of the Censorship Act of 1963 to ban their works. The Reverend K. Vorster, brother of the Prime Minister, found Brink's *Kennis van die Aand* (translated into English as *Looking on Darkness*) to be especially disgusting, giving his opinion that 'If this is literature, then a Sunday school is a brothel'. Brink himself, writing in the bilingual journal *Standpunte*, argued that revolution was the function of art – 'not the easy political revolution, but the type which continually rebels against everything that makes life unbearable'. He and his colleagues were undeterred by official disapproval. Indeed, in 1975 they formed the Afrikaans Writers' Guild, open to writers of all races and languages. All this was a long way from the 'healthy unanimity' which the Broederbond had once held up as the aim of 'right-thinking' members of the *Volk*.

There was, for the moment, no healthy unanimity in the Cabinet. Three ministers, including Albert Hertzog, the veteran of right-wing causes, were dismissed in 1968; and in 1969 Hertzog and Jaap Marais left (or were extruded from) the National Party; they formed their own party, optimistically named the Herstigte (restored) National Party. They did not win a single seat in the general election of 1970; but their presence was a warning to Vorster not to be seen as 'soft on liberalism'; 'no enemies on the right' had long been an axiom of Nationalist politics. Vorster's hand now fell on student movements, both in the English and the African universities; passports were withdrawn from those judged to be subversive; decisions of the Publications Control Board were placed outside the scope of judicial review; and the English-language press was constantly urged to put its own house in order if it wished to avoid censorship. A Prohibition of Political Interference Act made membership of multiracial political parties illegal. Faced with this prohibition the South African Liberal Party, which had long been a voice crying in the wilderness, dissolved itself; the Progressive Party carried on, shorn of its small non-White membership. An Affected Organizations Act empowered the State President to declare as 'affected' any organization which he deemed to be dangerous to the security of the State; those 'affected' were prohibited from receiving foreign funding. This was used against the Christian Institute, founded by the Reverend Beyers Naudé, once a member of the Broederbond and Moderator of the Southern Transvaal Synod of the Dutch Reformed Church and now the most celebrated of ecclesiastical rebels, who had declared that there was a conflict between the Christian conscience and the means used to promote Afrikaner survival: *apartheid*, he said, had been elevated above the word of God. By 1976 Naudé's Christian Institute was campaigning for sanctions and boycotts on South Africa as a means of pressing the Government to end apartheid and was declaring its support for 'liberatory' movements. It was banned in 1977.

By then South Africa's international position had changed markedly for the worse. In 1974 General Spinola took power in Portugal and committed himself to the granting of independence to Portuguese colonies in Africa. By 1975 Mozambique had a black government under Samora Machel, who announced himself as the leader of a people's democracy which he would turn into a 'revolutionary base against imperialism and colonialism in Africa'. The end of Portuguese rule in Angola precipitated an indigenous power struggle in which South African troops briefly and unsuccessfully intervened to prevent the victory of a faction backed by the Soviet Union and assisted by Cuban 'volunteers'. What had happened in Lisbon in 1974 meant that the cordon of buffer states around South Africa had been breached.

Vorster ran his Cabinet on a slack rein, allowing considerable independence to ministers and even to deputy ministers. This means of doing business was a contributory cause of the two disasters of his premiership, the Soweto 'uprising' and the scandal arising from the Department of Information's misuse of public money.

'Soweto' is an acronym for 'South-western Township', the huge African segregated area near Johannesburg. There were grievances in plenty in Soweto, most of which were common to the other concentrations of Africans in urban areas – housing shortages producing improvised shanty-towns on the outskirts which swiftly became slums; organized and casual crime; streets made dangerous by young hooligans or feuding gangs; and the continual tensions produced by the attempts by the Government to control the influx of Africans into the townships and the arrest and banishment of those without papers to prove authorized rights of abode. Among the predisposing conditions making for discontent should be added the effects of the Black Consciousness movement, probably an importation from the United States, which was gaining converts among Africans all over the country. Sympathy for the African National Congress was reinforced by the hopeful examples of the collapse of white rule in the Portuguese territories to east and west. The trigger which detonated all this explosive material was an act of administrative insensitivity – the insistence of the equal use of Afrikaans with English as a medium of instruction in secondary schools. On 16 June 1976 about 15,000 young Africans took part in an illegal protest march. They were stopped at police road blocks; stone throwing began; the police opened fire. This pattern was to be repeated over and over again in a prolonged period of urban violence which spread all over the country, accompanied by school burnings, turbulence and attacks on township dwellers accused of collaboration with government authorities within the *apartheid* system. The original march had been organized by a body which called itself the Soweto Students' Representative Council: in its youth, its self-confidence, its radicalism, its disdain for its elders and its effective intimidation of those who did not obey its instructions it represented something unexpected and ominous: it was the revolt of a new generation. Violence continued into 1977. The Government declared a state of emergency, which enabled the police to arrest suspects at their own discretion – nearly 6,000 of them, of whom about 370 were detained. A commission under Mr Justice Cillié which investigated the whole cycle of violence calculated that 575 people had been killed between June 1976 and February 1977 in more than thirty separate areas; many believed that the number of the dead had been understated. Killing bred killing: funerals took on the aspect of political defiance, and the police tended to open fire at any signs of mass protest.

The Government used its extensive statutory powers to ban any organizations and persons considered to be subversive, especially those connected with the Black Consciousness movement. The death that received world attention was that of Steve Biko, who died in horrendous circumstances while in custody – transported naked, after prolonged interrogation, in the back of a police vehicle for 600 miles from Port Elizabeth to Pretoria, where he died. Biko's name was added to the growing list of martyrs, and the Sixteenth of June, the day of the Soweto uprising, took its place next to the Twenty-first of March (the anniversary of the Sharpeville shootings in 1960) in the calendars of anti-*apartheid* movements.

The Government's exhibition of *kragdadigheid*, or ruthless determination, in suppressing disturbances by force did it no harm at all with the electorate: in the general election of 1977 the National Party increased its seats to a record number of 134. But this electoral success was no measure of the shock to its own confidence. Were the disturbances organized or spontaneous? If they were organized, it might be asked why the elaborate internal intelligence services – including the much-publicized Bureau for State Security – had failed in detection; if they were spontaneous, they demonstrated a depth of hatred which made nonsense of any claims that *apartheid* would eventually be accepted by Blacks as in their own true interests. It was also evident that the creation of 'autonomous homelands' was no remedy whatsoever for the increase of the African population in and around the cities and industrial areas.

The last months of Vorster's political career were clouded by public scandal over the malversation of funds by the Department of Information. In 1969 Parliament had voted to create a Securities Services Special Account which could be used at the Prime Minister's discretion. The practice developed by which individual ministers could draw off funds for use by their own departments under the broad heading of national security. In 1977 rumours began to spread about the irregular use of these funds by the Department of Information. The ensuing scandal probably denied the premiership to Dr C. P. Mulder, Minister of Information, leader of the Transvaal branch of the party and generally regarded as the favoured candidate when, in September 1978, Vorster chose to resign and take the purely dignified office of State President, vacant since the death of Dr N. Diederichs. Instead, after a particularly bitter contest, the leadership of the party and hence the premiership went to P. W. Botha, the Minister of Defence and leader of the party in the Cape Province. Protracted judicial enquiries into the misuse of funds – which the press had now called 'Muldergate' – eventually discredited President Vorster, who resigned in disgrace in 1979.

The manœuvres which brought P. W. Botha to the premiership were of unusual and complicated intricacy. Once in office Botha made it clear that his style of government would be autocratic rather than collegiate. None of South Africa's prime ministers could have been described as bubbling founts of merriment, but even by those austere standards Botha was a grim figure. He was called – though not perhaps to his face – the Great Crocodile; his temper could be thunderous; and his normal facial expression was one of solemn disapproval. His leadership was full of contradictions as he swayed between reform and reaction. He had already, as Minister of Defence, produced in 1975 a White Paper proposing novel methods of security; in 1977, in the aftermath of Soweto, this had been reissued with embellishment, propounding a 'total strategy' for the defence of South Africa against what was described as a 'total onslaught'. This 'total strategy' would embrace new attempts to construct an urban policy which Africans would accept, initiatives to improve industrial relations across the colour line, and fundamental changes in the constitution of the State; all these were portrayed as steps towards racial conciliation, but at the same time they were accompanied by a strengthening of the State apparatus of security and intelligence. Accommodation, it was asserted, did not mean capitulation, but it did take account of the accelerating transformation of South Africa.

Perhaps the most far-reaching of these transformations was progressive urbanization, which affected both Afrikaners and Africans. Since the electoral victory of 1948 the Government had deliberately used state power to benefit the economic condition of the Afrikaner. Although they numbered scarcely more than one- twelfth of the total population of the country, Afrikaners by 1980 firmly controlled the state machine – the Cabinet, the higher ranks of the ever-growing bureaucracy, television and radio, and the security services. The State itself had been described as a *Boereplaas*[11] (a tautological phrase meaning 'the Boers' private pasture'). But the word 'Boer' now needed to be used with circumspection: he had moved a long way from his rural origins and was now predominantly urbanized. Furthermore, he had risen significantly higher on the economic ladder; thanks to the patronage of the State, the Afrikaner had been able to overtake the economic lead which the English had for so long enjoyed. He had moved into the managerial classes. The proportion of Afrikaner white-collar workers had gone up from 29 per cent in 1946 to 65 per cent in 1977. Metropolitan prosperity had loosened the old tribal ties: it was increasingly difficult to interest the new generation in the folk ceremonies which had fortified the spirits of their elders by summoning the ghosts of past tribulations and triumphs. Even the choicer suburbs of Johannesburg, for so long regarded as the lair of Hoggenheimer, his co-conspirators and other enemies of the *Volk*, were no longer English preserves. The prosperous suburb of Linden, for instance, had been colonized by the affluent Afrikaner, with his swimming bath, the patio for his *braaivleis* (barbecue) and his two-car garage. Indeed, the Afrikaner had embraced Hoggenheimer as an ally with the acquisition of Federale Mynbou and his enrolment among the ranks of gold-mining capitalists. A consequence of all this was that the Afrikaner businessman was no longer insulated from his English counterpart. He, too, became increasingly aware of the economic consequences of *apartheid* – the waste of human resources at home and increasing hostility abroad, with the deepening threat of sanctions. P. W. Botha, it seemed, had a more sympathetic ear than his predecessor for the grievances of businessmen. Vorster had warned business off the turf of politics. 'You cannot ask me', he had said in 1976, 'to implement policies rejected by the electorate, and in which I do not believe.'[12] Botha, by contrast, called a conference in Johannesburg in 1979 in which he committed the Government to an alliance with business interests on a basis of free enterprise. But free enterprise and *apartheid* were antithetical, as Afrikaner entrepreneurs came to realize as more and more of them found themselves constricted by the myriad regulations which, intended for the protection of the white man, now appeared to be an impediment to his advancement. Manufacturing industry had already supplanted the old staples of mining and agriculture as the principal contributor to the gross national product. The conditions that inhibited further development of manufactures were the artificially constricted size of the market – differential wages at home and political hostility abroad – and the shortage of trained

PLATE 18 *P. W. Botha, 1988* (Courtesy of Popperfoto).

operatives. South Africa had already passed the point at which Whites alone could meet the demand for skilled workers. One of the most significant indications that *apartheid* might be dangerous for national security came from the high command of the armed forces. In 1974 black volunteers were permitted to carry arms. This was an early indication that aspects of apartheid might be subjected to piecemeal challenges from within the state apparatus. Indeed, it was increasingly realized how dependent the apparatus of government had become on its black components.

> The core state remained dominated by Afrikaners, but the extended state with its black bureaucrats and policemen was a multi-racial one which the Afrikaners could not control by pretending to be a people apart or refusing forever to share power.[13]

It was increasingly evident that Bantu education, designed to keep Blacks out of white preserves, had now become a danger to the very values which it had been designed to protect. Now, when the black man was needed, he was not there. South Africa possessed the highly unstable combination of a first-world infrastructure and a third-world labour force.

The beginning of Botha's premiership seemed to point to a new departure in official thinking. *Apartheid* itself seemed to be rejected; Botha himself referred to it as a recipe for continual confrontation and warned the National Party that it must 'adapt or perish'. However, this was rather a matter of semantics than of reality. There was talk of 'multi-nationalism', of South Africa as a country composed of minorities, of the scrapping of what was rather oddly described as 'unnecessary discrimination', and of a future 'constellation' of South African states (which entailed the promotion of the 'homelands' to national status). He was the first prime minister to visit Soweto. There remained, however, the matter of the Cape Coloured people and the South African Indians, for whom there was no possible territorial sovereignty. What Botha was doing was searching for new collaborators without conceding the principle of white rule. In this he was following the direction of thought in the 'enlightened' section of the National Party, which had for some time been discussing alternative constitutional forms to the Westminster model of parliamentary government which entailed the principle of majority rule. This, it was now contended, was unsuitable for a country in which no majority existed, but only blocks of minorities. Proposals for a new constitution were tinctured by ideas of 'consociational democracy', through which a universal franchise could be combined with the rejection of majority rule. The work of Arend Lijphart seems to have been particularly influential. In his book, *Power Sharing in South Africa* (published in 1985, after the new constitution had come into force) Lijphart set out the 'four basic elements' of consociational democracy: executive power-sharing among representatives of all significant groups; a high degree of internal autonomy for these groups; proportional representation to be applied to the distribution of seats in the legislative assembly, positions in the public service and the allocation of public funds; and, finally, the granting of a veto on vital issues to each minority group. All this, it was claimed, would lead to consensus rather than adversarial politics. What it lacked was a body of experience from countries where it had previously been practised; Lijphart could cite only the Lebanon between 1943 and 1975, which was not everyone's idea of an encouraging precedent.

The movement towards constitutional change provoked the most serious splits within the ranks of Afrikanerdom since the Second World War. The point at issue was whether there should be an attempt to win collaboration from the Cape Coloured and Indian people within a new structure of government. What P. W. Botha referred to as 'a healthy form' of power sharing was rejected by a faction within the party, led by Andries Treurnicht, as a betrayal of Nationalist principles. A complicated struggle ended with the expulsion of Treurnicht and his followers from the party; their response was to form themselves into a new Conservative Party, which claimed to have widespread support and to represent the convictions of 'right-thinking' Arikaners who had not been led astray by 'liberalistic' heresies. Conflict and controversy were compounded by the appearance of a paramilitary organization, led by a former policeman named Eugene Terreblanche, which called itself the Afrikaner Weerstandsbeweging (the Afrikaner Resistance Movement). It adopted Nazi-style regalia, including banners with swastika-like insignia formed of combinations of the figure 7 (declared by Terreblanche to be a Christian symbol) and announced its

PLATE 19. *E. Terreblanche addressing his supporters, 23 April 1994* (Courtesy of Popperfoto).

intention of fighting for an independent 'people's state' when the time was ripe.

This time, however, the National Party was not deterred by the appearance of these formidable enemies on its right. A new constitution, which abandoned the Westminster model, came into being, ratified by a majority of two-thirds in a referendum put to the white electorate. There was now to be an executive president, chosen by an electoral college for a seven-year term; there would be a multiracial cabinet, responsible to him; and a tricameral parliament, consisting of a House of Assembly for Whites, a House of Representatives for the Cape Coloured people, and a House of Delegates for Indians, each house to be elected by voters on separate ethnic rolls and each to control its own affairs (such as education, health and community administration). It was evident to all but the simple-minded that effective power sharing would be minimal: executive power would lie with the State President, and legislative power with the white House of Assembly. There was no place in this scheme for Africans; it was hoped that they would be placated by the attractions of the 'national states' for those in tribal areas and by municipal self-government under the Black Local Government Act of 1983 for the townships.

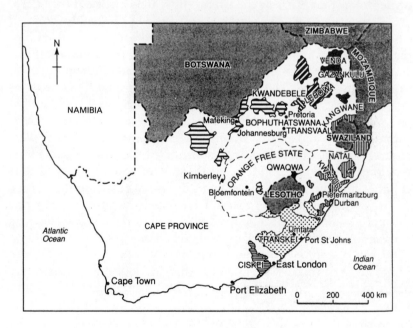

MAP 2. *The Bantustans (Homelands), 1987.*

(The substitution of 'Black' for 'Bantu' in legislation referring to Africans was a significant shift of language.)

It was soon clear that ethnic representation without effective power would not be enough to satisfy those whom it was intended to appease. The forced removals of peoples under the Group Areas Acts was evidence that the Government had no intention of abandoning the essential elements of 'grand *apartheid*'. Instead of reconciliation, the Government found itself opposed by new extra-parliamentary organizations, the most important of which were the United Democratic Front and the (black) Congress of South African Trade Unions. The United Democratic Front claimed to speak for over 500 organizations. It was too diffuse in its membership to have any coherent aim other than opposition to the existing regime and rejection of its constitutional arrangements. There was, however, considerable potential for industrial action in the trade unions, where Cyril Ramaphosa, leader of the black National Union of Mine Workers, was demonstrating sophisticated talents of leadership.

Chronic political violence became acute in 1985 after police in the Eastern Cape Province opened fire on a funeral procession that they regarded as menacing; it was not clear whether the security authorities knew that this was the twenty-fifth anniversary of the Sharpeville shootings of 21 March 1960, a day of highly charged emotions for Africans. The incident touched off a cycle of killings that spread throughout the country, provoking the declaration of a state of emergency which continued, with some interruptions, for the next five years. This time the African National Congress was able to operate close to South Africa's borders, well within what had once been a cordon of buffer states. It issued instructions to its supporters to make the townships ungovernable. There were attacks on the homes and persons of black town councillors, municipal policemen, and on all those who could be regarded as collaborators with the Government. Lynch law came to the streets, with or without the interposition of 'people's courts'. A horrible form of popular execution appeared, called 'necklacing' – placing a rubber tyre around the neck of the living victim and setting it alight. (This received an endorsement from Mrs Winnie Mandela, Nelson Mandela's estranged wife, in words that are not easy to forget: 'We are going to dismantle *apartheid* ourselves. That programme will be brought to you by the African National Congress. Together, hand in hand, with that stick of matches, with our necklace, we shall liberate the country.') As in Soweto in 1976, radicalized and violent children played a significant part in street-fighting. School buildings became prime targets for fire raisers – over 920 were destroyed or damaged between September 1984 and December 1985, along with over 2,500 private houses, 33 churches, 639 shops and more than 10,000 buses and cars.[14] The damage to property within the townships was estimated at over 100 million rands. According to *The Times* of 20 December 1985 there had been 965 political killings in the past fifteen months, about half of them through police action, the other half as a result of black feuds and assassinations.

One journalist expressed an all-too-justified fear of 'a hideous human harvest in the children who have grown up with this limitless violence around them'.[15] That harvest was already being gathered in, for children themselves were responsible for some of the violence and it seemed that the townships were breeding a generation that would be both lawless and unlettered; the slogan appeared: 'Liberation before education'. One of the child heroes of the liberatory movement was Stompie Moketsi, who at the age of thirteen had become the 'general' of a guerrilla army of 1,500, all of them under fourteen; the youngest was said to be eight. They fought battles with the municipal police and with right-wing vigilantes (who were believed, with justification, to have the backing of the South African Police).

Under the state of emergency the Government used to the full its powers of detention without trial and deployed both police and troops in strength. Murder and arson in the townships was compounded by the African National Congress's campaign of bombings: the Institute of Strategic Studies of Pretoria University calculated that there had been 398 incidents of what it termed 'guerrilla warfare' since 1976, 136 of them in 1985. The South African Defence Force made retaliatory raids on suspected bases in neighbouring countries. These had little discernible effect on the level of African National Congress action but they added to the chorus of international condemnation. Thus far South Africa had not had to face the effect of mandatory sanctions, in spite of the activities of the network of anti-apartheid movements abroad fortified by support by black leaders at home, but the inward flow of capital was contracting. The word 'disinvestment' entered the vocabulary of politics as foreign firms disposed of their South African assets, often as a result of pressure from their own shareholders. Among Commonwealth countries only Mrs Thatcher's Government in the United Kingdom stood out against comprehensive economic action, holding that it would be of no benefit to anyone if the South African economy were destroyed and that to treat white South Africans as pariahs was no way to persuade them to come to terms with their black fellow-countrymen. None the less, those with capital to spare had come to regard South Africa as an investment zone that had moved from one of moderate risk to high risk and might soon move again to prohibitive risk. In spite of restrictions on the reporting of unrest, television screens all over the world showed pictures of the aftermath of bloody conflict in townships and the deployment of troops and armed police in warlike vehicles. The black, green and gold flags of the banned African National Congress were flaunted at political funerals which had now taken the place of illegal rallies. Demands increased for the release of Nelson Mandela, by now probably the most celebrated political prisoner in the world. In 1985 Mandela was diagnosed as suffering from tuberculosis and was moved from the bleak confines of Robben Island to a prison hospital on the mainland. There were many who warned of the catastrophic consequences if Mandela were allowed to die in custody. P. W. Botha reiterated that there could be no negotiations with the African National Congress until it had repudiated violence; the reply was that violence would not be repudiated until the apparatus of *apartheid* had been dismantled and the Government had committed itself to elections under universal suffrage. Deadlock seemed complete.

However, public expectations were whetted by reports that P. W. Botha was contemplating a change of policy, to be announced at a speech which he was due to make to a National Party conference on 15 August 1985. That may have been Botha's first intention; a draft of the original speech which came into the hands of journalists hinted at the release of Mandela and announced that South Africa had 'crossed the Rubicon' on the way to a programme of 'cooperation and co-responsibility' on the principle 'that all our population groups must be jointly responsible for decision-making at all levels of government in matters of common concern, without domination by any one population group over another.'[16] That speech was never delivered; Botha either had second thoughts, or was deterred by right-wingers within his own entourage who warned him that he was inviting desertions to the Conservative Party: Nationalists could no longer avoid the existence of political enemies on their right, but they need not act as their recruiting agents. Instead, Botha said that he was 'not prepared to lead white South Africans and other minority groups on a road to abdication and suicide'.

This defiance was received with dismay by such friends as the South African Government still possessed, and with a certain grim satisfaction by its enemies: it had shown itself, finally it seemed, to be immune to argument. International confidence plunged further downwards. The value of the rand was nearly halved against European currencies. Bankers refused to renew South African loans. (There was a moratorium on repayments, which lasted for four months.) The European Community banned new investment and various South African imports; the Scandinavian countries restricted trade; and the United States Congress enacted the Comprehensive Anti-Apartheid Act of 1986. Botha had dared the world to do its damnedest, and much of the world had taken him at his word; he now turned to repression. The national state of emergency, which had been briefly lifted, was reimposed. Nearly 1,000 people died in political violence in 1986, over 20,000 were detained, and there were about two hundred guerrilla attacks by Umkhonto we Sizwe, the military arm of the African National Congress. Botha was unrepentant about the stand of the National Party *contra mundum*. South Africa, he said, was where the first and third worlds met, 'where the historical hatred of the third world, and the historical guilt complex of the first world, interface in the vendetta against South Africa. Our unity must not be sacrificed for the sake of a discordant world.'[17] Those who had argued that sanctions would merely harden white intransigence saw their warnings come true when the Conservative Party, fighting its first election, won twenty-two seats on a platform attacking the Government for being soft on terrorism and became the official Opposition. The National Party had lost seats but still had a comfortable majority; it had 52 per cent of the popular vote, but it was ominous for the unity of Afrikanerdom that the Conservatives had 26 per cent. The Conservative temper was shown when it captured several municipal councils; in Boksburg, on the East Rand, it attempted to reimpose petty *apartheid* in all its former rigour. The council changed its mind after a well-organized African boycott had impoverished shopkeepers as well as holding the town to ridicule.

How coercive was the imposition of sanctions likely to be? Those who thought that this, unaided, would bring down the Government were pleasuring themselves with wishful thinking. For one thing, sanctions would never be complete: South Africa was linked to the world economy through dozens of countries and thousands of connections. It would require a common will, a disposition towards sacrifice and an extraordinary exercise of co-ordination among many states and a myriad corporations to cut off South Africa's links with the wider world. What sanctions could and did do were to contract those links and weaken export markets, with consequent effects on the balance of payments. On the other hand, some who clamoured loudly for others to take punitive action were open to the charge that their behaviour did not match their rhetoric; the so-called 'front-line states' on South Africa's borders, whatever their leaders might say for public consumption, were often only too glad to retain trading links that were essential to their own well-being, if not to their viability. What was more damaging was the shortage of capital and the extreme difficulty of raising loans in the international money markets in consequence of a loss of confidence in South Africa's stability.

Here were the outlines of a vicious circle. Some, at least, of the unrest in the black townships and in the squatter camps that grew up around them could be traced to poverty, to unemployment, overcrowding and the effects of inflation. Miserable living conditions increased the willingness to listen to calls for action in the streets. Township unrest, especially when the police responded in heavy-handed fashion, fortified perceptions abroad of instability at home. The main threat came from the slow starvation of the economy. But however bleak the economic outlook, there was no chance that the South African regime could be overthrown from within. Those who believed that mass action might have the same effect in South Africa as in Eastern Europe were deceiving themselves. A comparison with the Chinese reaction to events in Tiananmen Square would have been more appropriate. The essential point was that the army and the police were strong enough, in capacity and determination, to subdue any mass action that they were likely to encounter. Indeed, there were some who thought that danger to the Government lay in another direction altogether – that the security apparatus had become a political force in its own right, independent of the authority of the Cabinet. This, if true, was an unforeseen consequence of President Botha's 'total strategy'. Investigative reporters revealed the existence, for example, of the Civilian Co-operation Bureau, a mildly-named organization which appeared to be immune to civilian control as it operated in the shadows against those whom it deemed to be the enemies of *apartheid*, in and out of South Africa.

In September 1985, too late to stem the avalanche of international condemnation, Botha said: 'I finally confirm that my party and I are committed to the principle of a united South Africa, one citizenship, and a universal franchise.' He was speaking in code: universal franchise did not mean that each vote would have an equal value. Botha was still hopeful of gaining acceptance for some scheme that would give Blacks the sensations of self-government while retaining the essentials of power in white hands, probably by means of group representation and the retention of a minority veto. But the reference to a single citizenship suggested a change of policy towards those who lived 'outside the national states'. This in itself was an admission of the failure of *apartheid*. F. W. de Klerk, who had been the National Party's leader in the Transvaal since the departure of Treurnicht in 1982, said in 1987:

> The denial of a political power base to the ten million blacks who live outside the national states will drive those who seek political change into the hands of revolutionaries . . . There are blacks who have been living in South Africa all their lives, and they and their children will remain here . . . They cannot stay in South Africa, year after year, without political representation.[18]

But what sort of political representation? The device of elected municipal councils had failed because militants had destroyed them by force; it was a brave candidate indeed who would take office and thus risk the burning of his house or, it might be, himself. African National Congress symbols were to be seen everywhere in the townships, illegal though it was to display them under the banning regulations. The Congress itself was beginning to take on the air of a government in exile – not surprisingly, considering the number of eminent South Africans who were now visiting its representatives abroad to try to find common ground for what would amount to a peace treaty. The African National Congress not only had international sympathy; it also believed that time was on its side. Officially, the Government disapproved of the 'Lusaka trek', as these visits came to be called. The National Party already had a formidable rival to its right; there was now some evidence of disintegration on the left, with the resignation from the party of two highly respected professors of Stellenbosch University. In 1988 a group of Afrikaner liberals travelled to West Germany to meet Congress representatives. In 1988 Botha himself visited Mozambique, Zaire, Malawi and the Ivory Coast, with little discernible result. At the same time, in another change of direction, he authorized private discussions with Mandela, now recovered but still under restraint, although now accommodated in comfort in a house within the precincts of a Cape Town prison. Mandela himself had no doubt about the part which P. W. Botha had played in his eventual release.

Indeed, considering his experiences, he showed an astonishing lack of bitterness. When, in 1990, he was asked by a reporter from an Afrikaans newspaper what he thought about Afrikaners, he replied: 'For the past three years I have been negotiating with Afrikaners. The progress that has been made so far has been with Afrikaners. That is sufficient comment on what I think of them.'[19]

Botha was not a man to run ahead of opinion within the governing circles of the National Party; talks with Mandela meant that he and his intimate colleagues had made up their minds that the exclusion of Blacks from the political process was no longer in the interests of white survival. Discussion papers circulated by the Broederbond by 1989 were suggesting that there might be a black head of government in the near future and that this would be acceptable provided that a new constitutional system was in place which guaranteed the political rights of minorities – universal suffrage without majority rule. The test of acceptibility of a new constitution might be: 'what will be in the interests of Afrikaners in the event that we end up in the opposition seat?'[20]

Thus plans were being made behind the scenes for another change in direction on the Afrikaner's long trek in search of survival. This change appeared the more dramatic since it was implemented under a new leader. In January 1989 P. W. Botha suffered a mild stroke. It was not enough to incapacitate him, but he thought it prudent to resign from the leadership of the Party. There was a disputed election, which F. W. de Klerk won in the end by a margin of eight votes. But Botha retained the office of state president and made it clear that he would expect to lead the government into the general election, which was necessary that year under the constitution of the tricameral parliament. This was too much for his followers, and after a brief and angry confrontation Botha resigned with an ill grace, and de Klerk became acting state president.

The general election of 1989 to the white House of Assembly was a lively affair in which both the Democratic Party (a development of the old Progressive Party, now fortified with new allies) and the Conservative Party had high hopes of cutting into the National Party's majority. In the event the Nationalists lost twenty-seven seats, sixteen to the Conservatives and eleven to the Democrats. Their own numbers came down to ninety-four, a sufficient majority for the time being although they had been warned that there was stormy weather ahead; the Conservatives had increased their percentage of the Afrikaner vote from the twenty-six of the election of 1987 to something like forty, and still seemed to be on an upward curve. If de Klerk were to lead his party into the ways of radical reform, the sooner he acted the safer he was likely to be.

Frederik Willem de Klerk was fifty-three when he was elected State President in his own right in September 1989. Thus he was twenty years younger than Botha. Nothing in his previous career had marked him out as a man of radical sentiments. His reputation was that of a genial and courteous party *apparatchik* of moderate abilities. He was a member of the Doppers, the most conservative of the Afrikaans churches; he had opposed integrated sport, mixed marriages and black trade unions; he had castigated English universities for liberalism. There was, therefore, no forewarning of the dramatic events of his first few months in power. By the end of the year the first steps had been taken both to repeal laws enforcing *apartheid* and to dismantle the National Security Management System which Botha had elevated to a position scarcely inferior to that of the Cabinet. Walter Sisulu and other survivors of the sentences of life imprisonment passed in 1964 were released unconditionally from Robben Island. In February 1990 de Klerk ended the restrictions on the African National Congress, the South African Communist Party, the Pan African Congress and all other banned organizations. On 11 February 1990 Nelson Mandela was unconditionally released from prison.

It was pardonable for the African National Congress to claim that these momentous actions were the fruits of their victory in the armed struggle. But this was too simple an explanation for the complicated events which had induced the National Party to take this leap in the dark: rulers are not often induced to change deeply ingrained attitudes by sporadic bomb explosions, nor by popular demonstrations, and still less by barricades and 'no-go' areas in places which are indifferent to national administration. National party intellectuals had, for some time, been discussing different modes of survival in a changing society. De Klerk, then, was not a lone pioneer; he would not have carried his party with him if he had been. He was moving with the grain of opinion. As a prudent politician, he acted swiftly, in the honeymoon period immediately after his election to the presidency. P. W. Botha's attempts at winning the hearts and minds of his opponents had clearly failed; there were no significant collaborators to be had – even black recruitment to the Defence Force, for instance, had practically ceased. It was evident that Blacks would negotiate only through their own leaders, and that meant talking to the African National Congress. A glance at demographic trends was enough to show that time was on the side of the Blacks; if that were so, then there was no point in watching the economy crumble into ruin merely to delay the inevitable. If bargaining there must be, it was in the interests of the National Party that it should begin at once. De Klerk was quoted in *Die Burger* of 31 March 1991 as saying: 'We have not waited until the position of power dominance turned against us, before we decided to negotiate a peaceful settlement.' It was clear that economic stagnation would need a political dimension in its relief. International assistance would not be forthcoming until South Africa's Government had been recognized as legitimate. That meant that the structure of *apartheid* must go, bag and baggage, by whatever name it had been known – the Department of Native Affairs, or Bantu Administration, or Plural Relations, or Co-operation and Development. The Government had repeatedly asserted that it would never deal with terrorists and that the African National Congress must repudiate the armed struggle before negotiations could begin. It was now prepared to accept a general commitment to a search for peace instead of a specific assurance, and it could find some justification for its change of attitude in events in Eastern Europe; with the collapse of communist regimes there it could be argued that, despite its alliance with the South African Communist Party, the African National Congress was no longer an agent of the Soviet Union.

In 1991 the last remnants of *apartheid* were legislated out of existence with the repeal of the Group Areas, Land and Population Acts. Exiles came back from their refuges abroad; what was said to be the largest crowd ever assembled at Jan Smuts Airport welcomed the return of the ailing Oliver Tambo, President of the African National Congress. But it was evident that it was Mandela who was the hero of the hour, and he received royal receptions as he travelled abroad, ostensibly to thank those who had helped his movement. Meanwhile, there was high euphoria as South Africa was welcomed back into the comity of nations. South African athletes were invited once more to the Olympic Games; South African cricketers were for the first time ever playing in India; the All Blacks of New Zealand were seen once more on the rugby fields of Ellis Park and Newlands. Some sanctions were lifted at once, and there was a loan of 850,000 rands from German banks. The National Party threw open its membership to men and women of all races. This was loathsome enough to the extreme right, and the Conservative Party showed its strength when it beat the National Party candidate at a by-election at Potchefstroom. But this was a

Pyrrhic victory, for de Klerk retaliated at once by calling a referendum of the white electorate, asking for a simple yes or no to the question whether the process of reform should continue. On this issue de Klerk believed that he could count on the votes of most of the English electorate – a novel dependence for a Nationalist politician. He was right; the result was a majority of two to one for reform, and de Klerk could now argue that he had a popular mandate behind him.

Twenty organizations sent representatives to the Convention for a Democratic South Africa (CODESA) which began what became a seemingly interminable set of meetings in the World Trade Centre at Kempton Park, near Johannesburg. Those who hoped for a speedy outcome were disappointed. De Klerk had begun a process which neither he nor anybody else could fully control. Tragically, so far from passing into a period of peace, South Africa now entered the most murderous period in her peacetime history.

Prophecies of a blood bath had long been part of the rhetoric of South Africa's critics. The prophecy now became reality; but what was unexpected was that most of the victims were Blacks killed by other Blacks. The reasons were complex but they included tribal feuds. The bitterest conflicts occurred where Zulus were concerned, either between Chief Buthelezi's Inkatha movement and African National Congress supporters in Natal, or in the townships of the Witwatersrand where Zulus living in the hostels for single men moved into the streets to kill Xhosas or anyone else who looked like an enemy. This hostility had existed for generations, but it took on a new edge at the prospect of non-racial elections as both the African National Congress and its opponents jockeyed for position. Zulus feared to be at the mercy of a Xhosa-dominated legislature. Buthelezi may well have wished to demonstrate the strength of his own following, to support claims for self-determination for the Zulu homeland. But there was a still more sinister side to the killings – the suspicion that a 'third force' was at work, drawn from the official security services which supported Inkatha with money and weapons and protected its members from reprisals by those whom they attacked. Evidence of this was revealed by a Commission of Inquiry under Mr Justice Goldstone which, unlike some other commissions, was bold enough to dig beneath the surface of public scandal rather than skate over it. It is not clear whether President de Klerk was responsible for what the press called 'Inkathagate'; there were those who thought that the security services were displaying an independence that could be checked only by a

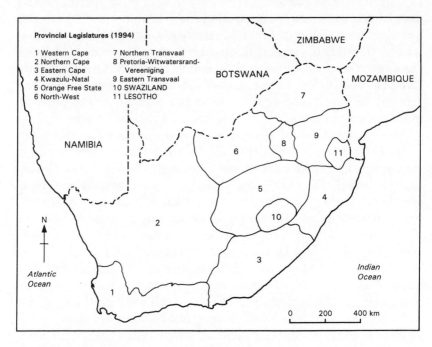

Provincial Legislatures (1994)

1 Western Cape
2 Northern Cape
3 Eastern Cape
4 Kwazulu-Natal
5 Orange Free State
6 North-West

7 Northern Transvaal
8 Pretoria-Witwatersrand-
   Vereeniging
9 Eastern Transvaal
10 SWAZILAND
11 LESOTHO

ZIMBABWE

BOTSWANA

MOZAMBIQUE

NAMIBIA

Atlantic
Ocean

Indian
Ocean

N

0   200   400 km

MAP 3. *Provincial Legislatures, 1994.*

purge of their leadership, which de Klerk dared not risk lest he lose control completely.

The National Party was not, at first, looking for quick agreement with the African National Congress. It was no simple matter to negotiate away a system of white supremacy which had lasted for nearly three and a half centuries. It was clear enough that both sides would have to retreat from their original positions since neither had the naked strength to subdue the other. The African National Congress was not going to get agreement on a prompt and complete transfer of power under majority rule; the National Party was not going to get agreement on 'consociational democracy' with majorities negated by minority vetoes. At first, the National Party seems to have thought that it need not necessarily be in the minority at all, that it might actually win an election if it had time enough to build up a coalition – the English, Zulus, Indians and Cape Colour-eds, and some at least of the Conservative deserters – while discre-diting the African National Congress and retaining control of the South African Broadcasting Corporation. Meanwhile, the killings continued; 1992 was the worst year of all, when three and a half thousand people died, mostly in fighting between Inkatha and supporters of the African National Congress. In the middle of 1992 constitutional negotiations broke down and the Congress then turned to what it called 'rolling mass action' – strikes, boycotts, 'stayaways' (a form of passive resistance in which Africans simply did not turn up for work), meetings and demonstrations. The *toyi-toyi*, a sort of shuffling war-dance, became a familiar feature of African gatherings. Meanwhile the Afrikaner Weerstandsbeweging was threatening to begin a civil war if it were not granted a *volkstaat* for Afrikaners, in which Blacks would have no political rights. The Pan African Congress was ploughing a deadly furrow of its own, with the slogan 'one settler, one bullet'. There were repeated scenes of disorder in the House of Assembly, where Conservatives denounced de Klerk as the 'hangman of the Afrikaner' and the National Party as traitors to the people and (more obscurely) betrayers of the Covenant of Blood River. All this was a display of bare hatred that went well beyond the habitual abuse that characterized South African debate.

De Klerk's parliamentary following held together, fortified by their leader's assurance that there would be no more general elections under the existing dispensation, so that they no longer need fear the wrath of their constituents. But what was happening in Parliament became less and less significant. In September 1992 it seemed that the African National Congress's programme of mass action might provoke civil war. A 'peaceful' march on Bisho, the capital of the Ciskei homeland, was fired on by Ciskei troops, with loss of life. Worse would certainly have followed if plans had been executed for a march on Ulundi, the capital of Zululand. What brought the Congress back to the negotiating table was a sombre confidential report made to their leaders by the Minister of Finance, which showed just how precarious was the state of the economy. By this time the African National Congress had supreme confidence in its ability to win an election; it had no wish to inherit an empty exchequer.

Public confidence revived with the resumption of negotiations, which now took a new turn: it seemed that the Government and the African National Congress would seek for agreement between themselves, with the other parties to be faced with the accomplished fact. It was now clear to the National Party that whatever chances the prestige of de Klerk might once have had of attracting black support no longer existed and that the danger was that its own core support might disintegrate. It seemed possible for a while that there might be an alliance between Inkatha, the leaders of the homeland and the white movements of the extreme right, on the basis of a common distaste for subordination within a unitary state and a consequent demand for some form of self-determination. The most important element of the Afrikaner right wing consisted of the Conservative Party, the neo-Nazi Afrikaner Weerstandsbeweging, and a loose gathering of individuals and groups that looked for leadership to General Constand Viljoen. He was a highly respected soldier, formerly chief of staff of the South African army, who at one time had the backing of over fifty retired generals of the security forces. What the right lacked was coherence and, it became evident, discipline. There were ugly scenes when cohorts of the Afrikaner Weerstandsbeweging forced their way into the World Trade Centre, having used an armoured car to break through the plate-glass doors. They terrified the staff and uttered threats; but no lives were lost. But in April 1993 there was a major crisis when Chris Hani was murdered outside his house on the East Rand. Hani had been both a leader both of Umkhonto we Sizwe and of the South African Communist Party; he was also a man of great influence with the youth of the townships, and there was evidence that, whatever threats he had uttered during his warlike past, he was now committed to a constitutional settlement. For a moment the country seemed likely to plunge still deeper into violence. The murder certainly brought a new sense of urgency to the negotia-

PLATE 20. *Voters in Milnerton queueing to cast their vote in the first all race democratic elections, 28 April 1994* (Courtesy of Popperfoto).

PLATE 21. *South African President Nelson Mandela and Second Deputy President F.W. de Klerk hold their hands high as they address a huge crowd of people in front of the Union Building after the Inauguration ceremony, 10 May 1994* (Courtesy of Popperfoto).

tions. By the middle of 1993 it had been agreed that there would be a election on 27 April 1994.

Most of the concessions in the end had been made by the National Party. There would be a National Assembly of 400, elected for five years by proportional representation; there would be nine provinces instead of the existing four, with ten senators from each. The two houses together would form a constituent assembly, charged with the task of drawing up a definitive constitution. In the meantime there would be be an executive president, two deputy presidents and a composite cabinet drawn, in proportion to their electoral strength, from those parties which had polled more than 5 per cent of the popular vote. A vote of two-thirds of the members of the National Assembly would be needed for changes to the provisional constitution. Otherwise there were no political guarantees for minorities; but there would be a constitutional court, somewhat on the French model, to which appeal might be made.

The announcement of the election date was greeted with relief by most of the English. Since they had voted in the referendum they had been on the sidelines of politics, looking on events with anxious apathy. There had been remarkably few Whites killed; but what was now evident was the lack of confidence in their personal safety, not because of the violence of politics but because of the deluge of crime that had lapped over the white suburbs, where elegant houses were now protected by barricades of razor wire, electronically controlled gates and prowling guard- dogs, and patrolled by private security firms promising 'immediate armed response'. It was not only the Afrikaners who now possessed the *laager* mentality. Many of the English community were quietly making plans to emigrate – no easy task, considering the diminished value of the rand and official barriers to the export of private capital.

As the election approached there was little doubt, on all sides, that Nelson Mandela would be the first president of the new South Africa. At the end of 1993 he and de Klerk were jointly awarded the Nobel Peace Prize. There were those who thought this gesture of international confidence to be premature. The leaders of the homelands, the Conservative Party, the Afrikaner Weerstandsbeweging and the medley of organizations that called themselves the Afrikaner Volksfront all announced their intention of boycotting the election; there were muffled threats that some extremists would disrupt the whole process. There were rumours of bombings to come and terrorists of the far right opening fire on election queues from speeding cars. What, though, would happen if there were massive abstentions – by the Zulu millions who supported Inkatha and by the Conservative Party and its allies? What if they refused to abide by the result of the ballot? Would those Afrikaners of the far right who declared that they would fight rather than submit to black rule be as good as their word? Would Inkatha submit to a government led by Xhosas? Would the election see the end of political violence, or would it be the prelude to something worse?

In the last days of the old South Africa it was evident how much depended on the actions of individuals. There were no immediate substitutes, in 1994, for Nelson Mandela and F. W. de Klerk. One might say, too, that there were no substitutes for Chief Buthelezi and General Viljoen. At almost the eleventh hour Viljoen broke with the extremists on his right and registered his own party, which he now called the Freedom Front, as an electoral contender. Buthelezi waited much longer, indeed until fighting in Natal had reached a pitch that justified the imposition of a state of emergency. Then, and only then, did Buthelezi announce that the 'Inkatha Freedom Party' would offer itself to the electorate. The official date of registration had passed; the ballot papers had been printed without the new party, so that stickers had now to be printed in haste and glued to the end of a ballot paper that was already of formidable length; Buthelezi's party was the nineteenth to register.

What characterized the election was not violence but inefficiency and malpractices that would certainly not have been tolerated by the international observers had they occurred in their own countries. Arrangements were in the hands, not of the Government, but of an independent electoral commission which had hugely underestimated the task before it. There were polling stations that failed to open, electoral officers who did not turn up, stocks of ballot papers that ran out and ballot boxes which, when opened, showed bundles of completed papers neatly stacked and showing a remarkable unanimity of voter-sentiment. De Klerk, in what was one of the last acts of his state presidency, declared a public holiday to give an extra day of polling. Yet, notwithstanding the chaos, at the end of the process all serious contenders agreed to accept the published figures as definitive. If there was a miracle, this was it.

In all, 19.5 million votes were cast. Only seven parties polled sufficient votes to gain seats in the Assembly (see **Table 1**).

	Votes	*Percentage*	*Seats*
African National Congress	12.3 m	62.65	252
National Party	3.9 m	20.39	82
Inkatha Freedom Party	2 m	10.54	43
Freedom Front	425,000	2.17	9
Democratic Party	338,000	1.73	7
Pan African Congress	243,000	1.25	5
African Christian Democratic Party	88,000	0.45	2

Table 1. Voting Figures for parties elected to the Assembly, 27 April 1994

In the simultaneous elections for the provincial legislatures the African National Congress won in six and shared in the control of one; the Inkatha Freedom Party won in Kwa-Zulu-Natal, and the National Party won in the Western Cape, where it picked up most of the Cape Coloured vote.

Mandela was elected as Executive State President, with F. W. de Klerk and Thabo Mbeki (of the African National Congress) as Deputy Executive State Presidents. Mandela's cabinet of twenty- seven was made up of eighteen members of the African National Congress, three from the National Party and one from the Inkatha Freedom Party.

In May 1994 the 'new South Africa' formally came into existence. Before the year was out, South Africa had been readmitted to the Commonwealth.

EPILOGUE

One election does not create a new society, and the multi-racial government that took office in South Africa in 1994 was confronted with colossal difficulties of transition and adjustment. Among them were the conflicting claims of social justice, which would entail massive redistributions of wealth, and the need to maintain an economy which would attract the foreign capital denied to the previous regime by reason of its racial policies. The first of these requirements pointed to the rapid absorption of Blacks into the structures of government, industry and business, entailing a high degree of positive discrimination; the second suggested a slower process during which white experts would still be needed in most of the higher positions until enough Blacks had acquired the skills and experience to replace them on merit. Meanwhile the African National Congress, as the majority party, would be under pressure from those of its own supporters who had been encouraged to believe that to the victors belonged the spoils. The government produced by the election of 1994 would remain in power for five years, during which it would not only have to govern but also to direct a constituent assembly charged with drafting a definitive constitution. One of its immediate concerns would be the creation of new security forces, which meant the transformation of those who had been trained as guerrilla fighters into keepers of the peace, who in their new capacity would be confronted by widespread lawlessness, especially among the radical black youths of the townships, exacerbated in all probability by the opportunities which the new South Africa would offer to domestic and foreign drug pedlars. Moreover, with an executive state president well into his seventies, the problem of the succession would present new strains and open the way to discordant ambitions. Most important of all, South

Africa's new rulers would have the gigantic task of changing the attitudes towards authority of the majority of the people and persuading them now to regard as legitimate the authority of government.

The election of 1994 demoted the Afrikaner Volk, at a stroke, to a permanent political minority. As a governing class, it seemed now to be confined to the Western Cape, the area where Jan van Riebeeck had established the first settlement.

In 1990 the National Party had presented to the world the rare spectacle of a governing class deliberately voting itself out of power. The underlying motive, it has been suggested in this book, was that its leaders considered that this, paradoxically, gave the Afrikaner people their best chance of survival. They were able to carry out their purpose because of the ingrained loyalty of the majority of the Volk and their willingness to follow their leaders, even down strange and perilous paths which seemed to take them away from all their previous traditions.

Those who had studied the Afrikaner past might have reflected that this was a repetition, in new circumstances, of an old choice. At the deliberations in Vereeniging in 1902 the Boer commandos had been required to choose between the bitter-enders' demand that the war should be continued, no matter at what sacrifice, and those, like Botha and Smuts, who had argued that for the sake of the future of their people the time had come to make terms. 'We must not', Smuts had then said, 'sacrifice the nation itself on the altar of independence.' In those words Smuts had repudiated the tradition of Kruger.

One might carry the analogy further. Botha and Smuts after the Peace of Vereeniging, were faced with the task of mending the broken unity of the Boer people and bringing back into the fold those false brethren reviled as 'hands-uppers' and traitors to the *Volk*. De Klerk in 1994 likewise faced the problem of healing the *broedertwis* and restoring the unity between his own followers and those who had called him the hangman of his people. It would be tempting to argue that the Afrikaner was now faced with a choice between the spirit of the old Cape tradition of 'liberalism' and the spirit of Kruger's insistence on the racial exclusiveness of a people determined to fight for the independence which they had so hardly won. The murder, in November 1994, of Professor Johan Heyns, an anti-apartheid Afrikaans theologian, bore an ominous resemblance to the assassination of those in Weimar Germany who were held to be responsible for the mythical 'stab in the back'.

The National Party could claim, with some justice, that the election results of 1994 had shown that it was the most representative party of them all. It had brought in the Cape Coloured people, some at least of the Indians, probably the majority of the English and perhaps some Blacks as well. It was not, then, beyond the bounds of possibility that it would never be relegated to an insignificant minority, but would remain a force, within a democratic system, strong enough to preserve its language and at least some of its traditions. The hope remained. What would matter in the future was whether the majority of 'new South Africans' would be ready to forgive what *apartheid* had done to them and their forebears and whether Mandela's successors would show the same magnanimity as he had demonstrated.

NOTES

CHAPTER 1

1 Quoted in I. D. MacCrone, *Race Attitudes in South Africa* (Oxford, 1937), p. 11.
2 Ibid., p. 13, n. 2.
3 Ibid., p. 16.
4 Ibid., pp. 17–18.
5 Ibid., p. 19.
6 Genesis, 9: 25.
7 MacCrone, *Race Attitudes*, p. 43.
8 George M. Fredrickson, *White Supremacy. A Comparative Study in American and South African History* (Oxford University Press, New York, 1981), p. 93.
9 J. S. Marais, *The Cape Coloured People* (London, 1939), p. 3.
10 Ibid., p. 1.
11 R. Elphick and H. Giliomee (eds), *The Shaping of South African Society, 1652–1820* (Cape Town, 1979), p. 131.
12 Andrew Sparrman, *A Voyage to the Cape of Good Hope*, Vol. 1 (London, 1786), p. 12.
13 John Buchan, *The African Colony* (London, 1903), p. 60.
14 Quoted in MacCrone, *Race Attitudes*, p. 48, n. 2.
15 W. K. Hancock, *Survey of British Commonwealth Affairs*, Vol. 2, p. 2 (Oxford University Press, Oxford, 1942), p. 21.
16 E. G. Malherbe, *Education in South Africa*, Vol. 1 (Cape Town, 1925), *passim*.
17 Quoted in MacCrone, *Race Attitudes*, p. 69.

CHAPTER 2

1 James Bryce, *Impressions of South Africa* (London, 1897), p. 9.
2 Marq de Villiers, *White Tribe Dreaming* (London, 1988), p. 176.

3 Monica Wilson, in *Oxford History of South Africa*, Vol. 1 (Oxford, 1969), p. 235.
4 De Villiers, *White Tribe Dreaming*, p. 62.
5 Quoted in Richard Elphick and Hermann Giliomee, *The Shaping of South African Society, 1652–1820*, (Cape Town, 1979), p. 377.
6 I. D. MacCrone, *Race Attitudes in South Africa* (Oxford, 1937).
7 J. S. Marais, *The Cape Coloured People* (London, 1939), p. 113.
8 Quoted in W. M. Macmillan, *Bantu, Boer, and Briton* (Oxford, rev. edn, 1963), p. 41.
9 Slagtersnek is discussed at length in L. M. Thompson, *The Political Mythology of Apartheid* (Yale University Press, New Haven, CT, 1985).
10 J. P. Fitzpatrick, *The Transvaal from Within* (London, 1899), p. 230.
11 Marais, *Cape Coloured People*, pp. 156–7.

CHAPTER 3

1 John Locke, *The Second Treatise on Civil Government*, section 121.
2 *The Times*, 7 March 1851.
3 Quoted in G. H. L. Le May, *Black and White in South Africa* (London, 1971), p. 19.
4 T. R. H. Davenport, *South Africa. A Modern History*, 4th edn (London, 1991), p. 170.
5 Le May, *Black and White in South Africa*, p. 19.
6 W. P. Morrell, *British Colonial Policy in the Age of Peel and Russell* (London, 1930), p. 302.
7 James Bryce, *Impressions of South Africa* (London, 1897), pp. 392–3.
8 F. A. van Jaarsveld, *The Afrikaner's Interpretation of South African History* (Cape Town, 1964), *passim*.
9 *Round Table*, No. 23, June 1916, p. 574.
10 Genesis 13: 8–11.
11 C. 1961, p. 34.
12 CO 879/11, African No. 117, Shepstone to Carnarvon, 6 March 1877.
13 C. J. Uys, *In the Era of Shepstone* (Lovedale, n.d. [1934]), p. 262.
14 CO 879/11, African No. 117.
15 Uys, *In the era of Shepstone*, p. 248.
16 CO 879/11, African No. 117.
17 Ibid.
18 H. Rider Haggard, *Cetewayo and His White Neighbours* (London, 1882), pp. 141–2.
19 CO 879/13, p. 20.
20 Uys, *In the Era of Shepstone*, p. 381.
21 C. J. Uys, 'Shepstone's Letters and Diary', *Natal Witness*, 10 July 1930.

CHAPTER 4

1 CO 879/12, African No. 142.
2 CO 48/482, f. 573.
3 CO 879/11, African No. 123, 4 June 1877.
4 C 1961, Nos 7 and 9.
5 CO 879/13, African No. 151.
6 CO 879/13, African 154, No. 101.
7 C 2144, No. 75.
8 Ibid., No. 80.
9 CO 48/485, f. 369.
10 The formal exchanges between the Colonial Secretary and the deputation are in C 2220, Appendix 1.
11 W. Basil Worsfold, *Sir Bartle Frere* (London, 1923), p. 78n.
12 CO 2220, Appendix 1.
13 C 2302.
14 CO 291/2; Lanyon to Frere, 13 April 1879.
15 Transvaal Government Gazette Extraordinary, 17 April 1879.
16 CO 879/15, African No. 15.
17 CO 291/2.
18 Alfred Milner, *England in Egypt* (London, 1897), pp. 290–1.
19 CO 879/15, African No. 204, p. 138.
20 *De Volksstem*, 15 July 1879.
21 CO 291/3.
22 J. G. Kotze, *Cases decided in the High Court of the Transvaal Province*, 1877–1881 (London, 1885; 2nd edn 1912), pp. 115–23.
23 CO 291/3, Lanyon to Wolseley, 15 July 1879.
24 W. F. Butler, *George Pomeroy Colley* (London, 1899), p. 243.
25 C 2482, No. 121, 29 September 1879.
26 CO 291/3, Minute of 5 September 1879 on Transvaal 14,166.
27 Public Record Office. CAB 37/1/5
28 Ibid.
29 Command Paper, C.2842, No. 145, 20 November 1879.
30 House of Commons Debates, 5 November 1880, c. 92.
31 C.O. 291/3.
32 War Office printed papers: 0878, No. 140, 14 February 1881.
33 Butler, *George Pomeroy Colley*, pp. 294 sqq.
34 Quoted in Ronald Robinson and John Gallagher with Alice Denny, *Africa and the Victorians* (London, 1961), p. 70.

CHAPTER 5

1 W. E. H. Lecky, *Moral Aspects of the South African War* (London, 1900).
2 J. S. Marais, *The Fall of Kruger's Republic* (Oxford, 1961), p. 6.

3 Ibid., p. 7.
4 Ibid., p. 10.
5 Ibid. p. 125.
6 John Hays Hammond, *The Transvaal Trouble* (London, 1900), p. 13.
7 Bryce, *Impressions of South Africa*, pp. 511–2.
8 The most comprehensive account of the Raid is Elizabeth Longford, *Jameson's Raid* (London, 1960).
9 Marais, p. 117.
10 House of Commons Debates, 8 May 1896, *c.* 914.
11 Thomas Pakenham, *The Boer War* (London, 1979; paperback edn, 1982), p. 41.
12 Salisbury Papers, 3 February 1897, quoted in G. H. L. Le May, *British Supremacy in South Africa, 1899–1907* (Oxford, 1965), p. 7.
13 Quoted in *A Century of Wrong*, English edn (1900), pp. 49–50.
14 J. P. Fitzpatrick, *The Transvaal from Within* (London, 1896), p. 81.
15 J. L. Garvin, *The Life of Joseph Chamberlain* (London, 1932–4, 3 vols), iii, p. 141.
16 Marais, p. 205.
17 Le May, *British Supremacy*, p. 9.
18 C. Headlam (ed.), *The Milner Papers* (2 vols., London, 1931–3), Vol. i., pp. 252–3
19 Ibid. i, p. 445.
20 James Gustavus Whiteley, 'The Relation of England to the Transvaal in International Law', *Forum*, October 1899.
21 John Buchan, *Memory Hold-the-Door* (London, 1940), p. 470.
22 C 9530, quoted in Pakenham, p. 103.
23 Parliamentary Debates, 4th series, vol. lxxviii, cc. 378, 71.
24 *British Supremacy*, ch. 1, 'Sir Alfred Milner's War'.
25 I am grateful to Dr I. Smith for showing me his manuscript on the origins of the war, where this point is emphatically made.
26 Speech at the Lord Mayor's banquet; *The Times*, 10 November 1899.
27 Courtney Papers, vol. vii, f. 121.
28 Ibid., f. 208.
29 W. K. Hancock, *SMUTS. The Sanguine Years* (Cambridge, 1962), pp. 109–10.
30 Deneys Reitz, *Commando* (London, 1929), p. 17.
31 Ibid., p. 21.
32 Howard C. Hillegas, *With the Boer Forces* (London, 1900), p. 60.
33 Ibid., pp. 90–1.
34 Ibid., p. 100.
35 Pakenham, p. 572.
36 Churchill's reflections in captivity are in his *London to Ladysmith via Pretoria* (London, 1900) dated 24 November 1899.
37 Le May, *British Supremacy*, p. 87.
38 *With Rimington* (London, 1901), Letter of 23 November 1900.

39 Le May, *British Supremacy*, p. 97.
40 Pakenham, p. 498.
41 John Wilson, *C.B. A Life of Sir Henry Campbell- Bannerman* (London, 1973), p. 348.
42 Pakenham, p. 571.
43 J. D. Kestell and D. E. van Velden, *The Peace Negotiations between Boer and Briton in South Africa* (London, 1912), p. 85.
44 CO 417/51, f. 394 (Public Record Office).
45 Christiaan de Wet, *Three Years' War*, Popular edn, (London, 1903), pp. 495–8.
46 David Butler and Gareth Butler, *British Political Facts, 1900–1985* 6th edn, (London, 1986), pp. 475–6.
47 Le May, *British Supremacy*, p. 214.

CHAPTER 6

1 C. R. de Wet, *Three Years War* (Popular edition, London, 1903), p. 506.
2 For conditions in the camps, see Emily Hobhouse, *Report on a Visit to the Camps* (London, 1901) and the Report of Dame Millicent Fawcett's Committee of Ladies (Command Paper, Cd 893).
3 Cecil Headlam (ed.), *The Milner Papers (South Africa), 1899–1905* (London, 1933), Vol. 2: p. 134.
4 W. K. Hancock, *SMUTS. The Sanguine Years. 1870–1919* (Cambridge, 1962), p. 184.
5 *The Aftermath of War* (London, 1906).
6 Cf. Milner MSS Vol. 26: 'The average Boer really is the most good-natured manageable creature in the world as long as he clearly realizes that you have got the thick end of the stick.'
7 John Buchan, *The African Colony* (London, 1903), p. 343.
8 G. H. L. Le May, *British Supremacy in South Africa* (Oxford, 1965), p. 35–6.
9 Ibid., p. 169, quoting Colonial Office papers in the Public Record Office, CO 291/74.
10 *Johannesburg Star*, 13 February 1905.
11 S. G. Millin, *General Smuts* (London, 1936), Vol. 1, p. 213.
12 House of Commons Debates, 5 April 1906, c. 848.
13 Quoted in L. M. Thompson, *The Unification of South Africa* (Oxford, 1960), p. 226.
14 Lord Milner, *The Nation and the Empire* (London, 1913), pp. 90–1.

CHAPTER 7

1 On 'Hoggenheimer', in his various manifestations, see W. K. Hancock, *SMUTS. I. The Sanguine Years* (Cambridge, 1962) pp. 202 sqq.

2 Michael Roberts and A. E. G. Trollip, *The South African Opposition, 1939–1945* (Cape Town, 1947), p. 9.
3 Hancock, *SMUTS. I.*, p. 324.
4 Ibid., p. 383.
5 Quoted in A. D. Harvey, *Collision of Empires* (London, 1992), pp. 260–1.
6 For reactions to the rebellion or 'armed protest', see Marq de Villiers, *White Tribe Dreaming* (London, 1988), pp. 252 sqq.
7 Hancock, *SMUTS I.*, p. 392.
8 Harry Lawrence in *Dictionary of National Biography, 1951–1960,* (Oxford, 1971) p. 681.
9 Hancock, *SMUTS I.*, p. 397.
10 Journal of Parliaments of the Empire, Vol. 2 (London, 1921), p. 686.
11 Ibid., Vol. 7 (1926), p. 639.
12 Ibid., Vol. 8 (1927), p. 649.

CHAPTER 8

1 T. R. H. Davenport, *South Africa. A Modern History*, 4th edn (London, 1991), p. 274.
2 Michael Roberts and A. E. G. Trollip, *The South African Opposition, 1939–1945* (Cape Town, 1947), p. 6.
3 Ibid., p. 9.
4 W. K. Hancock, *SMUTS. The Fields of Force* (London, 1968), p. 257.
5 Roberts and Trollip, *Afrikaner Opposition*, p. 12, n. 1.
6 J. H. P. Serfontein, *Brotherhood of Power* (London, 1979), ch. 1.
7 L. J. du Plessis, quoted in Davenport, *South Africa*, p. 290.
8 Serfontein, *Brotherhood*, p. 41.
9 Dan O'Meara, *VOLKSKAPITALISME. Class, capital and ideology in the development of Afrikaner nationalism, 1934–1948* (Cambridge, 1983), p. 75.
10 *Report of the Carnegie Commission of Investigation of the Poor White Question in South Africa,* (5 vols, Stellenbosch, 1932), Part I, p. 18.
11 Ibid., p. vii.
12 Ibid., pp. xvii, xix.
13 Ibid., pp. 109–10.
14 Ibid., Part II, p. 83.
15 Hancock, *Fields of Force*, p. 287.
16 Private information from the recipient of the advice, the late Professor Olaf Wagner (who spoke English at home).
17 Hancock, *Fields of Force*, pp. 295–6.
18 Quoted in T. Dunbar Moodie, *The Rise of Afrikanerdom* (University of California Press, 1975), p. 13.
19 Roberts and Trollip, *Afrikaner Opposition*, p. 231, note to p. 64.

20 Nicholas Mansergh, *Documents and Speeches on British Common-wealth Affairs, 1931–1952. Vol. 1.* (Oxford, 1953), pp. 498–9.
21 B. K. Long, *In Smuts's Camp* (London, 1945), pp. 16–17.
22 *Die Transvaler*, 1940.
23 Quoted in E. G. Malherbe, *Education in South Africa*, Vol. II (Cape Town, 1977), p. 106.
24 Roberts and Trollip, *Afrikaner Opposition*, p. 51.
25 Ibid, pp. 159–61.

CHAPTER 9

1 Hancock, *SMUTS. The Fields of Force*, p. 330.
2 Ibid., p. 481.
3 Hancock, quoted in *A Survey of British Commonwealth Affairs* (Oxford, 1937), Vol. I (3 vols), p. 189.
4 Quoted in L. M. Thompson, *The Political Mythology of Apartheid* (Yale University Press, New Haven, 1985), p. 29.
5 Quoted in Hermann Giliomee and Lawrence Schlemmer, *From Apartheid to Nation-Building* (Cape Town, 1989), p. 47.
6 Quoted in E. G. Malherbe, *Education in South Africa* (Cape Town, 1977), Vol. II (2 vols), p. 101.
7 Ibid., p. 102.
8 S. Marks and S. Trapido, *The Politics of Race, Class and Nationalism in Twentieth-Century South Africa* (London, 1987), p. 15.
9 Quoted in Le May, *Black and White in South Africa*, pp. 73–4.
10 Hancock, *The Fields of Force*, p. 507.
11 Quoted in D. L. Keir and F. H. Lawson, *Cases in Constitutional Law*, 4th edn (Oxford, 1954), p. 521.
12 Le May, *Black and White*, p. 93.
13 Keir and Lawson, *Cases*, p. 343.
14 T. R. H. Davenport, *South Africa*, p. 339.
15 Ibid., p. 339.
16 H. M. Robertson, *South Africa: Economic and Political Aspects* (Cape Town, 1957).
17 Quoted in Davenport, *South Africa*, p. 354.
18 Quoted in Alistair Horne, *MACMILLAN, 1957–1986* (London, 1989), p. 193.
19 Ibid., p. 194.
20 Ibid., pp. 196–7.

CHAPTER 10

1 Quoted by David Welsh, 'The Executive and the African Population – 1948 to the Present', in *Malan to De Klerk* ed. Robert Schrire (London, 1994), p. 139.

2 Ibid., p. 138.
3 Quoted in Robert M. Price, *The Apartheid State in Crisis*, (New York, 1991), p. 31.
4 Quoted in Davenport, *History . . .*, p. 337.
5 Quoted in E. G. Malherbe, *Education in South Africa*, Vol. 2 (Cape Town, 1977), p. 106.
6 P. Randall (ed.), *Apartheid and the Church* (Johannesburg, 1972), and *Not Without Honour* (Johannesburg, 1982).
7 Quoted by Welsh, 'The Executive and the African Population', p. 165.
8 For a subtle exposition of the Marxist interpretation, see Dan O'Meara, *VOLKSCAPITALISME. Class, capital and ideology in the development of Afrikaner Nationalism, 1934–1948* (Cambridge, 1983) and 'The Afrikaner Broederbond, 1927–1948: the class vanguard of Afrikaner Nationalism', in *Journal of South African Studies*, Vol. 3 (1977).
9 J. H. P. Serfontein, Brotherhood of Power (London, 1979), p. 240.
10 André Brink and J. M. Coetzee (eds), *A Land Apart* (London, 1986), p. 2.
11 Hermann Giliomee, 'Broedertwis: Intra-Afrikaner conflicts in the transition from apartheid, 1969–1991', in N. Etherington (ed.), *Peace, Politics and Violence in the New South Africa* (London, 1992), p. 162.
12 Price, *The Apartheid State . . .*, p. 90.
13 Giliomee, 'Broedertwis . . .', pp. 189–90.
14 *The Annual Register* (London, 1986), p. 965.
15 Shaun Johnson, *Strange Days Indeed* (London, 1994), p. 14.
16 Helen Suzman, *In No Uncertain Terms* (London, 1993), p. 250.
17 *Annual Register* (1986), p. 513.
18 Price, *The Apartheid State . . .* p. 139.
19 Johnson, *Strange Days . . .* p. 69.
20 Giliomee, 'The Last Trek? Afrikaners in Transition to Democracy' in Etherington, op. cit.

INDEX